GLOBAL RACISM

GLOBAL RACISM

A CHALLENGE FOR THE WORLD

ANNA SPAIN BRADLEY

Professor of Law and MacArthur Foundation Chair in International Justice and Human Rights, University of California, Los Angeles

OXFORD
UNIVERSITY PRESS

OXFORD
UNIVERSITY PRESS

Oxford University Press is a department of the University of Oxford.
It furthers the University's objective of excellence in research, scholarship,
and education by publishing worldwide. Oxford is a registered trade mark of
Oxford University Press in the UK and in certain other countries.

Published in the United States of America by Oxford University Press
546 Fifth Avenue, New York, NY 10036, United States of America

Library of Congress Cataloging-in-Publication Data
Names: Spain Bradley, Anna, 1978– author
Title: Global racism : a challenge for the world / Anna Spain Bradley.
Description: New York : Oxford University Press, 2026. |
Includes bibliographical references and index.
Identifiers: LCCN 2026013939 (print) | LCCN 2026013940 (ebook) |
ISBN 9780197778388 hardback | ISBN 9780197778395 epub |
ISBN 9780197778401 updf | ISBN 9780197778418 online
Subjects: LCSH: Race discrimination—Law and legislation | Racism
Classification: LCC K3242 .S6575 2026 (print) | LCC K3242 (ebook)
LC record available at https://lccn.loc.gov/2026013939
LC ebook record available at https://lccn.loc.gov/2026013940

DOI: 10.1093/oso/9780197778388.001.0001

Printed by Integrated Books International, United States of America

MIX
Paper
FSC FSC® C183721

The manufacturer's authorized representative in the EU for product safety is
Oxford University Press España S.A. of Parque Empresarial San Fernando de Henares,
Avenida de Castilla, 2 – 28830 Madrid (www.oup.es/en or product.safety@oup.com).
OUP España S.A. also acts as importer into Spain of products made by the manufacturer.

Note to Readers

This publication is designed to provide accurate and authoritative information in regard to the subject matter covered. It is based upon sources believed to be accurate and reliable and is intended to be current as of the time it was written. It is sold with the understanding that the publisher is not engaged in rendering legal, accounting, or other professional services. If legal advice or other expert assistance is required, the services of a competent professional person should be sought. Also, to confirm that the information has not been affected or changed by recent developments, traditional legal research techniques should be used, including checking primary sources where appropriate.

(Based on the Declaration of Principles jointly adopted by a Committee of the American Bar Association and a Committee of Publishers and Associations.)

In memory of my father, William G. Spain, and our ancestors,
whose Black struggle for human rights has paved new roads for humanity.

Contents

Preface

Ten Years, One Book

"[N]o problem of human relations is insoluble."

—Dr. Ralph J. Bunche[1]

On September 8, 1943, in the small town of Sebring, Florida, not far from the swamps of the Everglades, a boy was born in the late summer heat. It was the height of World War II and the boy's father was enlisted as a soldier at a nearby Army base. There the father had met and married the boy's mother, a local woman whose own mother had taken the train down from rural Georgia to find work following World War I. The new parents named their firstborn after his father but called him "June" for short. After the war, the family moved eight hundred miles north to Virginia where June's father got work in the Norfolk Naval Shipyard. Soon to be the oldest of ten siblings, June was a dark-skinned colored kid growing in a nation where segregation was the law of the land. In addition to going to school, he had to learn the unwritten rules of survival for Black people living in the racist caste system of the Jim Crow South. Foremost among these were to keep quiet around people and never to look them in the eye. On rare trips to the white side of town, he made sure to use the entrances and water fountains labeled "For Colored Only." In the summers, June's father would drive him and his siblings back down to the family farm in North Carolina to help sharecrop tobacco, faithfully following the Green Book routes and avoiding sundown towns. June, and many kids like him, grew up in a nation built on the foundations of slavery, where the noble ideals of equality and dignity were no more than notional for Black people. But change was going to come.

Five years after June was born, on December 10, 1948, nations of the world agreed that those ideals of equality and dignity should be enshrined as human rights for all. At the United Nations, the General Assembly adopted the Universal Declaration of Human Rights, a milestone in human history, establishing universal and inherent fundamental human rights to which every person in the world is entitled. But the lived experience of millions still fell well short of the document's high ideals. Among the most pernicious and persistent forms of oppression that challenged the call for universal human rights was racism.

Back in America, racism-fueled oppression ran deep and proved difficult to overcome. Legalized segregation permeated everyday life. In addition to oppressing Black people, it also harmed millions of others deemed not white, including people of Chinese, Japanese, Jewish, and Mexican descent. Children grew up attending segregated schools, separate and unequal. Redlining meant that local laws often prohibited non-whites from owning houses in certain neighborhoods. The government played a central role in perpetuating racism. Three particularly egregious examples are the forced relocation and internment of over 120,000 Japanese Americans during the war, the medical experimentation infecting Black American men with syphilis in the Tuskegee study, and the forced removal of Native American children to military-style schools. Following centuries of outright massacres, forced displacement, and cultural erasure, this was yet another step in the ongoing genocide of America's Indigenous peoples.

The oppression that racism fed extended across the world, embedded in societies after centuries of slavery and colonialism. South Africa's system of apartheid, blatantly antithetical to the new framework of universal human rights, nevertheless endured for four decades more. Of course, the origins of racism's harms ran much deeper. Throughout the world, European monarchies in search of riches and territory had empowered their agents—like the British East India Company, the Dutch West India Company, and Portuguese traders—to carry out violent forced labor and resource extraction in the name of colonial expansion. More than four hundred years of the transatlantic slave trade resulted in the forcible transfer and subsequent enslavement of some 12.5 million people from Africa to the Americas, with millions dying during the Middle Passage. In these English, French, Dutch, Portuguese, and Spanish colonies turned countries, various European identities began to converge into the singularity of being white or *blanco* or *les blancs*. Whiteness afforded access to the top of political, economic, social, and cultural hierarchies. Other so-called races were deemed inherently inferior, with Black people, in the words of legal scholar Derrick Bell, becoming "the magical faces at the bottom of society's well."[2]

Back in Chesapeake, June was growing up as a bright, brave, and fun-loving boy with a thick Southern accent and a round, shiny head shaved bald. But he was deemed a colored, dark-skinned Negro, born into Jim Crow segregation, a face at the bottom of society's well. His natural tendencies for leadership—standing up to bullies and ensuring those around him had a good time—ran headlong into a world committed to racism and a nation that excelled in enforcing it. Even in his all-Black community, colorism—racism turned in on itself—ensured that he was near the bottom. Many of his teachers and elders made that clear—on account of his dark skin, he was not destined for much success. As the bluesman Big Bill Broonzy used to sing, "They say if you was white, you's all right / If you was brown, stick around / As you's black, oh brother, get back, get back, get back."[3]

By the time June reached adulthood, however, this old era had slowly begun to give way to something new. The war had broken open the start of a new world order. Monarchies ended, maps were redrawn, and the rules within and among nations began to change. In the postwar reckoning, highlighted by the Nuremburg Trials, public sentiment rejected Adolf Hitler, the Nazi Party, and the hatred for which they stood. Calls to end antisemitism and prevent future genocides took hold. The United Nations was born under the aspirational banner that a peaceful world required a more equal one.

In the United States, Black soldiers, who had risked dying for their country, demanded their fair share of these new human rights. By the time June turned twenty, America's Civil Rights Movement was in full effect.

In defiance of his father's fears, June was a part of it—participating in sit-ins and boycotts, and joining the 1963 March on Washington, where Dr. Martin Luther King Jr. delivered his historic "I Have a Dream" speech. Most of all, June redefined himself, not as a colored boy or as a Negro but, proudly, as Black.

Soon after, as American involvement in the Vietnam War expanded, June was called up to enlist, just like his father some twenty years earlier. That same week, he received a letter of acceptance into President John F. Kennedy's new Peace Corps. The Army let him go, and he deployed to Malawi along with a group of volunteers who identified as Americans with different racial and ethnic backgrounds, including Asian, Black, Jewish, Mexican, and white, all idealistically committed to the Peace Corps' "cause of world peace and human progress."[4] In Malawi, he met Mary, a British Volunteer from a coal-mining Catholic family in the north of England. She became the love of his life. Mary was white, and their interracial love was illicit. They got married anyway and made a life together across three continents and six decades, raising two daughters along the way.

Seven decades after he was born, June, now known as Bill, was sitting on his porch in Boulder, Colorado, reminiscing about days past with his younger daughter, a law professor at the nearby university. He recalled how he had always believed that world peace and friendship would prevail, but, given America's dark turn under then newly elected President Donald Trump, he wasn't so sure anymore. His eyes misted as he recalled the pain of his younger years and the sacrifices so many made just to end up back here. "We tried," he said to his daughter. "My generation tried. It's your turn now." That boy from Sebring, Florida was my father and I, his daughter. His life and his call to action on that day inspired me to write this book.

*

I started writing this book ten years ago, but its origins go back to my own. Born in England and raised in America, I came from a mix of cultures and nationalities. But in the small Ohio town where I grew up, I was simply a Black American girl. Racism, intertwined with sexism, was an everyday experience. My sister and I were among the few Black kids at our elementary and middle school. Our family integrated the all-white neighborhood we called home.

My earliest memory of racism came when I was about four, in a grocery store, where a woman yelled at my mother, pointing at me, and said, "How could you! How could you give birth to *that*!" A year later, I was playing in my friend's sandbox when another kid said, "Hey, you nigger, get out. You can't play here." I didn't know then what that word meant, but I knew by the kid's contorted face exactly what he felt when saying it; I knew what I felt hearing it, too. When I was 12, my best friend's mother showed up at our door to angrily announce, in front of both her daughter and me, that her white child could no longer be friends with a Black girl like me. My dad made the face he usually did in situations like this—his jaw set firm and his dark eyes piercing. That was the day I began making that face, too.

As I grew up, I started to notice how entrenched and widespread racism really was. It was the early 1990s at my large public high school, and fights often broke out at lunch between white boys with steel-toed boots who called themselves neo-Nazi skinheads and hockey-jersey-wearing Black boys. In these formative years, a Confederate flag was staked in my family's yard, and I was called the n-word more times than I can count. Even though it was common knowledge that the Ku Klux Klan, an old and dangerous white supremacist hate group, was active in our area, I was still surprised when I first saw them myself one day in the woods, in ghostly white robes, chanting around a livid flame. This kind of racism was blatant—explicit and undeniable. But racist experiences like these are only part of the problem. The other part has less to do with what people do and more to do with what they believe: the ideology of white supremacy.

In my small Ohio town, where the railroad tracks still divided the Black side from the white, the racial discord grew so concerning that the National Association for the Advancement of Colored People intervened. As a teen, I joined their efforts. There I met Dr. David Woodyard, a professor of religion from the nearby university. Leading by his own courageous example, he taught me and generations of others the meaning of liberation theology. A small group of my high school classmates and I, convinced of the power of conflict resolution to address racism, volunteered as mediators. We received training through a new peer-mediation program at our school. Calling our group Students Together Against Racial Tension, or S.T.A.R.T., we soon began mediating small dialogues about racism by invitation among the people of our town, students and parents alike.

Each week, we met in a high school gym or church hall, sitting in folding chairs around circular card tables. There was a water fountain, coffee, and, on a good week, some cookies. That was about it. Many people in that room entered with a fixed worldview: they believed that people are born into different races and that the white race is superior to all others. Some departed with a different view. Despite our Spartan surroundings, the simple act of bringing people together around those tables—to share, to listen, perhaps to understand—conjured a small magic. The one thing that proved more powerful than the isolated allure of racial superiority was the call to belonging rooted in our shared humanity.

Those days spent listening in stuffy rooms convinced me that racism isn't immutable and that conflicts, even those rooted in identity, can be resolved. People are capable of change, even us older ones. The key to eliminating racism, however, lies not in individual transformation alone but in communal efforts to undo *ideologies* of supremacy that block our shared sense of humanity. The key to doing that involves building a culture of dignity: the universal human right that we all have inherent value and deserve to be treated as such.

After high school, I went to that nearby university, Denison University, and studied with Dr. Woodyard, later focusing on environmental science and how ecosystems work. After graduation, I took a job with the US Environmental Protection Agency to work on climate change policy where I first fell in love with the United Nations and the promise of diplomacy. I went on to Harvard Law School and commenced my legal career back in government as an attorney-advisor for the US State

Department. In a stroke of luck in my early career, I was appointed as a US delegate to the United Nations, deepening my passion for international law and diplomacy. Life circumstances moved me to California and then to Colorado, where I started the long journey of becoming an academic—advancing as a tenured law professor and, after years of scholarship, publishing, and teaching, becoming a full professor of international law. Along the way, I kept mediating everything from divorces and neighborhood spats to post-conflict crises as a founding member of Mediators Beyond Borders International.

In a world that urged people to specialize, I remained a persistent outlier, seeing people and life through the lens of ecosystems and global connections. That integrative perspective drove my scholarship on protecting the environment, promoting peace and human rights through law, and combating the persistence of racism as a barrier to these noble ideals. It was often a lonely path. I was one of only a handful of Black American women in the field of international law and among fewer in leaderships roles, including as a Vice President of the American Society of International Law and as a life member of the Council on Foreign Relations. At every turn, I tried to ensure that even if I was the first Black woman in a space, I would not be the last.

It was around this time, in 2016, that my dad tapped me on the shoulder that day on the porch, passing the baton to fight against racism and to fight for humanity. Those struggles became even more important as I raised my two Black daughters. Had I done enough to make my dad, my children, and my ancestors proud? As he looked at me that day, I felt a twinge of guilt for the relative comfort of my life, recalling all he had sacrificed, all my grandparents had suffered, and the forgotten stories of my ancestors' survival.

That's when I picked up my laptop and began researching and writing about racism in my fields of expertise: human rights and international law. For all the good that the postwar world order had achieved, with its universal human rights and treaties and tribunals for nations to settle their disputes peacefully, something perplexed me. Racism wasn't on the agenda in the centers of power, making international law, forging peace and security, or crafting world order. Racism was not mentioned by name in key treaties, or discussed by judges in decisions at the International Court of Justice, or deliberated at the United Nations. The UN Charter itself doesn't even use the word "racism." International treaties only define "discrimination on the basis of race" in vague terms. Few casebooks of international law consider racism; in some of legal education's most prominent texts the word does not even appear in the index.

How could this be? Why was racism missing from the discourse of international law and human rights, areas that had examined so many other kinds of harms to the world? I knew from my many travels and experiences working with communities across the globe that racism was a persistent and prevalent threat to millions of people in most places. It was an affront to the noble ideals of human rights, peace, and world order. So why was it silenced? I began to write.

International law has a racism problem.[5] This was the opening sentence to a short piece I wrote in 2019 about how the international legal community had long been complicit in promoting racism and had done too little to bring about its elimination. It was based on a longer article built upon years of research, which I had published the same year titled *Human Rights Racism.*[6] In it, I argued that racism should be explicitly recognized as a human rights violation under international law. After reviewing the legal history and doctrinal development of racism within international law, my field of scholarly expertise, I articulated how vital it is to understand that racism manifests as more than acts of discrimination on the basis of race, color, or descent, as the current legal framework defines. I also argued that international law misses something. Racism is not just how we behave; it is also deeply rooted in what we believe, emerging as aggressive ideologies of superiority that threaten the purposes and principles of international law: namely, peace, security, equality, and human dignity. I challenged the field of international law, and those of us in it, to do more to prevent systemic racism, acknowledging how law had empowered apartheid, segregation, slavery, and the transatlantic slave trade for far too long. In doing this work, there was one challenge that really troubled me. The world—inclusive of the people and the nations therein—did not agree on what was and what was not racism.

This concern formed the original idea for this book. The success of *Human Rights Racism* and the conversations it helped spark about the relationship between racism and international law led to a book contract with Oxford University Press (OUP). The aim was to extend my research, originally intended for a scholarly audience, into a book for a public audience. But this book is not that book. Soon after signing the contract with OUP in 2020, three things happened that changed the world, changed me, and changed the course of this book.

First, on May 25, 2020, a hate crime took place in America that shocked the world. A Minnesota police officer named Derek Chauvin murdered a man named George Floyd, Jr. by kneeling on his neck, in broad daylight and in front of a horrified crowd, for over nine minutes. Because of a video that went viral online, people everywhere watched Floyd Jr.'s final moments of life, gasping for air and, with his last breath, pleading, "I can't breathe." They watched a white man in a police uniform mercilessly kill a Black man in America. Soon, the Black Lives Matter movement took hold, leading to national and global reckonings with racism at the United Nations and beyond. Racism was more than individual acts of discrimination for the US government to address. Racism was a systemic harm, violating universal human rights, and a matter of concern for international law.

Second, that same month, I accepted a new leadership role at the University of California, Los Angeles as the Vice Chancellor for Equity, Diversity and Inclusion, after a national search that had begun in January. By the time I started in September, racism was a hot topic within the 100,000-person university community of students, faculty, and employees. Different groups of people came forward seeking specialized responses to their particular concerns. Longer-term systemic changes that would lift all boats were much less satisfying than immediate attention for particular groups' needs by the university's leadership in the form of resources and public statements. Competition over limited resources and discord complicated efforts to create anything close to a university-wide approach to combating racism, made all the more complicated by the COVID pandemic happening at the same time. Overnight, I became a public spokesperson for the university's values and a target of hate-filled threats by people in the community and through anonymous social media accounts online. These experiences led to valuable, firsthand lessons that inform this book. First, racism is broader than racial discrimination, yet our laws and policies are centered around nondiscrimination, supporting penalties but not prevention. Second, racism lives in an ecosystem; it is connected to other forms of oppression and to cultures in which oppression thrives. Any effective strategy for combating racism requires the power necessary to change an ecosystem, such as buy-in from leadership and transformative cultural change. Finally, combating racism is a team sport. A community must reach some shared consensus about what racism is in order to determine what everyone is prepared to do differently to stop it.

Third, in 2021, I was appointed Legal Expert to the United Nations Ad Hoc Committee on the Elaboration of Contemporary Standards, a subsidiary of the United Nations Human Rights Council, to provide advice on the prevention of racial discrimination and xenophobia.[7] This experience emphasized the many ways in which the challenge I wrote about in 2019 and saw at UCLA in 2020 was also a challenge for the world. Representatives from various nations agreed that racism was a problem, but only in certain places. A few were prepared to acknowledge that racism was a problem in their country. But, beyond that, the international community seemed stuck. Racism was not viewed as a serious threat to international peace and security. It had never been defined by a treaty under international law, which only bans certain forms of racial discrimination. It had never been acknowledged as a global challenge, like climate change or a pandemic. (It doesn't help that, being an invented construct, race as a concept is not universal.) In the end, I left troubled by the international community's limited approach to combating racism, treating it largely as a domestic challenged to be handled by each nation as they do, or do not, see fit. Some nations, in fact, claim to have no problems with racism within their borders. Such fragmentation in approaches and thinking meant that effective measures to address racism as a global challenge would go nowhere. In these exchanges, I saw the need for this book.

A fourth thing happened, just a few months before this writing, that has also shaped this book. On April 8, 2025, my father, William Spain, passed away. I sat with him in the hospital in his final hours, grateful for his life and for all that he had done to help the world. I am sad that I did not finish this book in time for him to read it, but my promise to him to do more is embedded in these pages and in the work that lies ahead.

Introduction

The Thief of Humanity

Introduction

Racism is a thief, one that harms millions of people around the world every day. From segregation of Roma children in European schools to housing discrimination against foreigners in Japan, from systemic anti-Black racism in policing in the United States to pervasive societal discrimination against the Twa in Burundi, this thief's many faces emerge in interpersonal, institutional, and systemic forms. Like a robber in the night, racism ambushes people, plundering opportunity, equality, and dignity. It can even steal away life itself.

But racism is not just the work of individual thieves. It also operates like a global syndicate. Complex and multifaceted, racism extends its influence across countries and cultures. This is paradoxical given that race, a human construct, is not globally agreed upon. Racism also moves around, often in society's shadows, interacting with global forces that shape world order. More than a local problem affecting some people in some places, racism seems connected to our very human ecosystem. Its dangers lie in its ubiquity and in its potential universality. Racism is possible everywhere and anywhere people are, including online.

In its most damaging forms, racism is the thief of humanity. History reveals it as a threat to international peace and security and a persistent

Global Racism. Anna Spain Bradley, Oxford University Press. © Anna Spain Bradley 2026.
DOI: 10.1093/oso/9780197778388.003.0001

root cause of atrocious crimes. From genocide centered in dangerous ideologies of racial superiority to barbarity legalized by colonialism and slavery, racism is grounded in a depravity that has fueled the most pernicious injustices. It has the potential to make evil of us all.

We know less than we should about a thief so old, widespread, and dangerous. What are the root causes of racism? When does racism spread? How do we explain its global presence? What might account for racism's persistence over centuries? Why has it been hard to eradicate? And what new insights can we glean about racism's modern manifestations by taking a global view? In essence, humanity still needs to address the fundamental question—what is racism?

A Small Book About a Big Subject

This book is about this ubiquitous and universally available form of oppression I call *Global Racism*. It is widely understood that racism causes harm to millions of people in ways already recognized as internalized, interpersonal, institutional, structural, and systemic. But this book explores racism as something more. It investigates the global prevalence of racism as a connected phenomenon, operating *across* nations and cultures, not just within. Global racism names this phenomenon as a complex and multifaceted danger existing in the human ecosystem and interacting with world order.

To examine global racism, the book travels through stories about people and nations told through histories of human rights and international law in an effort to better understand what racism is from a global perspective and what it steals from us all. The book considers both acts defined as racial discrimination under international law and the more elusive ideologies of racial superiority sustained by what people believe. It traces how global racism emerges in the modern world and the role leaders play in weaponizing constructed distinctions to justify exclusion, domination, and inequality. It seeks to better understand how global racism emerges at such junctures, transforming human-created distinctions into durable ecosystems of oppression. The tragic histories of the racism wrought through slavery, colonialism, segregation, apartheid, and genocide—harms all banned by international law today—teach us a great deal about our species and ourselves. So, too, do the rare yet inspiring moments of human solidarity, where the world commits to naming and combating harms *together*.

As an imperfect analogy, consider another global phenomenon—climate change. Understanding climate change begins, for most people, with understanding the weather. When we are children, we learn about the weather every day. We go outside and experience sun or rain, heat or cold. Weather is immediate, local, and tangible. We first understand what weather is because we encounter it.

When I was young, we learned about weather in school. We learned how snow forms when particles and water vapor in the atmosphere fall to the ground as the temperature drops below freezing. We also learned that local weather patterns could be shaped by larger systems, such as jet streams and ocean currents. We relied on the local news to tell us what the weather might be that day. Even then, weather was presented as something discrete, observable, and mostly bound by place.

What I didn't learn about was climate change. Back then, some forty years ago, most people didn't have a framework to understand that local weather events were connected to and impacted by an even broader, invisible phenomenon now known as climate change. But today we do. Advancements in science connect what we once understood as local weather events with broader climate changes in sea surface temperature or ocean currents. As extreme weather events become more common, we even have new names to describe what is happening, like a polar vortex or heat dome, where extreme temperatures can become trapped over a region for an extended period. Science has also shown how human activity, notably the massive release of greenhouse gases into the atmosphere, is causing the climate to change. As a result, many people and most nations have come to recognize climate change as a global challenge that requires a global framework to address.

I worked on climate change after college in 1999 as a policy analyst at the US Environmental Protection Agency. Having majored in environmental studies, I spent my college years as a big-picture, comprehensive thinker, learning to address climate challenges through ecosystem analysis, blending insights from different areas of scientific research. I began to approach understanding racism through a similar, big-picture lens. What if racism is also a global, interconnected, yet poorly understood phenomenon?

Think of it like this. Racism is like the weather. Discrete experiences of racism are akin to localized weather events. Most people understand racism as something they can observe or something they have experienced. Racism is most often defined in laws as acts of discrimination and conceptualized as occurring between people, inside institutions, and within systems.

Global racism is akin to climate change. It names the broader contours of oppression within which racism operates across our human ecosystem. Like weather events, localized incidents of racism are shaped by larger, often unseen global forces operating in ways people don't directly see or know. In some parts of the world, people learn about racism as a relic of the distant past, taking place for centuries during the transatlantic slave trade and slavery, during colonialism, during segregation, and during apartheid. We lack much less common understanding about the forces that shape racism today. Such forces may operate through a global superstructure, circulating among institutions and transnational networks. Alternatively, they may function on a deeper substructure of humanity itself, embedded in human nature and giving rise to desires to feel superior to others that then attach to race. Perilous ideologies of racial superiority, like white supremacy, connect people all over the world under a shared belief system that one race is inherently superior to all others. This book undertakes a search to identify and to map these global connections.

Conceiving of racism as global is not new. W. E. B. Du Bois warned us about it in 1903 when he famously wrote that "the problem of the 20th century is the problem of the color line, the relation of the darker to the lighter races of men in Asia and Africa, in America and the islands of the sea."[1] His work shed light on the problem of racism as a collective one and examined how ideologies of white supremacy meant that those in power were able to embed in world order their own beliefs about themselves. Du Bois was inspired by Frederick Douglass's 1881 warning, in *The Color Line*, that "[f]ew evils are less accessible to the force of reason, or more tenacious of life and power, than a long-standing prejudice."[2] Douglass's vision, too, was globally inclined, stretching back in time, to note compassionate concern for the plight of the Saxons at the hands of the Normans. He called this evil "race-pride" and believed it to be foundational in justifying acts of indignity and violence around the world and throughout history. Later, after both world wars, Du Bois published *Color and Democracy*, which laid bare that for democracy to remedy inequality, it must sacrifice white supremacy.[3]

In those same years, United Nations diplomat and Nobel Peace Prize Laureate Ralph Bunche was working through institutions to address racism in world order. He wrote that "race is a universal social problem," and examined it as such in his 1936 book, *A World View of Race*.[4] In these pages I have endeavored to build on the foundations laid down by Douglass, Du Bois, and Bunche, all of whom warned of racism as a threat to the world. Such inquiries remain unfinished and, given the state of our world today, urgent.

This book names and examines global racism. It also calls for recognizing global racism as a challenge for the world to address. Nations must lead in taking full responsibility for combating racism in a globally systemic way, starting with explicitly recognizing racism as a human rights violation under international law. Within and across nations, people also bear responsibility for ending racism—all eight billion of us. In that spirit, the book identifies four pillars of a framework for combating global racism: emboldening moral leadership from world leaders in resisting ideologies of racial superiority, strengthening protections in international law rooted in the human right to dignity, elevating the power of education through inclusive pedagogy and equitable access, and adopting the principle of *humanitas* as our guiding norm for humanity. Why?

Because we define our humanity, in part, by that which we agree not to become.

Key Themes

Throughout its ten chapters, *Global Racism* seeks to understand racism on a worldwide scale, marking a phenomenon more complex and more interconnected than many realize. The following key themes emerge.

First, global racism is not just a problem for some people and some nations. It is a challenge for the world. An honest account of global racism's promulgation through slavery, colonialism, segregation, apartheid, and genocide—harms once legal but now banned by international law—reveals it as a globally interconnected form of oppression and a grave threat to international peace and security. By recounting the legal history of how nations around the world have approached the challenge of racism (and how they have not), the book reveals a significant international legal gap. There is no legal definition of *racism* under international law. Indeed, nations' attempts to specify what racism is beyond certain acts of racial discrimination have been fraught and contentious. Nations, today, still do not agree about what racism is nor the full extent of its harms. The international community cannot address a challenge it has yet to fully understand or define.

A second theme of this book is revealed through historical accounts and modern-day stories of racism, in all of its forms. Racism is a thief. It steals away the lives, rights and dignity of the people it harms. But global racism also steals away our humanity, as the painful histories of slavery, genocide, and other widespread atrocities remind us. The path towards humanity, towards the state of being human, requires us to fully understand global racism as its plague.

Third, the book examines how global racism survives and spreads throughout the human ecosystem. It is a universally available, yet uncharted form of oppression, that extends beyond discriminatory acts. Global racism is rooted in aggressive and destructive ideologies of superiority. It is advanced by leaders who espouse such ideologies. It can become viral, when fear and misinformation travel faster than facts, transforming difference into division into violence. Combating global racism requires dismantling dehumanizing ideologies of superiority at their roots.

Finally, this study of global racism also reminds us of reasons for hope. The most striking lesson *Global Racism* reveals isn't about challenge or hatred or that which divides us. It is the persistence of our humanity, found in those rare yet sustaining moments of human solidarity, when the world commits to naming and combating harms *together*. We've done it before, and we can do it again. This book highlights the power of education and the promise of human rights, through dignity and *humanitas,* as foundations for building a better future. In gaining knowledge about what divides us, we also find wisdom about what unites us and what can help advance our shared humanity.

Through this book, I invite you to explore one question above all others: What will we choose to become as a species? *Global Racism* is a call to action for people and nations alike to name and to acknowledge racism as a threat to the world and a challenge we must address together. The world cannot solve a problem it fails to define. Defining global racism requires global collaboration. Combating it effectively demands global commitment. Four pillars guide us: (1) resisting ideologies of racial superiority through strong moral leadership, (2) strengthening protections in international law rooted in the human right to dignity, (3) elevating the power of inclusive education, and (4) committing to the principle of *humanitas* as our guiding value. The way forward involves a globally coordinated response to a challenge that spans the world. It also requires acknowledging, with urgency, that the fight against racism is a fight for our very humanity.

*

Plan of the Book

This book's stories, explorations, and insights unfold over ten chapters. The first half journeys through history to consider how people and nations have understood racism, often through the lens of law and the international community. Chapter 1, "The Racism Question," centers on 1950, when a group of experts gathered under the auspices of UNESCO (United Nations Education, Scientific and Cultural Organization) to author a statement for the world about the challenges of racism, documenting its continued presence. Chapter 2 asks the central question "What Is Racism?" tracing the origins of the word and gathering ideas about what racism is while examining contemporary forms of racism from around the world to illuminate its complexities. Chapter 3, "An Old Enemy," turns to the deep past to recall how racism operated through colonialism, the transatlantic slave trade, slavery, segregation, and apartheid before revisiting the origins of the United Nations, the Universal Declaration of Human Rights, and the international order that followed. Chapter 4 revisits 1965 as "A Question for the World," when nations negotiated the first treaty calling for the elimination of all forms of racial discrimination. It charts these developments during a period in history that marked independence and the end of formal colonial rule in many nations and the rise of the Civil Rights Movement in the United States. During this time of rapid global change, nations banned racial discrimination through international law, raising disagreements during the negotiations that remain unresolved to this day. This journey informs Chapter 5, "The Non-Illegality of Racism," which charts the development of international law concerning racism, developments at the United Nations following the murder of George Floyd Jr. in 2020, and judicial approaches to racism by the International Court of Justice. In total, the first half of the book reveals how diverse peoples and nations have understood the challenge of racism over time and key questions that remain today.

The midpoint of our journey, and the book's central thesis, is found in Chapter 6, "Naming *Global Racism*," where I articulate global racism a yet unmapped layer of this problem, describing it as a phenomenon rooted in our human ecosystem that interacts with world order and spreads through ideologies of racial superiority.

The second half of the book outlines four calls to action essential to advancing a framework for combating global racism. Chapter 7, "Resisting Ideologies of Superiority," exposes how ideologies of identity rooted in racial superiority permeate societies and become central mechanisms through which racism manifests and sustains itself globally. Chapter 8, "Demanding Dignity," turns to the work of substituting such ideologies of racism with ideologies of dignity, grounded in universal human rights. Dignity offers a values-based counterideology to racial superiority. Chapter 9, "The Power of Education," explores why education—particularly inclusive and experiential education among people with diverse identities—is a powerful tool in the fight against global racism. It highlights how learning in racially diverse and experiential settings reduces bias and fear in our brains, a topic I spent years researching for my book *Human Choice in International Law*.[5] It also frames education as a political act, birthing ideas that challenge the status quo—and exposing to risk those who dare to learn and to teach. Chapter 10, "The Quest for *Humanitas*," revisits the historical origins of the principle of *humanitas* as a fundamental normative basis for world order and the law that helps secure it. The book concludes with a call to embrace the fact that eliminating global racism is fundamental to fully realizing our humanity and a reminder of an enduring reason for hope: "The Promise of Us." Along the way, *Global Racism* charts conversations among nations and leaders and families and communities, asking how the beliefs we hold within and the beliefs we spread to those around us become the ills we most fear and the hopes we most cherish.

Taking a global view of any topic has constraints. Admittedly, it isn't feasible to be inclusive of all nations in the world—not to mention the experiences of some eight billion individuals, for whom no nation can ever fully account. Weaving together lessons and insights from throughout the world and over great spans of time is necessarily an approximate task. Scholars from an array of disciplines have documented racism's harms, traced its structures, and theorized its persistence in ways that have built an extraordinary body of knowledge. Many have focused deeply on specific times, places, and contexts, yielding essential insights. This book takes a broad view, stepping back to investigate how racism travels, mutates, and persists across societies and centuries. Looking at the challenge this way reveals patterns and connections that a closer, more focused approach could not. Both approaches are necessary; I have chosen to pursue the broad view.

Many of the insights in the book are inspired by my two decades of working with globally diverse communities, including my recent experience as United Nations Legal Expert on the prevention of racial discrimination and xenophobia and as Vice Chancellor for Equity, Diversity and Inclusion for the University of California, Los Angeles. I have drawn on research and stories from various parts of the world, as well as the consensus views that emerge within the international community of nations, especially at the United Nations. I have also been inspired by my experiences with people during time spent in the Bahamas, Belize, Canada, Cyprus, Denmark, the Dominican Republic, England, Fiji, Guatemala, India, Japan, Malaysia, Mexico, the Netherlands, Paraguay, St. Croix, Sweden, Zambia, and across the United States, where I grew up. The ideas I have penned here are rooted in all of these experiences as well as in my decades of research and scholarship.[6] My ideas have been informed and inspired by the work of many scholars and authors who study racism's global dimensions.[7]

I've written this book to spark discussion and to generate dialogue about the challenge of global racism. The very act of naming global racism is a call to collective action, not only for nations but for individuals. To that end, this book is intended for a public audience. Although this book draws upon research, history and scholarship, its scope includes a broad readership. With this in mind, *Global Racism* does not attempt a comprehensive coverage of the vast research, scholarship and other books on racism from around the world throughout time. Readers will not find a comparative analysis of racism across nations or cultures or an extended analysis of racism in one nation alone. The book recognizes but does not deeply analyze other related forms of oppression based on human identity, a choice dictated by both scope and space.

Finally, on a personal note, this book has been a challenge to write. The topic is not merely one reached through research or legal analysis or history. Grappling with racism is a deeply personal endeavor for me. I have a lifetime of experiences with racism, both at home in America and in my travels around the world. Too many family members and friends have suffered as well, including my children. Racism is painful, and writing about it compounds the pain. I have not enjoyed the luxury of engaging with my subject at a dispassionate remove. Instead, writing this book has occasioned deep reflection on what I believe and what I am uncertain about, during a tumultuous period of human history. Writing during the COVID pandemic, during a resurgence in authoritarian rule, through war and genocide, and amidst economic and climate stressors that have brought humanity to the brink has been a labor.

But for all of these changes and challenges, I remain optimistic about humanity, about the promise of us. I believe in the possibility of our species, defined not only by what we have been, but by that which we resolve to become. With this intention in mind, I hope that you read this book with openness and curiosity. The most important questions do not yield easy answers, only complex human ones.

I

The Racism Question

The 1950 UNESCO First Statement on Race

In 1950, following the long end and longer sorrows of two world wars, eight eminent scientists gathered in Paris to formulate the first international response to "the great confusion on the notion of race."[1] Published under the auspices of the newly formed United Nations (UN), through its Economic, Scientific and Cultural Organization (UNESCO), *The Race Question* put the world on notice that "race is a social myth constructed by man," for all people "belong to the same species, Homo sapiens."[2] UNESCO's report, a now half-forgotten eleven-page booklet, was significant at the time because it refuted centuries of scientific racism, the belief that race was determined by nature. With it, UNESCO made clear what many had long tried to deny, that racism "directly affects millions of human lives and causes countless conflicts."

Such a bold project seemed unlikely even a few years before. During the terrible ordeals of World War II, plans began for ordering the postwar world. In 1945, the UN was born, ushering in a new era that promised peace, dignity, and equality for all nations. Yet its Charter stayed silent on the matter of racism. That was by design. The UN's "four policemen," so named by American President Franklin D. Roosevelt, consisted of the then Republic of China, the United Kingdom of Great Britain and Northern Ireland, the United States of America, and the Union of Soviet Socialist Republics. These four nations (along with France)

Global Racism. Anna Spain Bradley, Oxford University Press. © Anna Spain Bradley 2026.
DOI: 10.1093/oso/9780197778388.003.0002

would become the permanent five members of the UN's Security Council, afforded extraordinary powers in keeping with the vision that they would collectively guarantee world peace by safeguarding order within their territorial spheres of influence. At the time of the Charter's creation, these nations had domestic reasons for suppressing explicit agendas to name and address racism in the blueprint for the new world order. Japanese occupation and surrender deepened existing ethnic tension in China, which National Government Chairman Chiang Kai-shek sought to alleviate. Under Joseph Stalin, the Soviet Union had long criticized American racism while seeking to justify its own widespread use of ethnic cleansing—from the Balkans through Ukraine to the Caucasus Mountains. UK Prime Minister Winston Churchill's commitment to a "world family of Democratic Nations" did not temper his long-held belief in the inherent superiority of Anglo-Saxons and the British Empire.[3] American President Franklin D. Roosevelt, seeking to avoid the mistakes of President Wilson with the League of Nations two decades prior, was determined to ensure the Charter's ratification by the US Congress. To gain support and avoid angering certain powerful senators, he ignored the calls of many Black Americans to ensure that the United Nations decried racism and white supremacy, which remained rampant and systemic throughout America.

The choice to avoid addressing racism as a threat to international peace and security and a problem affecting world order at the founding of the United Nations in 1945 may have been viewed by some as a political necessity, but it was also a grave mistake. Racism, in one form or another, had underpinned some of the world's greatest evils, including four hundred years of the transatlantic slave trade and the institution of slavery itself, as well as the legalized horrors of colonialism and imperialism throughout Africa, the Americas, and Asia that followed. Racism had fueled the Nazi regime's ideology of racial supremacy and genocide against people identified as Jewish, Roma, Black, and anyone otherwise considered undesirable. Racism was at the root of the world's great evils—slavery, segregation, apartheid, and genocide—all banned by international law today.

Perhaps with this in mind, Mahatma Gandhi wrote to President Roosevelt in 1942 with the following admonishment: "I venture to think that the Allied declaration that the Allies are fighting to make the world safe for freedom of the individual and for democracy sounds hollow, so long as India and, for that matter, Africa are exploited by Great Britain, and America has the Negro problem in her own home."[4] Indeed, how could this new world order espouse equality for all nations and universal human rights for all peoples while disregarding the British Empire's atrocities in India, the United States' legally sanctioned segregation and violent Jim Crow racism, and the South African government's oppressive apartheid regime?

Concerns about racism troubled the United Nations from its very founding. Within the UN's first year of existence, India asked the UN General Assembly to address South Africa's racist treatment of people of Indian origin. The two-thirds majority vote needed to pass a resolution on the matter was not reached, so no official action was taken. Although many nations were uncomfortable with South African apartheid, some leaders feared that taking action on one kind of racism would open the floodgates to addressing all forms of racism. Similar thinking resulted in the omission of racism in the Universal Declaration of Human Rights, championed by American First Lady Eleanor Roosevelt, and adopted by all nations in 1948. The UN Economic and Social Council then tasked UNESCO—whose mission is to advance the cause of peace through education, science, and culture—with studying the problem.

It was within this historical context that the eight experts—hailing from Brazil, France, India, Mexico, New Zealand, and the United States—traveled to Paris to devise official UN answers to questions about the meaning of racism and its harms. Among the experts were the French Jewish anthropologist and ethnologist Claude Lévi-Strauss; African-American sociologist E. Franklin Frazier, later the author of *Black Bourgeoisie* (1957); and British-born (and American émigré) Jewish anthropologist Ashley Montagu. These men knew what racism was, for they had grown up with its ever-present harms, whether as Black, foreigner, or Jew. Together, the authors recalled UNESCO's

Constitution "that the great and terrible war which has now ended was a war made possible by the denial of the democratic principles of the dignity, equality and mutual respect of men, and by the propagation, in their place, through ignorance and prejudice, of the doctrine of the inequality of men and races."[5] This named racism as one of the root causes of World War II and the terrible suffering it wrought. Near its end, *The Race Question* issued a final, carefully worded, warning: "Racism is a particularly vicious and mean expression of the caste spirit. It involves belief in the innate and absolute superiority of an arbitrarily defined human group over other equally arbitrarily defined groups. . . . As an ideology and feeling racism is by its nature aggressive. It threatens the essential moral values by satisfying the taste for domination and by exalting the contempt for man."[6] With this, UNESCO put nations on notice that racism was not just a problem among some peoples; it was a problem for the world.

Racism Around the World Today

Even if it was disputed in 1950, today there is no doubt that racism threatens the rights and lives of hundreds of millions of people around the world. The United Nations recently reported that "among both women and men, racial discrimination, rooted in factors such as ethnicity, colour or language, is among the most common grounds" of discrimination in the world today.[7] In 2025, UNESCO published its Global Outlook on Racism and Discrimination, finding that "race accounts for 38% of reported discrimination cases globally," with sex and gender at 33 percent and ethnicity at 20 percent.[8] Of the reported cases of racism, 18 percent involved physical violence. A 2022 UN report found that one in six people around the globe had experienced some type of discrimination, with racial discrimination cited as among the most frequent.[9] UNICEF has documented similar concerns about the prevalence of racial discrimination against children, further finding that racism in childhood causes adverse impacts that last a lifetime.[10] According to the World Justice

Project Rule of Law Index, racism has gotten worse in 70 percent of all nations between 2021 and 2022, with a steady increase since 2015.[11] This rise in racism is occurring amidst an overall increase of inequality around the world and declining protections for human rights.

Regional and national data reveal similar concerns. In China, according to a 2023 Human Rights Watch report, anti-Black racism by state-sponsored TV, on the internet, and on Chinese social media platforms like Bilibili, Weibo, and Douyin is egregious and widespread.[12] Videos and image-based content show degrading anti-Black stereotypes, such as blackface and comparing Black people to animals, and condemnation of interracial relationships between Chinese women and Black men is commonplace. For a country in which the government exercises extensive control over internet use, there has been little to no acknowledgment of such racism or reforms to address it. These recent examples of contemporary racism exist in a complex context of Han-centrism in China, where the Chinese Communist Party's "Sinicization of religion" policy coercively establishes government control over religion, targeting Buddhist Tibetans, Muslim Uyghurs, and other ethnic and religious minorities.[13] In 2018, the United Nations put the Chinese government on notice that it had failed to comply with international law because it had yet to adequately define and outlaw racial discrimination under national law.[14]

Across Europe, racism remains a widespread challenge. As reported in a 2023 survey, racism manifests as "relentless and pervasive" racial discrimination in housing, employment, and healthcare; as verbal abuse and harassment; and as violence across thirteen European countries—Austria, Belgium, Denmark, Finland, France, Germany, Ireland, Italy, Luxembourg, Poland, Portugal, Spain, and Sweden. Of the 6,752 people of African descent who participated in the poll, 45 percent had experienced racial discrimination—an increase from 39 percent in 2016.[15] A 2024 report by the European Union Agency for Fundamental Rights found that 47 percent of Muslims in Europe experience racial discrimination, with the highest rates occurring in Austria, Germany, and Finland.[16] The European Commission against Racism and Intolerance has documented the surge in hate speech online, xenophobic and ultra-nationalistic politics across Europe, and an overall increase in racist hate crimes. Racist hate crimes reported to police in England and Wales reached their highest levels between 2021 and 2024, peaking at 109,843 in 2021–2022.[17]

Systemic forms of racism in policing, education, employment, and health sectors have long been a part of the public discourse in Brazil. Given Brazil's history with the extensive practice of slavery and colonialism, modern forms of racism are complex and nuanced. According to its 2022 census, 45 percent of Brazilians identify as multiracial, a category that has become the nation's new majority racial group.[18] Racism's relationship to race in Brazil is complex and closely intertwined with the nation's continued struggle with economic inequality, where the richest 1 percent account for nearly half of the nation's wealth, and gender inequality restricts women's rights.[19]

In Australia, racism causes acute and intergenerational adverse impacts for Indigenous Australians. According to a 2022 national survey of Indigenous Australians, including Torres Strait Islanders, 60 percent of participants reported experiencing racism in the form of racial prejudice within the last six months, also documenting an increase in racism since 2018.[20] One participant shared that "[j]ust being born Indigenous makes you feel second class."[21] People immigrating and migrating to Australia, whether for employment opportunities or to seek asylum, are also subjected to racism. Racism's prevalence in Australia today is linked to its colonial past. The nation's formal White Australia policy enacted by Parliament in 1901 was in effect until 1975, when the Racial Discrimination Act was passed as a landmark federal law banning discrimination on the basis of race and other categories.[22]

Racism in the United States remains pervasive. A 2022 Pew Research study found that 79 percent of Black Americans have experienced discrimination on the basis of race and/or ethnicity and report that racism is their top concern, followed by police brutality.[23] Fatal police shootings peaked at the highest recorded number of people killed in 2023 at 1,164, continuing long-standing systemic racism in policing and criminal justice.[24] Voter suppression, backed by recent changes in state law, has reduced voting rights and access for Black people as well as the elderly, students, and people with disabilities.[25] The US Congress has formally acknowledged "the growing prevalence" of "hate groups that espouse racism, extremism, xenophobia, anti-Semitism, and White supremacy" across America.[26] A 2024 Executive Summary issued by the White House documented how racism is responsible for mortality gaps and economic loss due to equity pay gaps that cost the US economy trillions of dollars annually, and racist property laws such as redlining that have barred family and intergenerational wealth.[27] By the numbers, racism is a major problem in America. This is also a widely held perception around the world. A 2021 survey found that the majority of people across fourteen nations believed that racism was most severe in America, with some survey takers also agreeing that racism was a serious problem in their society as well.[28]

This data provides a mere snapshot of the lived reality for millions of people around the world, where racism inhibits their lives, curtails their rights, and negatively impacts their health. However, these reports offer an imperfect metric for measuring racism globally. Data is not available for all nations. Even if it were, racism lacks a universal definition—meaning it often evades recognition where the vocabulary to name it is absent. For many nations and societies, racism has long been defined along a Black–white paradigm in contexts of white supremacy, slavery, and colonialism. Outside of such historical, social, and cultural contexts, some nations assert that they do not have any racism, sometimes claiming that all of their citizens are of the same race. In Russia, for example, the 2013 violence and unrest in Biryulyovo involving right-wing nationalist groups chanting "Russia for the Russians" was labeled as anti-immigrant, not as racism, even as the people targeted were othered as "illegals," "guest workers," and "Blacks."[29] In other countries, harms are not categorized as racism but variously as tribalism or being related to ethnicity, religion, and other identity factors.[30] Still, the available data makes one conclusion clear:

Racism is a problem that is global in scope. Wherever people are, racism is possible.

*

Why Is Racism Global?

Why is racism *capable* of being global? Is its prevalence a direct consequence of our globalized world, in which technology and trade connect many people in many places all at once? Or is it innate to humans and to the societies we build? To examine these questions, let's consider the following lessons from history.

A critical period in history for the study of racism concerns the rise of the transatlantic slave trade, connected to the expansion of European empires. In the fifteenth century, Portuguese traders started to expand their ventures beyond Morocco down the western coast of Africa in search of precious woods, spices, ivory, and gold to trade. They also traded enslaved peoples, taking captives of war and tapping into the trans-Saharan slave trade that had existed for centuries. The Portuguese expanded such trading practices beyond Europe across the Atlantic to modern-day Brazil, marking the beginning of what would become the transatlantic slave trade. This practice involved capturing and enslaving millions of people in various parts of Africa who were then taken to ports along the western coast of Africa before being forcibly shipped in inhumane conditions across the Atlantic Ocean in return for raw materials and manufactured goods. Those who survived the perilous journey were sentenced to a life of enslavement—a condition extended to any children they might bear. From the sixteenth century on, other European groups sought to profit by launching a race to conquer new territories and secure precious resources, even when those lands belonged to others. People indigenous to the Americas were enslaved, as were people taken from China, Japan, and elsewhere. During this period, slavery, which had long been practiced in various forms in the ancient world, became globalized into a multimillion-dollar transatlantic slave trade. The book explores this history and its role in developing ideologies of race and racial superiority used to justify the barbarism of slavery.

Another critical historical era concerns the rise of colonialism and the transition of some colonies to independent nations. Colonialism, largely through the expansion of European empires, gave way to ongoing occupations and widespread domination. Even when sovereignty was obtained by law, odious colonial practices remained. From caste systems in India to apartheid in South Africa to segregation in the United States, racism under slavery and colonialism remained a systemic feature after their formal end. Today, many of these practices and policies have been banned by nations of the world under international law. Yet the eradication of the racist societal cultures they have embedded remains a persistent challenge.

This book also considers the history of war and world order to better understand *Global Racism*. Looking at the wars of our lifetime and our grandparents' lifetimes, we learn more about racism's capacity for worldwide contamination. Wars involved the rise, conflict, and sometimes fall of various forms of governance—communism, democracy, fascism, monarchy, nationalism, and socialism have all played a role in racism's rise and, sometimes, its demise. Finally, within these historical eras we find mass ways of thinking—ideologies that fuel the powerful and those that follow them, convincing everyday people through the allure of racial superiority that their turn toward oppression is justified.

International legal history reveals further insights about how nations have and have not understood the challenge of racism. From the creation of the United Nations to the establishment of universal human rights to the negotiation of the world's first treaty banning racial discrimination, many of the debates nations have had about what racism is and how to define it remain with us today. Throughout these eras of human history, this book seeks to frame its exploration of racism as a global one. Following the wisdom laid down in 1950 by UNESCO's *The Race Question*, the book considers global racism in all of its forms: as acts of discrimination, as ideologies of racial superiority, and as a yet poorly understood phenomenon capable of spreading throughout our human ecosystem. Fundamentally, this book asks what we can learn when we examine racism globally, treating it as a challenge for the world.

To date, we have thin theoretical, empirical, and practical understandings of global racism. People and nations alike lack a universal conceptualization of what racism is and what it is not. International law has never defined racism by name or treated it as an explicit human rights violation. Racial discrimination, which is banned, is dependent on the concept of race. However, the lack of a shared global definition of race—and the fact that race is a concept without basis in human biology—hampers any global sense of its meaning. In recent years, racism has once against threatened global peace and security, yet nations remain unaligned about their obligations to prevent racism and their responsibility to protect the world from its harms.

The chapters that follow trace these eras and themes with the goal of better understanding what racism is through a global lens and considering what its persistence reveals about who we are as humanity. Developing a shared understanding of what racism is and the full extent of its harms provides the foundations for eradicating global racism. Doing so raises questions that speak to the very core of what human beings value and how we choose to live, together. It also challenges us to evolve as species, prioritizing value not through power over one another but through dignity for all. The book concludes by asking us to reevaluate that which makes us human, charting a practical path forward where racism's insidious seduction is no match for the universal desire for humanity.

2

What Is Racism?

Racism as a Word

Though the word "racism" is etymologically straightforward, its first appearance in English remains uncertain. The *Oxford English Dictionary* traces its origins to 1903, as published in the Proceedings of the 1902 20th Annual Meeting of the Lake Mohonk Conference of Friends of the Indian in New York.[1] At that conference, American Colonel Richard Henry Pratt gave an address stating that "[s]egregating any class or race of people apart from the rest of the people kills the progress of the segregated people or makes their growth very slow. Association of races and classes is necessary to destroy *racism* and classism."[2] The Conference was one of three annual gatherings hosted by twins Albert and Alfred Smiley at their Lake Mohonk vacation destination to discuss social matters of the day, concerning international arbitration and—using the language of the time—"the Indian" and "the Negro." These were forums for white men of means to conceive policies and make recommendations to the government, notably without meaningful participation from anyone identifying as Indian or Negro.[3] Paradoxically, it was at one of these gatherings in 1902 that the first known use of the word "racism" in English was documented.

Over more than a century, across continents and languages, the term "racism" has shifted shape to suit many circumstances. Commonly defined as a set of harms inflicted against people on the basis of race or

Global Racism. Anna Spain Bradley, Oxford University Press. © Anna Spain Bradley 2026.
DOI: 10.1093/oso/9780197778388.003.0003

the mindset and beliefs that support them, racism is, in its root sense, linked to the meaning of race—a notoriously slippery term in its own right, born of a biological fiction. Webster's *1947 Collegiate Dictionary* contains a definition of "racialism" as "racial prejudice, race hatred" but didn't define racism by name until 1974.[4] If you search in dictionaries today, racism is variously defined as "a belief or doctrine that inherent differences among the various human racial groups determine cultural or individual achievement, usually involving the idea that one's own race is superior and has the right to dominate others or that a particular racial group is inferior to the others" or as "a belief that race is a fundamental determinant of human traits and capacities and that racial differences produce an inherent superiority of a particular race."[5] Its usage has become commonplace in many parts of the world, and the word exists in other languages, appearing variously as 种族主义, 种族歧视, and 种族迫害 in Simplified Chinese; नस्लवाद in Hindi; okāàbụ̀rụ̀ in Igbo, and racismo in Spanish.[6]

This usage reveals two fundamental meanings associated with the word "racism." The first is a description of the deplorable kinds of harms done to people based on their race. The second is a description of the beliefs, feelings, or ideologies people have about the inherent superiority of some races over others and of antagonistic hatred or prejudice against people because of their race. Thus, racism conceptualizes both an outward-facing set of harms done to others and an inner set of emotions and beliefs rooted in ideologies of racial supremacy.

Racism and the Concept of Race

Racism is linked to the concept of race.[7] From a scientific perspective, the idea of race being rooted in our biology is a fiction. Every person alive today is a member of the same species, *homo sapiens*, descended from the same modern human ancestors who emerged some sixty thousand years ago, capable of complex language, spiritual beliefs, social organization, and technological discoveries. Humans are not born into some grouping of subspecies conceptualized as a race. Though it is true that each of us inherits our DNA from our parents and ancestors and that DNA dictates much about our physical traits and appearance, such traits are not categorizable into distinct groups of human races as a matter of biology. Race isn't real in the biological sense, a fact recognized by scientific communities around the world.

However, in certain countries and cultures, race is a social construct and, sometimes, a legal one. The United States Census Form, for example, has listed race as a form of group identification since 1790. The 2020 Census Form provided the following categories for race, in this order: white; Black or African American; American Indian or Alaska Native; Chinese; Filipino; Asian Indian; Other Asian; Vietnamese; Korean; Japanese; Native Hawaiian; Samoan; Chamorro; Other Pacific Islander; and Some Other Race.[8] "Hispanic," designated to include Spanish and Latino origins, is not listed as a race, but as its own category.

This approach makes problematic assumptions about identity. For instance, it conflates ancestry with race—assuming that if your family hails from Vietnam, you must be Vietnamese in a racial sense. It mixes nationality with racial groups, taking "Korean," for instance, to mean a race as well as a nationality. Its hyperspecificity when it comes to certain identities ("Chamorro; Native Hawaiian; Samoan . . .") only underscores its lack of specificity on others (e.g., white). The form is full of problematic presumptions, listing people with ancestry from Jamaica, a nation that boasts great diversity, as racially Black by default. Africa, a continent home to a vast array of diverse human identity groups, is presumed to correlate with Black as a racial category. The form asks people identifying as American Indian or Alaska Native to print the name of the enrolled or principal tribe or tribes, yet not all tribes have been enrolled or federally recognized. It does not provide an explicit recognition of indigenous identity from most other parts of the world. It doesn't recognize identities where a person is from a group that extends beyond one nation or is migratory, such as the Hazda or Nenets. The result is a legally sanctioned matrix of race and identity that is intrinsically incoherent and deeply problematic.

The taxonomy of race in other nations naturally differs in name, purpose, and practice. Zambia's census form, for example, does not ask about race, ethnicity, or tribal identity. The Census of Population and Housing has collected personal information on age, marital status, ethnicity, economic activity, education, and health data.[9] Zambia is home to over seventy distinct groups, including Bemba, Lozi, Ngoni, and Nsenga. When I lived there in the early 2000s, I saw that people noted their group differences, sometimes through jokes and stereotypes. Many also identified through their national identity as Zambian, perhaps a feature of Zambia's first president Kenneth Kaunda's "One Zambia, One Nation" campaign.

Japan's 2020 Census Form, as translated into English, does not mention race and asks only for one's nationality, offering one option for Japan and one option for Others, with room to write in the name of the country. Tellingly, it also asks where you lived five years ago, offering Outside of Japan as an option.

Questions often arise about the difference between race and ethnicity in this regard. Ethnicity is a concept used to describe group identity rooted in social, cultural, and language connections. In Fiji, for example, the major government-recognized ethnic groups are iTaukei, Indo-Fijian, and Rotuman.[10] Ethnicity conceptualizes shared group identity, something that has always been important to our species. A sense of one's individual identity often relies on affiliation with a distinct group rather than with the human whole.

However, attributing a person's group identity based on how they look or where they are from is an inherently flawed approach, especially in our increasingly globalized world in which people move far away from their ancestral home, giving rise to new generations with layered identities. Many people do not identify in ways that align with the category or concept of race. Colonialization has also disrupted and erased many group identities forcing divergent nationalities upon groups that share common bonds. For example, the people of the Tohono O'odham Nation have lived for generations on territorial and ancestral lands that are now divided by the U.S.–Mexican border.

Defining racism as linked to the meaning of the root word "race" poses obvious challenges, especially in the global context.[11] Race is a social construct, created and perpetuated to sort individuals into groups based on perceived differences. When people attach fixed value and hierarchy to those differences, racism is born. People are often racialized—a process sociologists describe as defining people according to race. Other aspects of identity intersect with race and racialization, including nationality, ancestry, ethnicity, language, and place of birth. Both governments and individuals often assume that race can be determined by how a person looks or by where they or their ancestors came from. These are just some of the ways our world constructs race into reality, even though science confirms race as a biological myth.

Race is thus a constructed concept—a biological fiction still assigned to people at birth, whether by law, by culture, or both. As a result, race as identity becomes a lived experience, shaped by geography, context, and time. For some, it is immutable: assigned at birth and unchangeable. For others, it is more fluid, shifting by virtue of economic or social means or migration to another part of the world. When the constructed nature of race bumps up against people's unassailable experience of racism, theory and lived experience diverge, complicating easy definitions of both "race" and "racism." In these moments, race and racism manifest themselves as both unstable constructs and ubiquitous realities.

In recent years, racism has increasingly been described through the lens of the racial identity of those experiencing the harm, as in anti-Asian racism and anti-Black racism. Harder questions arise when we try to describe racism directed at people who are not, or are not always, defined along racial lines, or against people who do not consider their group identity to involve race. Examples include people who identify as indigenous; groups defined by shared language and culture, such as Hispanic or Latino/a/x; those defined by common descent, such as Arab, Romani, or Tajik; and those with identities rooted in religion and ethnicity, who might be subjected to antisemitism, anti-Sikh bias, Hinduphobia, or Islamophobia. Indeed, racism can itself act as the catalyst for societal creation of "races" by lumping people of various identities into a targeted racial group.

Racism by Type

Racism is frequently categorized in one of five ways. First, it can be internal, which theories on explicit and implicit bias seek to explain. Second, it can be interpersonal, arising when a person or a group harms another. Third, it can operate within organizations as institutional racism, embedded in the policies and practices of workplaces, schools, and other entities. Fourth, it can manifest as structural racism, such as with redlining—the policy of restrictive racial covenants governing who can buy property in a particular neighborhood. Fifth, racism can take a systemic form, advancing beyond any single institution to pervade an entire system. Well-known examples of systemic racism include its virulence in the medical profession and within healthcare, in policing and criminal justice, and in the legal system. High maternal mortality rates among Black and Latina mothers and widespread imposition of harsher prison sentences based on race are but two current examples.

There are other forms of racism this book seeks to better understand. Racism can be embedded within the power centers of a nation or its government. This state-based or governance-driven racism includes systems founded on apartheid, caste, colonialism, and segregation. Such racist governing bodies enjoy the amplifying factors of social capital, legal authority, and military powers. Racism also occurs between nations, across nations, and globally. Examples include the transatlantic slave trade and colonialism—both global in scope and lasting for centuries—as well as South Africa's apartheid and the US system of segregation, which were legal until international law evolved to deem them otherwise.

Racism can be embedded within ethnic nationalism. Groups seeking to create a nation-state based on a shared ethnic identity are commonplace in human history. But when such groups become exclusionary, practicing identity-based membership, the dangers of racism can emerge.

Racism is also defined at times by the ideology of those advancing it, like Nazism. Such ideological racism seeks to justify and advance a racist worldview. What, for instance, motivates the Ku Klux Klan or the Aryan Brotherhood? Their ideologies are founded on a specious mythology of white supremacy. As a consequence, the US government has designated these two groups as white supremacist gangs.[12] Concerningly, as of 2024 the Southern Poverty Law Center has identified 110 active white nationalist groups in the United States.[13] Crimes like those committed by Anders Breivik, who murdered seventy-seven people at a summer camp in Norway in 2011; Brenton Tarrant, who attacked two mosques, murdering fifty-one people in Christchurch, New Zealand in 2019; and Patrick Crusius, who murdered twenty-three people at a Wal-Mart in El Paso, Texas in 2012 have been given a new label: *white supremacist terrorism*. This label seeks to categorize a complex set of harms comprised of acts of criminal violence motivated by racist ideologies rooted in white supremacy.[14]

Numbers are essential in telling the story of global racism. Equally important, though, are the testimonies of individuals across time, place, and culture. Both inductive and deductive approaches are needed when giving a definition to such a far-reaching concept. In that spirit, what follows is a series of accounts of racism from specific places around the world. Together, they provide a human-centric view that statistics alone might otherwise obscure.

Racism Around the World

Albania

In 2018, Albania authorities denied allegations of widespread racial discrimination against Albanian Roma and Balkan Egyptian communitites, including segregated schools.[15] Yet, in 2024, the UN body responsible for monitoring racial discrimination, the Committee on the Elimination of Racial Discrimination, determined that widespread structural racial discrimination was indeed occurring in Albania.[16] This finding followed an earlier European Court of Human Rights decision determining that Albania had violated the European Convention on Human Rights because it had failed to desegregate an elementary school in Korça, where 99 percent of the students identified as Roma or Balkan Egyptian.[17] Parents reported how poor the quality of education was at the school. Children enrolled there lagged behind their peers at other schools, and some children demonstrated particularly poor reading and writing skills. The UN recommended that Albania work to address the root causes of racial discrimination and segregation in their education system to ensure that all children enjoyed equal opportunities to access quality education. They also called upon Albania to improve access to birth registration and identity documents for Roma and Balkan Egyptians—as well as other minority groups, migrants, refugees, and asylum seekers—to prevent statelessness.

Australia

Late one summer, two teenagers, Ash and Tai, went shopping at the sporting goods store in Victoria, Australia.[18] The store was large and carried all manner of equipment students needed for school sports, from basketballs to swimming goggles. Ash and Tai, accompanied by their guardian, were excited to select just the right cricket bats for the new season. They made their purchase, and the store clerk put the items into bags. On their way out of the store, the security guard stopped them for a bag search without explanation. Ash and Tai's guardian reported the incident to the store manager, who stated that without CCTV footage there was nothing to be done. The guardian later reported the incident to Australia's Victorian Equal Opportunity and Human Rights Commission. She recalled, "[a]s we were leaving, the security guard deliberately singled Ash and Tia out for a bag search. He wasn't stopping anyone else, and I just knew that the only reason he stopped them was because they're Aboriginal." The Commission determined that the incident violated the law, which prohibits discrimination or harassment on the basis of race. The store manager agreed to conciliation with Ash and Tai and their guardian. The outcome: The store manager paid compensation, provided a written apology, and committed to having himself and his team participate in cultural awareness training.

China

In 2019, the *New York Times* reported that the Chinese government used artificial intelligence and facial recognition technology to racially profile, monitor, and locate people of Uyghur identity, screening residents 500,000 times in Sanmenxia, for example.[19] China's mistreatment of people of non-Han backgrounds, especially against Uyghur people, is widespread and well-documented. The harms include arbitrary detention, harsh sentences without due process, and secret abductions. Yet the government has long denied that racism exists in China. In 1987, the leader of the People's Republic of China, Deng Xiaoping, declared that "since New China was founded in 1949, there has never been any ethnic discrimination in the country." In 1988, former general secretary of the Communist Party of China, Zhao Ziyang, similarly claimed that racism is common "everywhere in the world except China."

Denmark

In 2018, Denmark launched a self-described set of "Ghetto Package" policies to reduce the number of people and family housing units in certain residential zones.[20] The program has demolished, sold, and caused evictions of thousands of homes and has mandatorily displaced families. The criteria for demolition applied to common family housing units with more than one thousand people in which 50 percent or more of the residents are immigrants from non-Western countries. It also included their descendants, even those born in Denmark. In 2020, twelve people living in the Mjolnerparken housing complex brought the first legal case against the Danish Ministry of Transport and Housing, alleging state-based racial discrimination in violation of

European Union Law and the EU Convention on Human Rights after they faced eviction. According to the group's lawyer, Eddie Khawaja, "[t]hey feel offended by the fact that in everyday speech, in legislation, in all the political proposals that surround this, they have been referred to as residents of ghetto areas." The controversial law categorizes people into groups. The category of "non-Western" can include people born in Denmark whose parents were from certain countries. Australia and New Zealand were not considered non-Western despite their geographical location, and refugees from Ukraine were also not treated as "non-Western." In December 2025, the European Court of Justice issued a preliminary ruling that Denmark's legislation may violate EU antidiscrimination laws.[21]

Guam

Early human settlement on the island nation of Guam in the Mariana Islands dates to 1500 BC.[22] Their descendants, the CHamoru, continue to live in Guam today. An unincorporated territory of the United States, Guam is governed by the US Constitution and local law. According to Guam's Public Law 25-106, people who are native inhabitants enjoy the right to join the Guam Decolonization Registry, which allows members to vote in matters regarding the island's future political status. In late 2011, Arnold Davis, an American resident of Guam, sued the government of Guam on the grounds that his inability to join the Registry was a violation of his Fifth, Fourteenth and Fifteenth amendment rights under the US Constitution because his exclusion from participation in political activities based on his status as a non-native inhabitant was an impermissible form of discrimination under US law. Guam's counterargument was that the Decolonization Registry and Guam Public Law was a remedy to restore rights taken away from native inhabitants and that the category of "native inhabitant" is open to various ethnic groups, not exclusively to the CHamoru, and is not explicitly race-based. In deciding this case, the courts grappled with the question of whether the CHamoru identity is a race. The US district court ruled in favor of Davis, finding that the Guam Public Law was unconstitutional, as the definition of "native inhabitant" violated the Fourteenth and Fifteenth amendments. The Ninth Circuit Court of Appeals affirmed the lower court's decision in 2019. In 2024, the governor of Guam, Lou Leone Guerrero, asked Guam Attorney General Douglas Moylan to investigate the possibility of creating a legal definition of "Native Inhabitants of Guam" that would allow for the continuation of the Public Law but would not violate the US Constitution. Attorney General Moylan's legal opinion was that "Native Inhabitants of Guam" cannot be redefined in a manner consistent with the requirements of the United States Constitution."[23]

Japan

On January 29, 2024, Maurice, Syed Zain, and Matthew filed the first-ever racial profiling lawsuit against the Japanese government, alleging they were targeted for racial profiling involving arbitrary policy stops, searches, and harassment by the police.[24] Matthew, for example, alleges he has been stopped and questioned by the police at least seventy times since he came to Japan in 2002. All three plaintiffs were foreign-born Japanese residents of different racial and ethnic backgrounds: African-American, Pakistani, and Indian, respectively. Though not citizens of Japan, they are legal permanent residents. Racial profiling by the police is on the rise in Japan, with a 2022 survey documenting that almost 63 percent of foreigners have experienced it. The case raises critical questions for a nation where 98 percent of the population identifies as Yamato. Xenophobia against foreigners is commonplace, as are preferences toward white skin deemed to be "pure" or Junketsu. Japan does not have a criminal law prohibiting racism and discrimination. However, the Japanese Constitution, under Article 14, does guarantee equality under the law. Certain distinctions against foreigners are legally permissible based on their lack of citizenship or nationality. This case raises legal questions for Japan about what racism is and whether the nation's laws will deem it illegal. As of this writing, the case is ongoing.

United States

> "I'm Mexican but was adopted by an all-white family in a white community. I don't speak any Spanish and nobody would know I was Mexican unless they looked carefully. When I married a white man, I never talked about my heritage with my in-laws, so they may have assumed I was just a very tan white person. One day driving home with my husband and sister-in-law, we saw a black woman being pulled over. Immediately the race jokes began. My husband looked his sister in the eye and asked, 'Are you a racist? Why would you say that?' She responded that she was and hated all people of color. It was her right to be racist. I remember my husband yelling at her. I remember feeling my body shake as I realized the family I married into hated me. I remember saying that if she ever spoke like that in the future, I wouldn't give her the opportunity again. But most of all I remember feeling sick. My whole life people assumed I was white, but I wasn't. I'd been living a lie. And now my in-laws knew I wasn't white. I knew they wouldn't like me now. It's troubling, to say the least. Now at family gatherings I can't help but feel insecure. I know nobody will forget that day in the car—the day they realized I wasn't one of them. But today . . . I'm proud. I'm proud to be Mexican. Sometimes I'm thankful for that night. I'm thankful because it allowed me to come out and be proud of who I am regardless of what some might think."
>
> —Anonymous, as reported to *The Atlantic*[25]

Uruguay

In May 2024, the Futbol Club Miramar Misiones faced a tough match against Liverpool Fútbol Club. They ultimately prevailed 2–1.[26] In the final minutes of the game, referee Javier Feres sent a player from Miramar Misiones off the field. Manager Ricardo Caruso Lombardi took issue with the ejection and called Feres a "negro de mierda," or "Black piece of shit." The incident was recorded on video, and it quickly spread on social media. The Uruguayan Football Association sanctioned Lombardi, who later resigned and made a public apology to Feres. He was also investigated by public prosecutors for incitement to hatred, which was later dropped. A national debate ensued in a country where Uruguayans of African descent are a minority group, constituting less than 5 percent of the overall population, along with the 3 percent of people of indigenous descent.

*

These stories articulate various forms of racism and its harms. Some are the firsthand accounts of people who have experienced racism caused by other people, institutions, and systems. Other stories reveal state-sponsored forms of racism. Whatever racism is, it is intrinsically tied to our human experience. Anyone who has experienced racism knows what racism is because they have lived it. Here, two central aspects emerge. Racism harms through its acts of violence and discrimination that violate people's lives and rights. But racism, through its ideology, also harms people's dignity.

But it is harder and, indeed, riskier to try to objectively assess and judge if what happened to someone else qualifies as racism or not. In places that ban racism by law, the harm is most often defined as racial discrimination. Here, one must have the evidence to prove to a court that there was a harm done with disparate treatment or disparate impact on the basis of race, ethnicity, and/or color. Of course, these categories of human identity differ greatly by country. What is seen as race in one country might be viewed as ethnicity elsewhere, or as a combination of hard-to-describe traits that include ancestry and culture. As between nations, what constitutes an unlawful action in one place does not necessarily transfer to another place. Ash and Tai in Victoria, Australia, had protections under a local law that the victims of racism in Japan did not. Even more concerning, some countries have denied that racism is a problem in their land and have claimed that all of their people are of the same race. Without a universal definition, can we say what is and what is not racism?

This Is Racism: Consensus and Collective Acknowledgment

Consider one last story about racism.

> This Negro soldier was sitting on a seat opposite to a white man. The bus was not crowded, and he wasn't sitting in front of any white. But the driver came back and told him to move. He refused. The driver shouted, "I'm gonna move you." The Negro took his coat off and said, "Well I'm fixing to go off and fight for democracy, I might as well start right now." And I want to tell you that bus driver backed down. It did me good to see it.[27]

The year was 1942. Stories like this one, recorded by the Black American poet and essayist Sterling A. Brown in "From Massachusetts to Mississippi," reveal real-life experiences of racism in America, told from the perspectives of Black people suffering the harms and white people witnessing it. Racism violates the right to life. After slavery, which killed an estimated four million people and cost many more their freedom, formally ended the inhumane practice of lynching intensified, particularly throughout the South. Between 1877 and 1950, documentation shows that at least 4,075 Black people were lynched, publicly murdered by a violent mobs.[28]

The inhumanity of these horrors lives on in James Cone's documentation of Mary Turner, who was "stripped, hung upside down by the ankles, soaked with gasoline, and roasted to death. In the midst of this torment a white man opened her swollen belly with a hunting knife and her infant fell to the ground and was stomped to death."[29] The inhumanity lives on in the remnants the two-day-long Tulsa Race Massacre of 1921, a coordinated act of white supremacist terrorism against Black communities, erasing generational prosperity, economic wealth, and culture along with the dream of racial equality. The inhumanity lives on in the untold victims of racism's wrath and their descendants who remember their pain.

Such harms are undeniable. People were murdered, a crime in its own right, and their human rights were violated. What, then, makes these violations racism as well? Simply put, the answer is collective acknowledgment and consensus. In America, there is widespread acknowledgment—backed by law—of the egregious crimes of the past committed by white people against Black people, rooted in slavery and entrenched during segregation. We name these crimes as racism. A white person calling a Black person the n-word with animus is interpersonal racism. A company categorically failing to promote any of its Black workers is institutional racism. A racial wealth gap where the average white family holds $184,000 in wealth as compared to $38,000 for Latino families and only $23,000 for Black families, with little to no change in two decades, is systemic racism.[30] The American Bar Association has estimated, for example, that racism and related oppression have caused a $14 trillion loss in wealth for Black Americans.[31]

Of course, racism's harms are not limited to Black people. Racist tropes in movies against Japanese and Chinese people, or naming a professional football team the "Redskins," are now widely acknowledged as outmoded and racist—evidence that the old ways should not become the new ways. But, racism in America has been largely defined through a process of cultural acculturation and legal acknowledgment—consensus forged through society's collective imagination solidified into law. Such understandings are rooted in a historical context. America's history of slavery, followed by segregation, is marked by a period of over four hundred years of racist ideologies. America's history of settler colonialism and genocide against various Native American and other Indigenous groups is marked by a period of over four hundred years of racist ideologies. Racism became an overt manifestation of the deeper evil of white supremacy, normalized by so many for too long. America's shared history, documented by the Civil Rights Movement, reflected in changes to the law and cemented in landmark human rights cases by the Supreme Court such as *Korematsu v. United States* (1944), overturning the legality of wartime internment camps of Japanese-Americans, and *Brown v. Board of Education* (1954), overturning the legality of segregation in schools, helped cement some consensus about what racism is and how it harms. The sins of the past have shaped today's narratives of racism in America, grounding them in both history and collective acknowledgment. Beyond the American white–Black context, however, there is much less certainty about what racism is and what it is not.

*

Different Histories, One Global Challenge

Globally, we lack a similar legal–cultural acculturation history. We lack shared consensus about what racism is and the full extent of its harms, despite the fact of racism's global reach.

There are, however, notable exceptions. Alongside segregation, apartheid as practiced in South Africa is a named form of racial discrimination in the treaty that calls for its elimination. Antisemitism, fueled by Nazi Germany's ideological hatred against and genocide of Jewish people, is recognized as a form of both religious and racial discrimination. These three specific ills—segregation, apartheid, and genocide—are all recognized as illegal under international law because they violate fundamental norms so essential to the international community that they cannot be allowed by any nation. In international law, we give this idea the Latin name *jus cogens*.

The centuries of slavery and the transatlantic slave trade also gave rise to wide recognition of the racial caste systems that existed in British, Dutch, French, Portuguese, and Spanish colonies around the world. Brazil, the territory that received the largest number of enslaved peoples and where the terrors of slavery were particularly egregious, is recognized alongside the United States for its present-day struggles with racism. Here, we see the makings of a pattern. Where human suffering is great and sometimes, but not always, long, consensus tends to form in the aftermath about the evils that must not stand.

For the global community, the consensus about what is and what is not racism tends to end here. We are left with a patchwork of coexisting but unorganized truths. Through international law, nations have outlawed slavery, genocide, and racial discrimination in the forms of apartheid and segregation. Nations are obligated to prevent such harms from occurring in their own domains, enacting laws, policies, and educational campaigns within their borders to provide equal protection, regardless of race. Many of racism's most serious harms would be banned anyway as crimes or as human rights violations. Discrimination "on the basis of a person's race" is also prohibited. Beyond this, however, we lack a global consensus about the fundamentals.

Linking the meaning of racism to discrimination on the basis of race is problematic when we start to travel around the world. The construct simply doesn't hold. Take a nation like Russia, which has declared that there is no racism among its citizens because Russians belong to the same race. Or consider Fiji, Tonga, and Samoa, each with its distinct culture forged over thousands of years, where waves of earlier human travelers arrived in succession. Today's ancestors of those earlier peoples do not fit into the constructed categories of race that include white, Black, or Asian. The same is true for the many people of the world like me whose parents are of different races.

This construct of racism that relies on race is challenged by the vast diversity in our human species. It leaves little room for racism to be recognized in cultures or countries where race is not acknowledged as a group identity in the public imagination, in government practice, or in the law. This construct often obfuscates how racism can be waged by one person against another who is deemed to be of the same race. It also struggles to recognize racism built into the very design of our institutions and societal systems. It fails to account for the ways that governments weaponize racism or seek to justify it by labeling a person a terrorist or invoking the need to protect national security.

Answering the question of racism is a task for the world and humanity to take up together. The following chapters dive into its history, tracing the contours of racism, international law, and world order over the past several centuries through today. Along the way, there are glimmers of consensus among nations and peoples about what racism is, what it is not, and how it harms humanity. These glimmers are revealed most clearly in moments of immense and widespread suffering.

3

An Old Enemy

Pope Urban II's Call to Arms

In November 1095, Pope Urban II issued a dispatch, calling on cardinals, archbishops, and bishops to gather at the Council of Clermont in what were then territories under Frankish rule. After enacting various religious decrees and settling some local disputes, Pope Urban gave the speech that would launch the First Crusade. He called upon the Frankish people, nobles and serfs alike, to take up arms against the Seljuk Empire "to destroy that vile race from the lands of our friends. . . . Christ commands it. . . . O what a disgrace if such a despised and base race, which worships demons, should conquer a people which has the faith of omnipotent God. Let those who have been accustomed unjustly to wage private warfare against the faithful now go against the infidels and end with victory this war which should have been begun long ago."[1] In those days, the Seljuk Empire controlled Jerusalem, spreading Islam along with Turkish and Persian culture throughout the region. The Seljuks were adversaries of the Byzantine Empire, viewed as a threat to its Christian rule.

Pope Urban II's command was not only a call to arms but also a declaration to defend Christianity itself. He had to convince the Frankish people to stop fighting one another, an ongoing reality in those days, and instead turn their ire against a people far away whom they had never met. To do so, he ideologized Frankish Christians as inherently superior to the people of the Seljuk Empire, whom he reimagined as foreigners

Global Racism. Anna Spain Bradley, Oxford University Press. © Anna Spain Bradley 2026.
DOI: 10.1093/oso/9780197778388.003.0004

from a vile and despised race, less than human and unworthy of life itself. The First Crusade led to eight more, ending with the Ninth Crusade of 1271–1272 before that era of history would give way to another. In all, anywhere between one million and nine million people are believed to have died during those wars. Christians lost Jerusalem and the region, but Pope Urban II ensured that an ideology of racial superiority lived on.

*

From Gods to Kings to the Rule of Law

Long before history recalls Pope Urban II and the era of the Crusades, earlier civilizations had waged bloody wars and had forged means to mitigate their inhumanity. In Ancient Egypt, for example, there were early restrictions on the use of force in war. Considered one of the first peace treaties, the Treaty of Kadesh, forged around 1259 BC, helped end a long conflict between the Egyptians and the Hittites by defining borders, returning prisoners of war, and forging agreements for friendly relations and mutual defense.[2] More than three thousand years later, peace treaties still follow this blueprint.

In Ancient Greece, the virtue of *philanthropia*, "to love mankind," was demonstrated through kindness and service to the greater good.[3] Myths hold that this kind of love inspired Prometheus to steal fire from the gods to help humankind.

Roman law introduced the concept of *humanitas*, defined as "the human tendency as an ethical commandment, benevolent consideration for others."[4] Cicero argued that *humanitas* was a key quality of an ideal leader, admonishing that "if fate had given you authority over Africans or Spaniards or Gauls, wild and barbarous nations, you would still owe it to your *humanitas* to be concerned about their comforts, their needs, and their safety."[5] In fifth-century BC China, Confucius introduced the idea of humanity through the virtue of Ren 仁, "to love the people," as humaneness and benevolence to others.[6]

Such values, virtues, and ideals have been present throughout human history. They would be tested in new ways at the dawn of the Age of Enlightenment, following centuries of religious conflict, political fragmentation, and social upheaval that had marked the post-Roman Middle Ages. From 1618 to 1648, a devastating era of war known as the Thirty Years' War spread throughout Central Europe, following the earlier Eighty Years' War, which began in 1568. Both arose from ongoing religious and political conflicts within the Holy Roman Empire and beyond, fueled by the fragmentation that followed Martin Luther's Protestant Reformation in the early sixteenth century. Driven by their naval powers and an unrelenting thirst for wealth, Portugal—soon followed by Spain, France, the Netherlands, and England—began a long period of European colonization that would eventually extend across much of the world. It was an era of destruction, death, and a global reordering of power on a massive scale. It is in these tumultuous years that some historians locate the origins of international law.

In 1625, a Dutch jurist named Huig de Groot, or Hugo Grotius, published his now-famous treatise, *On the Laws of War and Peace*.[7] Having lived through extreme and widespread violence, Grotius believed that war should have limits, delineated and enforced through law.[8] He was also concerned about the lack of *humanitas*. Grotius wrote "[f]ully convinced, by the considerations which I have advanced, that there is a common law among nations, which is valid alike for war and in war, I have had many and weighty reasons for undertaking to write upon the subject. Throughout the Christian world I observed a lack of restraint in relation to war, such as even barbarous races should be ashamed of."[9] Published when Grotius was forty-two, his book was read widely in Europe and would influence intellectual thought, political theory, and philosophy for generations. Many scholars attribute this "Grotian Moment" as a paradigmatic shift in Europe about war, law, and humanity, although such temperance was not widely applied by European nations in their colonial endeavors elsewhere.

Grotius's ideals were noble, but not without compromise. As an attorney before the Dutch courts early in his career, Grotius once argued that his client and cousin, Captain Van Heemskerck, was legally right in waging war against Portuguese ships in order to protect his own ship and crew.[10] He defended this assertion of right to private war, in part, by characterizing Portuguese traders as brutish and uncivilized in their murderous treatment of the Indigenous peoples of Indonesia.[11] According to Grotius, his cousin's seizure of a Portuguese trading vessel was not only legally permissible but morally defensible in its alleged protection of the Indigenous people from Portuguese atrocities.[12] Yet Grotius's concern about atrocities seems not to have extended to his cousin Van Heemskerck's own engagement in holding captives aboard his ships, purportedly for purposes of slave trading.[13] Slavery and the transatlantic slave trade would prove a consistent challenge to the emerging world order, where the early principles of international law and human rights would not extend to protections for enslaved peoples and victims of European colonization.

While Grotius laid the philosophical groundwork for certain nations to wage war more humanely, the reality of Europe's wars and empires complicated that vision. Back in Europe, with an estimated eight million people dead, a landmark series of treaties forming The Peace of Westphalia brought an end to both the Eighty Years' War and the Thirty Years' War in 1648.[14] Negotiated over several years between various delegations representing the Imperial Estates of the Holy Roman Empire and Spain, Switzerland, the Netherlands, France, and other nations, the resulting treaties formed the first pan-European peace agreement. This agreement called for a "Christian and Universal Peace" and introduced a new concept that would become the foundation of world order, the concept of state sovereignty.[15] The doctrine of sovereignty shifted the authority to rule over dominions, peoples, and lands from the ruler, a king, or the Holy Roman Emperor to a nation-state. This was a paradigmatic new way of thinking. The authority, legitimacy, and power to rule were reimagined, originating not through the divine right of a king but emanating from the state, which was now entitled to rule over its domain, territory, and subjects without external interference in its internal affairs. As sovereigns, states now had the authority to determine the religion of their domain under the principle *cuius regio, euis religio* "whose realm, his religion." Of course, strife for religious freedom had only just begun, as people sought the freedom to be Protestant in Catholic domains or to be Catholic in Protestant domains. But these treaties and the ideas they cemented marked the start of a new order for certain European monarchies and empires of the day, establishing a principle of Westphalian sovereignty as the foundation for the Law of Nations and international law that followed.[16]

Even as a recourse toward *humanitas* was taking shape in Europe, European powers were far less willing to extend such virtues to peoples in other parts of the world. The practice of enslaving people, particularly as spoils of war, had long been practiced in many parts of the world. Due to their naval prowess, the Portuguese excelled at exploration by sea, traveling along the coast of West Africa and the Canary Islands. The search for gold in West Africa led to slave trading by sea, competing with the longer-established trans-Saharan trade routes. One record from 1442 documents the purchase of enslaved peoples by a Portuguese trader named Antão Gonçalves, who traveled past Cabo Branco near the Bay of Arguin in present-day Mauritania. There, he reportedly traded for gold dust, salt, ostrich eggs, and ten people described as Black Africans presented to him by an "Arab mounted on a white camel," as a gift for Portuguese Prince, Henry the Navigator.[17] Within the century, the increased demand for enslaved people from West Africa by prominent Portuguese families in exchange for cloth, silver, and grain became a system, all before Christopher Columbus sailed across the Atlantic in 1492.

By the 1500s, Portugal and Spain had established a system of trading goods for enslaved peoples from West Africa across the ocean to their new domains and colonies. This system would last for nearly four hundred years. All told, it is estimated that close to two million people perished during the Middle Passage alone. The opportunity for European nations to colonize unfamiliar lands and take dominion over new resources would fundamentally shape world order, international law, and the disparities in who was—and was not—entitled to the rights those systems purported to uphold.

Early on, there were concerns regarding the violent practices of enslaving Indigenous peoples in the Americas and, later, the emerging transatlantic slave trade. In the early 1500s, Pope Leo X stated, "[N]ot only the Christian religion but nature herself cried out against a state of slavery," and Pope Paul III proclaimed the abolition of slavery in the *Veritas Ipsa*.[18] In 1554, Portuguese Dominican friar and explorer Fernando de Oliveira denounced Portuguese slaving practices as "such an evil trade" as the "buying and selling of peaceable freemen as one buys and sells animals" in his book, *Art of War at Sea*.[19] A Spanish Dominican priest named Fray Domingo de Soto published *Ten Books on Justice and Law* in 1557, arguing that slavery was immoral and wrong.[20] However, the economic benefits the new colonies took advantage of would soon overwhelm any efforts to constrain slavery.

By the late 1600s, the slave trade had become internationalized, with the English and the Dutch overtaking the trade initiated by Portugal and Spain. The profits to be found in the sugar market alone drove an insatiable greed for unregulated trade in slave labor. The inhumanity of it all grew too, requiring an ideology that could justify atrocities within the doctrines of Christianity and Islam. People were no longer simply enslaved as prisoners of war or spoils of war. They were transformed from people into property. In the lands of what is now Peru, a Dominican friar, Fray Francisco de la Cruz, gave testimony to the Inquisition in Lima that an angel of God revealed to him that "the blacks are justly captives by reason of the sins of their forefathers, and that because of that sin God gave them that color."[21]

The practice of enslaving humans intensified over the next century. In 1607, the Virginia Colony was founded in Jamestown. In 1619, two private English ships, the *White Lion* and the *Treasurer*, arrived with much-needed supplies for the seven hundred colonists. Those ships also carried the first recorded enslaved Africans in North America.[22] Around twenty people, believed to originate from the Kongo and Ndogno kingdoms, were traded for goods. They are believed to be the survivors of some sixty people taken by force near Mexico from a Portuguese slave ship named *San Juan Bautista*. Several years later, a boy named William, born to Antonio and Isabella, who were among the twenty, would become the first known child of African descent born in America, free under the laws of the colony.

Almost a century later, blatant and brutal slave trading across the Atlantic gave way to an international system of slavery that spread across the new colonies in the Americas. An estimated twelve million children, women, and men were taken from Africa. Of those who survived the horrific Middle Passage, around five million were enslaved in Brazil, over three million were enslaved in the Caribbean, and about four hundred thousand were enslaved in the British colonies of North America.[23] Back in Virginia, laws were enacted to create an infrastructure to support slavery and protect slaveholders' interests. By 1660, Virginia enacted slave codes naming enslaved Africans as chattel, with no rights as subjects of the British Crown or in personhood. By 1662, a Virginia court established hereditary slavery, ruling that any child born to an enslaved mother became enslaved by birth as the property of the mother's slaveholder.[24]

Other British colonies, as well as French, Portuguese, and Spanish colonies, adopted various legal, economic, and cultural approaches designed to justify and maintain systems of slavery.[25] Many of the new colonists had themselves sought refuge from persecution, often religious and sometimes ethnic, across the sea. This did not stop many from adopting persecution against enslaved peoples and those whose lands they occupied, using law as their tool.

Rights, Liberties, and Freedom for Some

But, as is true in the course of human history, ideas spread. By 1775, a war for independence was underway in America, where British subjects sought a democracy founded on "life, liberty and the pursuit of happiness." By the late 1700s, the ideals of the French Revolution—*liberte, egalite, fraternite*—replaced a long season of rule by absolute monarchy with rule through a republic. These new rights were novel; they sought to have the sovereign authority uphold certain rights of man based on the rule of law. They were also limited, applying only to males, and only to certain males.[26] These noble ideals and the new governments that they initiated did little for the rights of children, women, the millions of enslaved people, Indigenous peoples, and anyone deemed racially inferior and unworthy of such "inherent" rights.

A few years later, a third revolution, neglected by history, took place: the vitally consequential Haitian Revolution of 1791–1804. Led by Toussaint Louverture, Jean-Jacques Dessalines, as well as "Gran Toya" Victoria Montou, who had trained Dessalines in combat when he was a child, slave revolts turned into an organized armed resistance by *gente de color*, both free and enslaved. By 1804, their efforts had ended centuries of slavery and colonial rule in the highly prized colony of Saint-Domingue.[27] The heroines and heroes united in this struggle for independence and self-rule were condemned by European and colonial leaders alike, all of whom were fearful that the spirit of liberation would spread across the Americas. The newly established nation of Haiti was to be severely punished for its freedom. In 1825, France levied an initial indemnity of 150 million francs on Haiti—a debt later enforced and backed by the United States—resulting in the extraction of billions of dollars of wealth and contributing to Haiti's structural underdevelopment.[28] Instead of being lauded as a landmark in the global history of human rights, however, the Haitian Revolution is often excluded entirely from histories of international law.[29]

These historical fights for freedom ushered in a new era of values and ideas as an early foundation for human rights.[30] In 1807, the United Kingdom passed a law banning the slave trade throughout the British Empire, with the United States passing a similar law soon thereafter prohibiting the importation of enslaved people.[31] Two years prior, President Thomas Jefferson, a slaveholder himself, delivered the sixth annual address to Congress congratulating them on efforts to ban the slave trade "to withdraw the citizens of the United States from all further participation in those violations of human rights which have been so long continued on the unoffending inhabitants of Africa, and which the morality, the reputation, and the best interests of our country, have long been eager to proscribe."[32] Because compliance with this ban was so poor, international tribunals were established in Sierra Leone, Brazil, and elsewhere to better enforce the new laws prohibiting slave trading across the Atlantic.[33] The law effectively made importation of enslaved peoples a hardship for US-controlled ships, which led to increased demand from foreign vessels. American slaveholders also found workarounds and alternate routes—for example, importing enslaved peoples to Cuba and smuggling them into the United States.

In 1820, Congress passed an amendment to the 1819 Act to Protect the Commerce of the United States and Punish the Crime of Piracy.[34] The updated law now declared that slave trading was a form of piracy that violated federal law and was punishable by death. Section 5, which provides the seminal language, reveals important historical context:

> *And be it further enacted*, That if any citizen of the United States, being of the crew or ship's company of any foreign ship or vessel engaged in the slave trade, or any person whatever, being of the crew or ship's company of any ship or vessel, owned wholly or in part, or navigated for, or in behalf of, any citizen or citizens of the United States, shall forcibly confine or detain, or aid and abet in forcibly confining or detaining, on board such ship or vessel, any negro or mulatto not held to service by the laws of either of the states or territories of the United States with intent to make such negro or mulatto a slave or shall on board any such ship or vessel, offer or attempt to sell, as a slave, any negro or mulatto not held to service as aforesaid, or shall, on the high seas, or any where on tide water, transfer or deliver over, to any other ship or vessel, any negro or mulatto not held to service as aforesaid, with intent to make such negro or mulatto a slave, or shall land, or deliver on shore, from on board any such ship or vessel, any such negro or mulatto, with intent to make sale of, or having previously sold, such negro or mulatto, as a slave, such citizen or person shall be adjudged a pirate; and, on conviction thereof before the circuit court of the United States for the district wherein he shall be brought or found, shall suffer death.[35]

Here we see that the law governs acts by citizens of the United States even if they are working for a foreign entity. Enslavement is described as using force to confine, detain, or aid and abet such actions. Notably, the law uses the words "Negro" or "mulatto" to describe a slave. The words "human being," "woman"' or "man," or "citizen" are nowhere to be seen. Nor is there any description of who might become a slave beyond words historically connected to people from Africa. Given the long tradition of enslavement throughout Europe, the Mediterranean, and beyond, this framing of US law reinforces slavery as a practice accounting for the enslavement and trading of people of African origin or ancestry deemed Black, who were not yet recognized as humans deserving of rights.

Despite these gains, challenges remained. The United States was reluctant to let go of the transatlantic slave trade and, later, of slavery. To avoid detection under the 1820 law, American slave traders used foreign vessels to smuggle enslaved people into the United States.[36]

Then, in 1854, the law was tested during the trial of James Smith. He was charged with engaging in piracy after shipping over six hundred enslaved people from Angola to Trinidad aboard an American ship, the *Julia Moulton*.[37] Smith was sentenced to two years in prison and later received a pardon from President James Buchanan in 1857. In total, at least seventy-four cases of slave trading were tried in the US courts with little penalty. The all-white, all male judges and juries in the US courts of the day were reluctant to criminalize violations against their white brethren for the benefit of enslaved people they viewed as property.[38] It was during the Civil War, on February 21, 1862, that an American named Nathaniel Gordon was executed by hanging in New York City for the crime of slave trading.[39] Less than a year later, on January 1, 1863, President Lincoln would go on to pass the Emancipation Proclamation declaring that all enslaved people held in Confederate states were to be freed.

The end of the Civil War and the ratification of the Thirteenth Amendment to the US Constitution formally abolished slavery in America.[40] It also marked the beginning of a new era of racism in America. The abolition of slavery under domestic and international laws was only the beginning of the many essential legal battles to come. In the United States, several legal cases arose seeking redress through the Thirteenth Amendment for continued racial discrimination against Black people.[41]

In *Plessy v. Ferguson* (1896), the Supreme Court determined that racial segregation and the legalized distinction of race in society were constitutionally permissible. In its decision, the Court upheld racial segregation under the doctrine of "separate but equal," reasoning that "a statute which implies merely a legal distinction between the white and colored races—a distinction which is founded on the color of the two races and which must always exist so long as white men are distinguished from the other race by color—has no tendency to destroy the legal equality of the two races, or reestablish a state of involuntary servitude."[42] Thus, even as the transatlantic slave trade and slavery had been banned under international law by the early twentieth century, white supremacy persisted, with impunity, for generations to come.[43]

The Law of Nations and Worlds at War

Though racial subjugation remained entrenched in domestic law, and notably so in the United States, the international community was beginning to explore legal mechanisms to address broader concerns about peace, sovereignty, and human rights. The abolition of slavery in the late nineteenth century was punctuated by efforts to establish slavery as a universally prohibited norm under international law, one that obligated states to prohibit and punish it. This growing consensus around the evils of slavery and the transatlantic slave trade helped to usher in a broader era of *jus cogens* norms, naming the compelling law that is universal and that all nations must abide.[44]

At the turn of the twentieth century, nations returned to the question of whether, once again, to forge an alliance for peace. Czar Nicholas II, Emperor of Russia, had become increasingly concerned about Russia's fate should war return to Europe. Due to mounting internal pressures and a series of external military losses that had considerably weakened the Russian Empire, he sought to engage nations in Europe in a pact for peace. He sent wax-sealed letters of invitation to some twenty-six heads of state to gather in pursuit of a peace, assembling the conference "by delicate compliment."[45] The resulting gathering was located in The Hague in the summer of 1899, resulting in the first of two Hague Peace Conventions.

Czar Nicholas II's aim was not entirely altruistic. He knew that Russia would be seriously disadvantaged should war erupt and he wanted a pact that would reduce armaments. While the parties did not agree to such, they did agree to several principles and institutions that sought to solidify the promotion of peace through law as a normative aim.[46] One important result was the establishment of the first Permanent Court of Arbitration to settle disputes between nations peacefully on the basis of law.[47] According to US Secretary of State Elihu Root, the Conferences helped "justify the belief that the world has entered upon an orderly process through which . . . there may be continual progress toward making the practice of civilized nations conform to their peaceful professions."[48] However, the recognition of only certain nations excluded much of the world and perpetuated the racialized agendas of the day, committed to protecting European superiority and entitlement to colonial rule.

Unfortunately, war did come to pass, causing the passing of twenty million people and shocking a generation with the cruelty of mustard gas and the senselessness of trench warfare. This Great War, later called the First World War, began in 1914 after Archduke Franz Ferdinand of Austria-Hungary was assassinated while visiting Sarajevo. Rooted in deeper causes, Austria-Hungary declared war on Serbia, and allied nations on both sides were drawn into the conflict: the Central Powers of the German Empire, Austria-Hungary, the Ottoman Empire, and Bulgaria against the Allied Powers of Britain, France, Russia, Italy, Japan, and ultimately the United States.

After US President Woodrow Wilson convinced an isolationist America to become involved in a foreign war, he set his sights on the future.[49] On January 8, 1918, Wilson delivered his *Fourteen Points* speech to Congress, outlining a blueprint for postwar peace. In his address, he drew upon age-old noble ideals rooted in *humanitas*, affirming the principles of national self-determination and sovereignty. He called for a "programme of the world's peace" established through open diplomacy and the creation of the League of Nations."[50] Despite Wilson's vision, Congress remained unconvinced, and the League of Nations was formed on January 10, 1920 without the United States. Wilson's caution, however, would prove all too true in the decades to come. Within two decades the Second World War, launched by Nazi Germany's aggression and Adolf Hitler's quest for absolute power rooted in an ideology of racial supremacy, would plunge the world into catastrophic conflict. After that, everything would change.

*

The World Inhumanity Made

On September 1, 1939, Nazi Germany invaded Poland, and a terrible war engulfed the world once again. Divided into Allies and Axis alliances, World War II would involve most nations and cross most continents. By its end, it had become the deadliest and most documented war in human history, claiming an estimated eighty-five million lives and giving rise to the Holocaust and other atrocities. Among the survivors were those who would go on to rewrite the rules of world order and transform geopolitics for generations to come. In this deeply troubled period of human history, we find enduring lessons to guide us today.

Global racism precipitated and permeated the war. Not unlike Pope Urban II a thousand years before him, Adolf Hitler espoused an ideology of racial superiority as a call to arms to amass power for his authoritarian rule. Nazism emerged as a sociopolitical fascist ideology based on a belief in the hierarchy of races and the supremacy of a Nordic Aryan master race. Antidemocratic, anticommunist, antisemitic, racist, homophobic, and ableist, this ideology of ultranationalism empowered untold atrocities.

Hitler's long-held beliefs about the inherent superiority of the German people and "the aims of our movement" first appeared in his book *Mein Kampf*, decades earlier.[51] In it, he claims that there was a

Jewish conspiracy to control the world and blamed Judaism, along with communism's faulty ideals, for Germany's decline in the years following World War I. He also imagined the genocidal practice the Nazi Party would later adopt, wishing that "twelve or fifteen thousand of these Hebrew corrupters of the people had been held under poison gas."[52] He concludes the book with a chilling warning about the future: "[a] state which in this age of racial poisoning dedicates itself to the care of its best racial elements must some day become lord of the earth."[53] In his own words, Hitler's ideologies of racial superiority formed the nucleus of what would become among the most dangerous eras in human history.

Another Axis power, Imperial Japan, also espoused ideologies of racial superiority to forge Japanese unity and solidify political power. In this context, the ideology of racial superiority rested on the concept of a Yamato master race with pure bloodlines and a divine mandate to rule. Imperial Japan propagated this existing idea into a full-blown ideology to build Japanese unity and justify atrocities against "racially inferior" peoples in China, Korea, and beyond—as well as against Ainu and Ryukyu peoples in Japan. The Imperial Japanese military's "Rape of Nanjing" in China, with estimates of the murder of 100,000–300,000 and the rape of 20,000 Chinese people came to represent the systemic nature of such violence. These crimes were later addressed at The International Military Tribunal for the Far East, established to prosecute Japanese leaders for war crimes.[54]

The collective documentation and acknowledgement of such wrongs through the postwar tribunals both shocked the conscience of the world and helped solidify consensus among nations about acts they agreed could not stand. In Germany and in Japan, the depth of racism-driven cruelty came to light after the war, when the defeated Axis powers were subjected to war crimes tribunals documenting their atrocities. How could entire nations descend into such evil? What drove not only leaders and militaries, but also millions of bystanders, to participate in—or passively witness—such inhumanity?

Such inquiries were not applied universally. No tribunal was set up to hold to account the war crimes committed by the Allied Powers during the war or to hold the US government responsible for using its novel atomic weapons to deliberately target, without warning, Japanese civilians in Hiroshima and Nagasaki. There was no similar moment of reckoning for the past crimes of the Allied powers, such as the British Empire's many atrocities against the Congolese or in India, nor an accounting of the United States's egregious policies to eradicate Indigenous peoples from the lands it sought to conquer by conquest.

Despite the irony of these nations ignoring their own atrocities over the years, efforts after the war intensified around preventing such horrors from happening again, particularly with regard to the Holocaust. Within the decade, new legal and political projects would eventually lead to the naming and banning of genocide alongside slavery as a crime that all nations are obligated to prohibit and prevent. Formalized as a treaty, the Convention on the Prevention and Punishment of the Crime of Genocide was adopted by the UN General Assembly in 1948.

That same year saw the adoption of another landmark document, the Universal Declaration of Human Rights. Spearheaded by former US First Lady Eleanor Roosevelt, this nonbinding agreement solidified international consensus that more was needed to protect individuals from such egregious harms. Adopted by the UN General Assembly in 1948, the Universal Declaration of Human Rights enumerated for the first time a set of inherent human rights owed to every person on the planet.[55] Among these are the rights to life, to liberty, and to be free from slavery and torture. This novel creation enshrined the idea of a world order that would protect human rights for all people, inspiring profound hope in the aftermath of global war and genocide.

However, the strength of such protections was notably absent from the new treaty that established the United Nations in 1945 ate the end of World War II. Many leaders shaping the postwar world order were concerned about how international human rights would influence politics and social movements at home. Early discussions about how to establish the United Nations raised questions about how to frame equal rights and self-determination.[56] The negotiation history leading to the final text of the United Nations Charter reveals a great deal about all that was at stake.

The final version was drafted by the Coordination Committee at the 1945 San Francisco conference. There, the decision was eventually taken to link the equal rights of nations and the right of self-determination of peoples as one principle, with the view that "[t]he Committee understands that the principle of equal rights of the peoples and that of self-determination are two complementary parts of one standard of conduct . . . ."[57] They were striking a comprise, for China and the Soviet Union wanted the Charter to reference independence, whereas the British argued for liberty instead. If the Charter asserted a right to independence, that would be disastrous for their colonial rule.[58] Herein, the issue of racial superiority was directly raised by the delegate from The Netherlands who discussed the "humiliation caused by the assertion of racial superiority."[59] This discussion of self-determination would influence subsequent negotiations on how to address the principle of trusteeship of non-self-governing territories and colonial rule

Many of the Charter's most important details had already been worked out in advance, particularly its arrangements around peace and security. In secret negotiations at the Tehran Conference of 1943, the Malta Conference of 1945, and later the Yalta Conference of 1945, Soviet Premier Joseph Stalin, US President Franklin D. Roosevelt, and British Prime Minister Winston Churchill outlined what would ultimately become the postwar security structure.[60] They agreed this postwar order would be enforced by the "four policemen" nations (later adding France), which are the five nations with permanent status and the power to veto in the UN Security Council today.

During these private talks, Roosevelt found himself at odds with UK Prime Minister Winston Churchill's desire to continue Britain's colonial agenda and sought to convince Stalin of his views about the postwar world order. [61]His altruism was based not on a categorial rejection of colonialism but on a strategic calculation: American hegemony would be less achievable if European colonial powers continued their global expansion. Determined to succeed where President Wilson's League of

Nations had failed, Roosevelt had long envisioned "the first great agency for the maintenance of peace," and proposed the idea of an international court of justice.[62]

To achieve his aims, he ceded to pressure by a strong bloc of US senators from southern states to avoid any mention of America's own race problems in the Charter. FDR was not keen to address African Americans' struggle against racism during the founding of the United Nations, risking congressional adoption of the Charter.[63] He sought to avoid what he saw as President Wilson's great downfall with the League of Nations twenty-five years earlier. But back home, racial tensions continued to mount, exposing the contradictions between America's international ideals and its domestic realities. The National Association for the Advancement of Colored People sent forth a delegation led by W. E. B. DuBois to the San Francisco conference appealing the United Nations to expressly address the problem of racism against African Americans.[64] Many who hoped that the United Nations would do more to protect people from racism would be greatly disappointed.

On October 24, 1945, the United Nations Charter entered into force with the signatures of fifty nations. A treaty with binding commitments under international law, it established the United Nations and the foundations for the postwar world order.[65] The Charter's central purpose is "[t]o maintain international peace and security, and to that end: to take effective collective measures for the prevention and removal of threats to the peace, and for the suppression of acts of aggression or other breaches of the peace, and to bring about by peaceful means, and in conformity with the principles of justice and international law, adjustment or settlement of international disputes or situations which might lead to a breach of the peace."[66] Across 19 chapters and 111 articles, the Charter established the United Nations General Assembly, the United Nations Security Council, the International Court of Justice, and many other aspects for governing and enforcing peaceful relations among nations.

In Article 1.3, the Charter "encourages respect for human rights and fundamental freedoms for all without distinction as to race, sex, language, or religion . . . ."[67] Article 13.1.b authorizes the General Assembly to study and make recommendations on international cooperation—again, without regard/attention to race and other factors. Similar language is found in Article 55.c, which discusses international economic and social cooperation, and in Article 76.c, which discusses the human rights objectives of the trusteeship system. Article 2.3 creates an affirmative obligation upon states to settle their disputes peacefully, and Article 33 provides a variety of methods for doing so.[68] Article 2.4 creates a general prohibition on nations from using force unless necessary for individual or collective self-defense as described by Article 51. The Charter tasks the Security Council with the primary responsibility for taking measures necessary "to maintain or restore international peace and security."[69] Yet, nowhere in its pages will you find the word "racism," nor does it discuss slavery, colonization, or apartheid—all of which were political concerns when the Charter was drafted.

Notably, the Charter does not mention racism nor include its elimination as an aim in its purpose to maintain international peace and security, despite the war raising these very concerns. Seeking to provide clarification about "international peace and security," the UN General Assembly adopted the *Essentials of Peace* resolution in 1949, which declared:

> [T]the Charter of the United Nations, the most solemn pact of peace in history, lays down basic principles necessary for an enduring peace; that disregard of these principles is primarily responsible for the continuance of international tension; and that it is urgently necessary for all Members to act in accordance with these principles in the spirit of co-operation on which the United Nations was founded.[70]

The subsequent development of UN bodies, organs, and subsidiary groups that serve the aim of peace promotion provide guidance as to how states, in practice, have observed their obligations and duties regarding peace.[71] Although "the concept of peace is firmly premised on the observance of fundamental principles of international law, and that compliance with international law is a condition for peace,"[72] the legal meaning of peace and related core terms, such as "collective security," were ambiguous.[73] As acclaimed jurist Theodore Meron inquired in

1985, is "the Charter of the United Nations adopted by a community really practicing the values stated in it? Or was it rather a code of *better* conduct of nations?"[74]

World War II had tested the principles of world order in unprecedented ways, and much about the prewar international system did not survive the aftermath. Weakened by the war, Europe's empires shrank, and former colonies gained independence. With seventeen countries gaining independence, 1960 was deemed Africa's "year of independence."[75] This wave of decolonization raised difficult questions for the newly established United Nations about the limits of sovereignty when a government violated people's fundamental rights. The United States and the Soviet Union emerged as the two dominant powers but soon entered into a long Cold War that would impede geopolitics and hinder the development of the newly minted United Nations system.

The challenge of global racism was present before, during, and after the creation of the United Nations. Its persistence and deep entrenchment continued to destabilize world order and human rights, even as it remained underacknowledged. These tumultuous years of human history proved true something W. E. B. Du Bois had long ago warned: oppression allowed to fester tends to spread like a disease.[76]

*

This brief glimpse into the deep history of racism reveals its endurance amid vast changes in human history. From its earliest origins, racism has been woven throughout the structures and ideologies that give rise to cultures and civilizations. Ancient dynasties with god-kings gave way to religious empires where kings were empowered by gods, expanding through monarchies into colonial regimes and empires. With each era came massive oppression that used racism to achieve economic, political, and ideological aims.

These painful histories reveal a central warning. The cost of racism is borne not only by its many victims but also by humanity as a whole. Colonialism, the transatlantic slave trade, and the genocide of Indigenous peoples are evidence of the deep inhumanity of an era steeped in ideologies of racial supremacy. Even as the extensive cruelty of this era finally gave way to human rights for some, racialized oppression persisted for many, with dehumanization not far behind.

From the beginning, law has remained one of racism's most effective accomplices. From natural law to the law of nations to modern international law and national laws, legal authority has long proved a powerful tool in maintaining and spreading the thief of racism into new places, often cloaked under the imprimatur of legitimacy and authority. This is a pattern humanity must fully acknowledge in order to break.

4

A Question for the World

1965

On December 21, 1965, at the United Nations General Assembly in New York, nations joined together to adopt the first treaty calling for the elimination of racial discrimination. Known officially as the International Convention on the Elimination of Racial Discrimination, or ICERD, it was hailed as a "landmark in the history of the United Nations," "a resounding victory," and a "solemn affirmation of the will of the peoples."[1] The treaty extended earlier efforts of the international community to ban slavery, outlaw genocide, and promote freedom and equality. It marked a moment of solidarity, if not complete consensus, in the early years of the newly established United Nations. Its passage birthed a sense of hope.

The treaty would not have been possible without a growing consensus among peoples and nations that the troubles owed to racism were troubles for the world. The promise of 1945 and the world the United Nations promised to build to "save succeeding generations from the scourge of war, which twice in our lifetime has brought untold sorrow to mankind," had not come to pass for most.[2] Despite its groundbreaking contributions, the Charter was silent on the question of racism. During its creation, proposals to include language expressing human rights and racial equality as central to the UN's mandate became polarized along Cold War lines, with the United States firmly against. In four instances,

Global Racism. Anna Spain Bradley, Oxford University Press. © Anna Spain Bradley 2026.
DOI: 10.1093/oso/9780197778388.003.0005

the Charter notes that states must fulfill certain obligations "without distinction as to race."[3] In the end, the terms "racism" and "racial discrimination" never appear in the Charter's 128 pages.

Yet racist oppression was a constant presence in those days. The generational impacts of the transatlantic slave trade had given way to the horrors of apartheid in South Africa, segregation in America, and untold varieties of racism wherever colonialism had taken root. Caste and Reishizumu and the erasure of Indigenous and ethnic minorities in Asia persisted with impunity. Colonialism ravaged Africa, Asia, the Caribbean, North and South America, and the Middle East.

By 1960, the colonial era was crumbling. Seventeen African nations broke from colonial rule amid a renewed wave of anticolonialist fervor that rebuked the white supremacy of the past.[4] South Africa's apartheid system was increasingly criticized as more and more nations called for its end.[5] The United Nations was beginning to acknowledge that racism, whether manifested through colonialism or apartheid or segregation, was a harm that international law must necessarily address.[6] Then, on November 20, 1963, the United Nations General Assembly adopted the Declaration on the Elimination of All Forms of Racial Discrimination.[7] In Article 1, the Declaration pitted "[d]iscrimination between human beings on the ground of race, colour or ethnic origin" as an offense to human dignity and antithetical to both the UN Charter and the Universal Declaration of Human Rights, as well as to peace and security. Nonbinding, yet powerful, its passage by the UN General Assembly laid the groundwork for what would come next, ushering in a new era for international law and for human rights.

By 1964, frustration over racism had reached a boiling point across the Atlantic in America. In the years following World War II, African American soldiers returning home increasingly demanded that the nation they had risked their lives to serve protect their constitutional rights in return. Soon, political protests, economic boycotts, and organized cultural resistance forged a Civil Rights Movement in the United States that would transform the fight against racism for generations to come.[8]

The time-honored idea that law could establish rights that give rise to freedom and equality was reborn one summer day when, on July 2, 1964, the Civil Rights Act became law. The *New York Times* hailed it "A National Victory"; the *Chicago Defender*, "A Significant Ruling."[9] A year before, in an address to the American people on June 11, 1963, President John F. Kennedy announced his intention to propose the Civil Rights Act, stating, "We are confronted primarily with a moral issue. . . . The heart of the question is whether all Americans are to be afforded equal rights and equal opportunities, whether we are going to treat our fellow Americans as we want to be treated. . . . Now the time has come for this Nation to fulfill its promise."[10] Five months later, he was assassinated.

As a consequence, it was President Lyndon B. Johnson who signed the Civil Rights Act into law. After its passage, he laid out in a public statement the road ahead for the American people: "It is the product, not of any man or group of men, but of a broad national consensus that every person is entitled to justice, to equality, and to an even chance to enjoy the blessing of liberty. It is in the highest tradition of a civilization which, from the Magna Carta on, has used the fabric of law for the fulfillment of liberty."[11] Johnson's framing links the Civil Rights Act to a deep tradition of legal reform stretching back to foundational moments in Western political history. By invoking the Magna Carta, he cast civil rights not as a radical innovation but as the latest expression of a centuries-long pursuit of liberty through law. In doing so, Johnson appealed to a shared civic heritage while subtly reinforcing the legitimacy of the federal government's role in enforcing racial justice.

Change came too slowly for some and too fast for others. Soon, "ugly pockets of resistance" formed.[12] In Mississippi, a state most resistant to civil rights protections and most feared for its deep racism, twenty-one suspects were arrested and later released in the killing of three civil rights workers. In the North, violence ensued from Rochester to New York City to Philadelphia, garnering national attention and concern.[13] A bitter irony, given that these locations were among the sites where the American Revolution began some two hundred years earlier.

Still, oppression would not hold. The words and deeds of one man in particular shaped these times. Dr. Martin Luther King Jr.'s vision for the future, powerfully enshrined in the pages of his 1963 Letter from Birmingham Jail and in the resonant tones of his voice echoing *I Have a Dream* across the National Mall, has become a symbol of freedom and liberty that rings through until this day.[14] In October 1964, the Norwegian Nobel Committee awarded Dr. King the Nobel Peace Prize "for his non-violent struggle for civil rights for the Afro-American population," cementing his place in history as a voice for peace and humanity.[15] Dr. King became increasingly outspoken about the link between the African American struggle for civil rights and the struggle of people around the world for international human rights.[16] Around the same time, Malcom X also sought to illuminate the connections between civil rights and the international human rights movement, particularly after his travels to the United Arab Republic, Sudan, Nigeria, Ghana, and his pilgrimage to Mecca in April 1964. In one of his final public speeches, in 1965, Malcolm X said, "[W]hen you call it 'human rights' it becomes international. And then you can take your troubles to the World Court. You can take them before the world. And anybody anywhere on this earth can become your ally."[17] Just a few days later, as he prepared to take the stage at the Audubon Ballroom in New York City, he was assassinated. Three years later, Dr. King was assassinated on the balcony of the Lorraine Motel in Memphis, Tennessee. Their brief intellectual convergence around the connection between international human rights and African Americans' fight for civil rights is largely forgotten in the histories that followed.

A Treaty to Eliminate Racial Discrimination

It was in the strife of these years that the world's first treaty banning racial discrimination was forged. On December 21, 1965, the General Assembly of the United Nations adopted a legally binding treaty called the International Convention on the Elimination of All Forms of Racial Discrimination.[18] With all but one nation agreeing to the treaty (Mexico abstained but later ratified), the moment was historic. ICERD became the first core international human rights treaty in the post-UN era, calling for nothing less than the elimination of racial discrimination everywhere. The Convention entered into force on January 4, 1969, and, since then, 182 of the 193 nations that are members of the United Nations have ratified or signed it. As a result, ICERD is one of the most universally adopted treaties in existence.[19]

Motivated by racist events of the day, namely, swastika paintings and antisemitism, and recognition of the harms of segregation and apartheid, the Convention's objective was as unequivocal as it was aspirational. Nations, for the first time, were now obligated to act affirmatively to bring about the treaty's aim of the "elimination of all forms of racial discrimination."[20] The Representative from Italy remarked that the treaty was "first and foremost a solemn affirmation of the will of the peoples."[21] The Representative from the United States characterized it as "more than a statement of lofty ideals."[22] The terms the nations ultimately agreed on became the binding law of the treaty.[23]

The Preamble reiterates principles established under the UN Charter and by the Universal Declaration of Human Rights, affirming equality and human rights and fundamental freedoms. It reaffirms the UN's condemnation of colonialism, segregation, and associated discrimination and its own condemnation of apartheid. The Preamble also addresses ideology, "[c]onvinced that any doctrine of superiority based on racial differentiation is scientifically false, morally condemnable, socially unjust and dangerous." Article 1 of the treaty provides a legal definition of racial discrimination:

> In this Convention, the term "racial discrimination" shall mean any distinction, exclusion, restriction or preference based on race, colour, descent, or national or ethnic origin which has the purpose or effect of nullifying or impairing the recognition, enjoyment or exercise, on an equal footing, of human rights and fundamental freedoms in the political, economic, social, cultural or any other field of public life.[24]

This definition links racial discrimination to an act (distinction, exclusion, restriction, or preference) that is connected to a harmful purpose or effect on the basis of race and also color, descent, national origin, or ethnic origin. This definition of racial discrimination does not extend protections against discrimination based on nationality or citizenship status.[25] Nations did not want international law to interfere with their own sovereign governance on citizenship and nationality, as long as national laws didn't discriminate against "any particular nationality."[26] Notably, the treaty did not fully echo the earlier concerns about belief and ideology that UNESCO had in 1950.

Another exception to racial discrimination concerns what are known as special measures, such as affirmative action in education. Article 1.4 provides that such measures are not racial discrimination when they serve the sole purpose of protecting the rights of people of certain racial or ethnic backgrounds, which "may be necessary in order to ensure such groups or individuals equal enjoyment or exercise of human rights and fundamental freedoms."[27] Such measures are meant to be temporary and are considered, by some, controversial, raising questions about whether the treaty is race-blind or race-neutral.[28] Special measures are associated with nations offering protections to ensure equal opportunity for people of African, Roma, or Indigenous descent. Adapting this to a nation in which much of the population can claim indigeneity, such as in Papua New Guinea, raises questions about when special protections for one group discriminate against another.

The treaty goes on to articulate the obligations nations must uphold. Article 2.1b forbids nations to "sponsor, defend or support racial discrimination by any persons or organizations." It also requires nations to take up preventive measures. Article 2.2 states:

> States Parties shall, when the circumstances so warrant, take, in the social, economic, cultural and other fields, special and concrete measures to ensure the adequate development and protection of certain racial groups or individuals belonging to them, for the purpose of guaranteeing them the full and equal enjoyment of human rights and fundamental freedoms. These measures shall in no case entail as a consequence the maintenance

of unequal or separate rights for different racial groups after the objectives for which they were taken have been achieved.

Legal requirements wrapped around the concept of racial identity beg practical, yet uncomfortable, questions. How does a nation designate the racial groups it recognizes by law? Who gets to say who belongs to which race?

To avoid these obligations and questions altogether, some nations simply do not recognize the existence of racial groups or use other identity markers as a proxy for race. Mauritius, for example, classifies people by religion and does not use race as a category. In Norway, expectations about assimilation lead to underreporting of certain groups, including Lapps and Roma.[29] In Panama, recognition of Indigenous identity has been linked to the requirement to live in government-designated areas.

The treaty also addresses the treatment of hate speech as a form of prohibited racial discrimination. Article 4 bans certain speech as racial discrimination, stating that nations shall "condemn all propaganda and all organizations which are based on ideas or theories of superiority of one race or group of persons of one colour of ethnic origin, or which attempt to justify or promote racial hatred and discrimination in any form." It further states that nations "[s]hall not permit public authorities or public institutions, national or local, to promote or incite racial discrimination." Nations are to take steps to stop the dissemination of ideas based on racial superiority or hatred, incitement to racial discrimination, incitement to violence of any kind and including that based on race.[30] The treaty does not use the terms "hate speech" or "racist hate speech" but subsequent discussions by the Committee on the Elimination of Racial Discrimination (CERD), the treaty's implementation entity, have done so, including the 2012 thematic discussion on racist hate speech.

Balancing rights of free speech with the right to be free from hate crimes and hate speech has proven challenging for nations.[31] In the Great Britain Race Relations Act, for example, the United Kingdom interpreted Article 4 as limited by the right to free speech and assembly articulated in the Universal Declaration of Human Rights. The United States interprets the treaty obligations as secondary to the rights enshrined in the US Constitution and law. Belgium has adopted legislation that aims to balance interests. Germany has made legal sanctions for racist hate speech contingent on the intent to discriminate. These differing approaches underscore the central challenge: Though nations have agreed through treaty that racial discrimination must be eliminated, they remain divided on how to reconcile that goal within the context of their peoples, laws, and nations.

*

What Nations Negotiated

In creating a treaty that would outlaw racial discrimination, the drafters struggled to define the harm and to conceptualize its meaning. In reviewing the negotiation history, known by its French name, *travaux preparatoires*, we learn about the key disagreements and nuances nations faced, many of which we still face today.

First, nations disagreed about whether the treaty should establish racial discrimination as a universal problem. The core question was about the prevalence and ubiquity of the problem. Representatives from many countries countered that racial discrimination was either not present in their country or did not apply to their minorities or Indigenous peoples.[32] The language in the Preamble ultimately aimed for a compromise, acknowledging racial discrimination as manifesting only "in some areas of the world," giving governments plausible deniability as a result.[33]

The discussion then turned to how best to describe various forms of racial discrimination. Colonialism, segregation, and related forms of racial discrimination were already banned by the UN, as was slavery. Should other specific kinds of racial discrimination be named? Jordan proposed a list: "fascist, colonial, tribal, Zionist."[34] Western states stressed the racial discrimination that emanated from Nazi ideology and antisemitism.[35] African nations and the USSR identified racial discrimination as integral to colonialism and apartheid.[36] Some sought to name racial discrimination more specifically, whether as antisemitism, Nazism, or fascism. The representative from Saudi Arabia voiced a common concern among delegates that "there were countless 'isms' which would have to be enumerated if any one was."[37] He inquired if antisemitism was best understood as religious intolerance not racial, raising the question of whether the animus against Jewish people aims at religion or at Semitic origin.[38] The representative from Israel responded that "[t]he Jewish people knew exactly what anti-Semitism was, for it had too long been its victim, whether for racial, religious or other reasons; to those who had suffered from racial discrimination, qualifiers were not important."[39] Ghana wanted the treaty to name apartheid, precisely to let South Africa know it was racial discrimination. Nigeria noted that apartheid was a state-sponsored policy that should be especially decried. Representative Morozov of the USSR stated that "[r]acism and racial discrimination are such shameful and odious products of imperialism and colonialism that all peoples and all decent human beings are resolutely demanding that they be ended."[40] Representative Verret of Haiti remarked, "[W]e share the distaste felt by the majority of the peoples of the world for all forms of racial discrimination, no matter by what means they are called: antisemitism, colonialism, nazism, apartheid and all such."[41]

In the end, the Third Committee, those responsible for drafting the treaty's text, did not open this question to debate. Instead, they adopted the Greece–Hungary proposal not to reference specific forms of racial discrimination.[42] There were two exceptions, "racial segregation and apartheid," both mentioned by name in Article 3 of the treaty.[43] Nigeria had argued that apartheid, which included segregation, was the official policy of a UN member state, and that the Union of South Africa had denied that it was racially discriminatory.[44] As is often the case, an effort to reach agreement among divergent views came at the cost of adopting specific commitments and definitions.

A third issue concerned how the ICERD treaty would address the question of racial differences among peoples. Ultimately, the Convention bans "any doctrine of superiority based on racial differentiation."[45] This was a departure from the language of the Declaration, adopted only two years earlier, which banned "any doctrine of racial differentiation or superiority."[46] As scholar David Keane has argued, this construction of language in the Convention suggests that there may be separate races instead of repudiating the entire concept of race, as science had already done.[47] He observes that this "departure from the position expressed by the signatories to the Declaration is similar to the difference between the first and second UNESCO statements on race, the second of which refused to deny the existence of . . . race in line with its predecessor, . . . condemning only the notion of racial superiority."[48] It proved far more difficult to push through language on more controversial questions of the day, such as the rights of Indigenous peoples and racial or ethnic minorities within a country.[49]

This political stumbling block is precisely what Du Bois had worked against. There was interest by some countries to avoid claiming that racism was ubiquitous in order to limit the treaty's scope and power. If the problem was cast as occurring only in certain contexts that were indefensible, such as apartheid in South Africa, the need for a universal treaty admitting that racism was possible everywhere could be avoided.[50] Although most countries had already acknowledged slavery, colonialism, apartheid, and segregation as illegal, many were unwilling to accept that racism was a matter of common concern to be governed by international law.

Nations had negotiated the text of the Declaration on the Elimination of All Forms of Racial Discrimination just a few years before settling on the text for the treaty, so many debates were fresh in the delegates' minds. Following the existing consensus found in the Universal Declaration of Human Rights of 1948, Article 1, which states that "[a]ll human beings are born free and equal in dignity and rights," the ICERD treaty centered on equality and nondiscrimination as its core aims.[51] But defining and achieving these aims has proved a complex exercise. Interpreting what the treaty means—how it did and did not define key terms such as equality, discrimination, and race, and how violations can be found as a matter of fact—has also proven complex. Does equality require the same for all, or special treatment for some? Are protections for individuals the same as for groups? Is equality under the law to be measured by intent or by effect?

As the ICERD treaty negotiations document, each nation had its own internal struggles to consider regarding the race question. India was concerned about caste. Ecuador was concerned about the growing awareness among various Indigenous groups of the protections they were owed under human rights laws. The United States was contending with internal claims of genocide against African Americans.[52] This legal history reveals the complexity of determining the meaning of racism then and now, rendering racial discrimination as a problem around the world both interconnected and yet distinct.

Agreements and Disagreements

Reading the ICERD treaty through the lens of its negotiation history reveals that each agreed-upon sentence raises other questions that remain unanswered. Behind the treaty's final text lay serious disagreements about the meaning of banning racial discrimination and what doing so under international law would require of nations. The final text represents the product of negotiations drafted and agreed upon by the representatives of various nations in the UN General Assembly. There was widespread consensus that racial discrimination was a barrier to the equality promised by the UN Charter and the Universal Declaration of Human Rights. The UN had already condemned slavery, colonialism, and segregation. But what more did this treaty condemn? Some of the key questions that the negotiation process raised continue to be asked to this day.

What constitutes racial discrimination? Nations agreed that it involved government policies that caused a distinction or separation and that these actions, upon causing harm, are linked to the human identity of the person or group harmed. Race, color, descent, and national or ethnic origin are all listed as identity factors at play in racial discrimination. The discrimination itself is described as a distinction, exclusion, restriction, or preference. Both documents list segregation and apartheid as examples of racial discrimination. The Declaration goes on to list, in Article 5, "separation resulting from such policies." This framing does not capture the fullness of the race question as envisioned by UNESCO in 1950. Is it racial differentiation? Or is it also the ideology and practices associated with racial superiority?

Turning to the purpose of the treaty, is discrimination the problem? Or is it the superiority of races? Or differentiation among races? The discrimination lens was intended to address the treaty's purpose in promoting equal rights. Within this framework, two categories of discrimination are discernible: purpose-based discrimination and effect-based discrimination, also known as indirect discrimination. Consider the following example. If the majority of people arrested in a city during a given year belong to one racial or ethnic group, a purpose-based test would look for evidence that the police had a specific policy or intent to do so. By contrast, the effect-based test would find racial discrimination even in the absence of such evidence. If the arrests had a disproportionate impact on a protected group, causing a disparate effect, that impact could constitute racial discrimination.

The language of purpose or effect muddies a deeper question. What about intent? Does the ICERD treaty make the intent to discriminate on the basis of race prohibited by international law? The *travaux préparatoires* reveal that the drafters of the treaty took account of antidiscrimination law in the United States at the time, questioning whether all discrimination should be legally prohibited or only that which discriminates on the basis of a protected class—in this case, race.[53] Later, in 1976, the US Supreme Court set the legal standard in *Washington v. Davis* that discriminatory effect alone, without evidence of discriminatory purpose or intent, did not violate the US Constitution.[54] In 1985, Meron argued that "Article 1 creates certain problems" because it defines discrimination as prohibited acts that "cause nullification or impairment of the recognition, enjoyment or exercise, on an equal footing, of human rights." He recalls the case of *Brown v. Board of Education* (1954) and asks us to consider if the "separate but equal" doctrine of racially segregated public schools in the United States that were law and practice at that time would have been permissible under ICERD. Meron argues that ICERD's basis is rooted in equality, not in antidiscrimination. According to this view, if equality is achieved, then the prohibition of racial discrimination under international law is achieved.

*

The final text of the 1965 treaty, for all of its groundbreaking ideas, failed to name or to define forms of racial discrimination beyond apartheid and segregation. Like the UN Charter before it, the ICERD treaty did not go so far as to name racism, only "racist doctrines and practices" in the Preamble and "racist activities" in Article 4.[55] Professor Patrick Thornberry, who served on the treaty's implementation Committee for thirteen years, remarked, "[I]t is not abundantly clear from the travaux how the experts and delegates involved in the drafting, who perceived racial discrimination as necessitating an enduring instrument to combat it, reflected on the fit between the title and the elusiveness of the target."[56] It is clear then and now that negotiating a treaty is a political matter. Its capaciousness hoped to contain and constrain the divergent aspirations of many nations and powerful interest groups into one treaty. However, the elusive definition of racial discrimination in 1965 plagues attempts to eliminate it today.

The world had changed between 1945 and 1965. The unifying urgency of the World War II era had given way to nations' disparate interests in an increasingly postcolonial Cold War era. UNESCO's 1945 Preamble noting "the great and terrible war which has now ended was a war made possible by the denial of the democratic principles of the dignity, equality and mutual respect of men, and by the propagation, in their place, through ignorance and prejudice, of the doctrine of the inequality of men and races" had given way to a new world order with new world priorities.[57]

After the Treaty, Changes, and Challenges

Even as the ICERD treaty named apartheid as racial discrimination that was prohibited under international law, the practice of apartheid by the government of South Africa continued on for decades. Recall that after the Boer War in 1910, the Union of South Africa was recognized as a nation-state governing parts of southern Africa. In 1948, the government formally legalized a long-standing set of racist practices, including segregation, into the system of apartheid.[58] Apartheid was designed to separate people into groups based on racial hierarchy, with white being at the top, a practice known and tolerated by the international community and under international law for years. As early as 1949, the UN General Assembly requested legal advice from the newly constituted International Court of Justice (ICJ) on the legality of South Africa's mandate to govern the territory of South West Africa (now Namibia), raising connected questions about the concern of South Africa's policy and practice of apartheid there.[59] In its 1950 Advisory Opinion, the ICJ found unanimously that "South-West Africa is a territory under the international Mandate assumed by the Union of South Africa on December 17th, 1920," failing to address the problem of apartheid.[60] The issue was brought before the ICJ again in 1966, but the Court determined that Ethiopia and Liberia lacked standing and dismissed the case.[61] In 1971, the Security Council asked the ICJ to issue an advisory opinion on the legality of South Africa's presence in Namibia, once again raising the ongoing tensions surrounding the government's continuation of apartheid.[62] The ICJ finally condemned apartheid, finding that South Africa's involvement in Namibia was illegal and upholding racial discrimination as a violation of the UN Charter.[63] Even though the government of South Africa ignored the ICJ's findings, the decision did further affirm apartheid and racial discrimination as violations of international law.

It wasn't until democratic elections were held in South Africa in 1994 that the government's apartheid rule was finally dismantled. People around the world celebrated this outcome as a human rights victory, marking the triumph of decades-long efforts by Nelson Mandela, other African National Congress (ANC) leaders, and countless other South Africans.[64] Their win was in spite of the many countries that had protected the South African government's legalized system of institutional racial segregation and discrimination since its inception in 1948, citing the doctrine of sovereignty as the international legal basis for respecting the government's choice of rule. Apartheid was defined as a crime under the 2002 Rome Statute as "inhumane acts . . . committed in the context of an institutionalized regime of systematic oppression and domination by one racial group over any other racial group or groups and committed with the intention of maintaining that regime."[65] This definition was built upon the earlier one provided in the 1973 Convention on the Suppression and Punishment of the Crime of Apartheid, the first binding treaty declaring apartheid and racial segregation as crimes against humanity.[66]

After the International Convention on the Elimination of Racial Discrimination treaty was adopted by the UN in 1965, it took several years for it to enter into force in 1969. The treaty established the Committee on the Elimination of Racial Discrimination, or CERD, to carry forward its charge.[67] This Committee consists of eighteen independent experts charged with monitoring implementation of the treaty in the following ways.[68] CERD conducts periodic reviews of how a nation is or is not complying with the treaty. Nations that have adopted the treaty are required to submit regular reports on how they are fulfilling their treaty commitments. The Committee makes findings, issues general recommendations, and imposes reprisals on states. The Committee's response ranges from inviting a state to provide an update to the Committee in the future to suggesting how the state should improve the application of its laws and policies.

One of CERD's central roles is to issue general recommendations providing an authoritative interpretation of the treaty. From its inception through 2025, CERD has issued thirty-nine general recommendations, addressing an array of themes including racial discrimination against people of African descent, racist hate speech, and racial discrimination in healthcare. In its report on combating hate speech, for example, the Committee recommends "that the criminalization of forms of racist expression should be reserved for serious cases, to be proven beyond reasonable doubt, while less serious cases should be addressed by means other than criminal law."[69] The Committee's limited authority and resources make it ill-equipped to address imminent and egregious threats caused by racism, such as Myanmar's discriminatory practices against the Rohingya people.[70]

Finally, CERD also addresses claims by individuals submitted directly to the Committee, pursuant to Article 14 of ICERD. Here, individuals can seek redress for violations of their human rights protected by the treaty. In 2011, the Committee published a report on selected decisions from 1988 to 2011, documenting allegations of racial discrimination in employment, inability to apply to a legal bar association, bias by jurors during trial, and reluctance to enforce laws preventing racial discrimination against renters or home buyers.[71] Each of these cases rests upon a nation's obligation to create and enforce laws preventing racial discrimination. In many cases, the alleged violation is also caused by individuals. The Committee's responses range from inviting a nation to provide an update in the future to suggesting how it should improve enforcing its laws. In this report, there are eight mentions of the word "racism," and, other than referring to an organization with the term in its name, the term is exclusively used by those individuals who submitted the facts as they recall their experiences.[72] For example, one person reported experiences of Islamophobia "as a form of racism."[73] However, the Committee, as author of the report, did not itself use the term "racism" or signal that its decisions addressed the complaints of racism.[74]

Lessons Learned

What does the ICERD era teach us about the challenge of racism in the world? Crisis begets change. Indeed, it was the great suffering of World

War II that helped usher in a rare moment of global momentum to take action to prevent another world war. The UN Charter, and the United Nations it established, laid down the blueprint for peace and security that changed the world. The result was a world order through international law that pledged to maintain peace and establish universal human rights, but not for all. This promise, however, would soon be tested. As Gandhi and many others warned, the sins of racism throughout the world would not simply disappear into history. Indeed, the pressure to address racism gave rise to the very first international human rights treaty calling for the elimination of racial discrimination throughout the world.

International law during this time sought to constrain nations from practicing or permitting the ills of slavery and the transatlantic slave trade, segregation, apartheid, and the racial discrimination they wrought. It sought to make these ways of the past odious—the marks of bygone times. The ICERD treaty's ambition was made possible through the strength of consensus reaching during the war years—years where humanity learned the hard way that the festering ideologies of racial superiority that gave rise to Nazism, ultimately brought disorder and suffering to the entire world. Banning racial discrimination alongside genocide, apartheid, segregation, and slavery was the salve that the nations applied to such a deep infection. Yet, this salve would not fully heal the wound.

5

The Non-Illegality of Racism

A Global Reckoning

Many years passed, during which the Cold War came and went and nations built multilateral trade agreements while navigating terrorism and a global pandemic, before the UN would once again turn its full attention to the cause of combating racism. Then, on Monday, May 25, 2020, a horrific act took place that shocked the world. George Floyd Jr. went into Cup Foods, a convenience store in Minneapolis, Minnesota, to buy cigarettes. The clerk, allegedly believing Floyd had paid with a counterfeit $20 bill, called the police. It was then that a police officer named Derek Chauvin made the fateful decision to force a handcuffed Floyd to the ground and kneel on his neck for over nine minutes, ignoring Floyd's pleas of "I can't breathe" and ending his life. The video footage of this horrific act went viral, reaching over 1.4 billion views in the two weeks that followed.[1] Certainly, watching any murder is difficult, but the image of a white police officer suffocating a Black man in cold blood in broad daylight invoked generational pain and united protesters around the world in the rallying cry of "Black Lives Matter."

Reaction at the UN, by its standards, was remarkably swift. On June 5, 2020, just over a week after Floyd's death, UN independent experts issued a response "condemning modern-day racial terror lynching" and called for systemic reform and justice to address "racial

Global Racism. Anna Spain Bradley, Oxford University Press. © Anna Spain Bradley 2026.
DOI: 10.1093/oso/9780197778388.003.0006

terror."[2] Within three weeks, on June 12, 2020, the Committee on the Elimination of Racial Discrimination (CERD) became the first official UN body to issue a formal statement, calling upon "the Government of the United States to fully respect its international obligations, in particular those arising from the International Convention on the Elimination of All Forms of Racial Discrimination to which it is a party," to investigate the death of George Floyd, "desist from calling on the military to ensure public order," and to "publicly recognize the existence of structural racial discrimination in the society, as well as to unequivocally and unconditionally reject and condemn racially motivated killings of African Americans and other minorities."[3] The CERD Committee—the very UN group responsible for monitoring the implementation of the treaty calling for the elimination of racial discrimination—did not use the word "racism" in its calls to action. Not even once.

The rest of the world did. The barbarity of George Floyd's murder at the hands of an on-duty police officer was something much more than just racial discrimination or discrimination of any kind. What happened to George Floyd Jr. was racism. Watching a police officer murder in cold blood and in broad daylight a human being, who was tall and strong and Black, brought back generations of trauma for so many and reminded the world how racism in America is older than the nation itself. Had none of the decades since the end of slavery, desegregation, the Civil Rights Act, the International Convention on the Elimination of All Forms of Racial Discrimination (ICERD), and the end of apartheid mattered? Were Black people still so unsafe, so disposable? Would there ever be reparatory justice for the untold human rights violations that stole life and liberty and equality and dignity for over four hundred years of enslavement and the transatlantic slave trade that built European empires and the foundations of new nations across the Americas? And most urgently, would racism—not just racial discrimination—ever become illegal?

The United Nations Says "Racism"

After George Floyd Jr.'s murder and the global cries for justice that followed, the United Nations began to employ the language of "racism" more frequently on its online and social media platforms.[4] By early 2021, the United Nations Human Rights Office of the High Commissioner launched its ongoing #FightRacism online campaign to raise awareness and gain support for "global action on racism, discrimination, xenophobia and other intolerances" marking a formal, highly visible shift toward official UN use of the word "racism."[5] The UN Human Rights Council held a special session on "systemic, anti-Black racism," resulting in a resolution focused on raising awareness about all forms of racism.[6] A year later, the UN High Commissioner for Human Rights, Michelle Bachelet, issued an "urgent call for States to adopt a 'transformative agenda' to uproot systemic racism."[7] In it, she spoke out against racism by name, again and again noting the pain as well as the anger it causes. Two months later, the UN General Assembly created the Permanent Forum on the People of African Descent by resolution.[8] Such a global response to the injustices of racism was felt with a force not seen since the 1960s, spurred on by a global public that was, once again, fed up with racism.[9]

Saying the word "racism" is one thing, defining what racism is under international law is much more difficult. One United Nations human rights body has taken up discussion about racism in this context extensively. The Ad Hoc Committee on the Elaboration of Complementary Standards, established by the UN Human Rights Council in 2007, has a mandate to "elaborate, as a matter of priority and necessity, complementary standards in the form of either a convention or additional protocol(s) to the International Convention on the Elimination of All Forms of Racial Discrimination, filling the existing gaps in the Convention, and also providing new normative standards aimed at combating all forms of contemporary racism, including incitement to racial and religious hatred."[10] The Ad Hoc Committee's ongoing work on racism over the years provides a rich source of official positions by various nations, expertise by independent experts, and unofficial dialogue that goes to the heart of disagreements and concerns about defining racism from a global perspective.

In 2020, I was appointed as a legal expert to this Committee, working to advise on how nations should best address contemporary forms of racism.[11] Among many issues, the Committee grappled with racism in sport, the lack of a definition of xenophobia, and whether or not to address concerns related to migration and refugee seekers together.

Here, old arguments that nations had hashed out during the treaty negotiations for ICERD resurfaced. What is racism, specifically? Does it include xenophobia, or is that a unique form of oppression in need of its own treaty? Should nations specify types of racism, particularly antisemitism and Islamophobia? How do racism and religious discrimination intersect? When should racism be criminalized as a hate crime, and should this include hate speech? What should be done about racism that takes place online? All of these questions go to the Ad Hoc Committee's broader mandate, to recommend whether the treaty should be amended to update its legal protections to account for modern-day manifestations of racism.

Responses varied by nation and over time. At the ninth session of the Ad Hoc Committee, the statement of support by the EU (European Union) centered on its commitment to two core human rights principles, equality and nondiscrimination.[12] Discussion ensued about legislation adopted by the EU to prohibit racial discrimination.[13] The representative stressed the importance of promoting equality and nondiscrimination through comprehensive legislation, such as banning workplace discrimination. Following the European Union Framework Decision of 2008, xenophobia and racism were viewed as describing different phenomenon, even though the words are sometimes used interchangeably. The representative from the United Kingdom acknowledged that hate crimes have no place in British society and discussed the problem of bias against black defendants in the criminal justice system.[14]

The representative from Tunisia, speaking on behalf of the African Group, recalled that "[t]he contemporary manifestations of racism included xenophobia, Islamophobia, anti-Semitism, propagation of racism and xenophobic attacks through cyberspace, racial profiling and incitement to racial, ethnic and religious hatred. . . . that victims of profiling required better protection from these manifestations. Maximum remedies should be applied and impunity for perpetrators of acts of racism should be eliminated."[15] Libya's representative called attention to root causes of migration, including poverty. The representative from South Africa called for solutions that would be "truly victim-oriented" and that "racism was not defined in the ICERD . . . and yet its meaning was understood" amid additional questions about how best to conceptualize racism and its relationship to xenophobia.[16]

The representative from Japan shared that Japanese law focused on equal rights and protected foreigners through antiracism legislation. The representative from Brazil noted that, under Brazil's Constitution, racism is a crime and stressed that measures were needed to protect migrants and refugees from racism, racial discrimination and xenophobia. The Russian Federation raised concerns about racism and neo-Nazism in sport elsewhere, noting a case in Ukraine involving Dynamo Kiev football club fans.

Many members of the Committee affirmed the importance of better understanding the meaning and causes of racism in order to combat it. For example, the Africa Group cautioned that the "Ad Hoc Committee could not afford to avoid its responsibility when it came to the protection of victims of racism, racial discrimination, xenophobia and related intolerance."[17]

Such wide-ranging conversations about racism also revealed foundational questions that were once raised in the context of negotiating the ICERD treaty itself over fifty years earlier. What is racism? How does racism relate to other forms of oppression? What are countries willing and able to say about combating racism in other countries and about racism that is more globally pervasive? What about governments that deny racism exists in their country?

In its final report of the ninth session, the Ad Hoc Committee explicitly names racism, concluding:

> The fight against racism, racial discrimination, xenophobia and related intolerance was a collective imperative that required the support and contributions of all Member States, if peaceful global coexistence was to be achieved. The way forward was for all to work together at all levels to combat the growing trend of xenophobia and racial profiling. Efforts must be redoubled to limit the contemporary forms of racism that were on the increase, particularly those forms targeting, among others, persons of African descent, immigrants and refugees. Those countries currently plagued by growing racism must take the Durban Declaration and Programme of Action seriously and ensure that it guided domestic policies.[18]

This passage from the report reveals both the moral urgency and the political difficulty of the moment. Though the language is unambiguous in naming racism as a collective global challenge, the report's persistent appeal to "member states" to act underscores a structural tension: international obligations continue to depend on the political will of sovereign governments. The statement's emphasis on the Durban Declaration reflects the enduring—but unevenly implemented—legacy of that framework in shaping global efforts to combat racism.

Throughout the Ad Hoc Committee's years of work, there is a palpable sense that the world must do more to combat racism, combined with bewilderment that solutions are not taking root. Independent experts invited to each session have shared views about why. There have been calls for the criminalization of racial discrimination under national laws. Independent expert and former UN Special Rapporteur Tendayi Achiume articulated this tension between treaty requirements that nations address racially discriminatory policies and national criminal laws that often require a demonstration of intent.[19] Independent expert Krassimir Kanev confirmed the serious discrimination against Roma and other ethnic minorities in Bulgaria, but noted that criminalization of racial discrimination has not worked in Bulgaria, "except in cases when private individuals are involved in severe forms of racial discrimination when there may be criminal prosecution."[20]

During my time as legal expert, I raised concerns about the lack of legal specificity regarding what constitutes racial discrimination as a substantive gap to the ICERD and the need for a stronger definitional framework that accounts for racism alongside racial discrimination—arguments I developed in *Human Rights Racism* in 2019.[21]

The Ad Hoc Committee's program of work continues to grapple with xenophobia, racial profiling, religious discrimination, and intersectionality.[22] Another area of inquiry concerns whether or not to criminalize racial discrimination. What kinds of acts in our present era constitute a crime? Where does hate speech fit in and what about participation in racist organizations?[23]

These modern debates about racism raise old questions. Is racism a crime because of the victim's identity based on "race"? Is racism a crime because of the hate or bias of the offender? Or should the law adopt a hybrid model, taking into consideration both the victim's identity and the perpetrator's motive? The variety of concerns raised throughout these Ad Hoc Committee sessions illustrates the ongoing complexities of defining and addressing diverse forms of racism and the lack of universal consensus on what approaches to pursue. Some nations called for comprehensive international standards, and others sought renewed efforts at national legislation. This demonstrates, once again, the continued challenges surrounding the definition of racism and its relationship to other forms of harm based on racial ideology.

The United Nations Security Council on Racism

On June 14, 2023, the UN Security Council (UNSC) gathered at UN headquarters in New York City for its 9,347th meeting. Established by the UN Charter in 1945 as the organ of the United Nations responsible for maintaining international peace and security, the Security Council has been behind some of the most historic moments in modern world affairs. It was the Security Council that set up the 1964 peacekeeping mission in Cyprus, still underway today. It was the Security Council that controversially authorized the North Atlantic Treaty Organization (NATO) to use force against Muammar Gaddafi's government in Libya in 2011, allowing "all necessary measures" to protect civilians. Yet the Security Council has also suffered from inaction in the face of major international crises, largely due to the veto powers of China, France, Russia, the United Kingdom, and the United States. These nations have used the veto to block Security Council resolutions responding to various threats to the peace over the years, notably China and Russia's veto against resolutions addressing the civil war in Syria, Russia's veto against resolutions targeting its own illegal annexation of Crimea and invasion in Ukraine and the US veto of resolutions seeking a ceasefire and end to Israel's war in Gaza.

Over the years, the Security Council's leadership regarding international peace and security has evolved. Perhaps, its most prominent role concerns terrorism. In the aftermath of the attacks on the United States on September 11, 2001, the United States has led and financed a number of efforts to combat terrorism through Security Council Resolution 2178, which set up international coordination requiring nations to take action to prevent terrorism, including through stricter airport controls. Terrorism, in this view, was named as groups affiliated with the Islamic State and associates of Al-Qaida.

What the Security Council has not been known for is combating racism—that is, until June 14, 2023, when it unanimously passed Resolution 2686 on "Tolerance and International Peace and Security Resolution." In this resolution, the Security Council explicitly recognized—for the first time—racism by name, distinct from racial discrimination, as a contributing cause of wars and armed conflict. The Resolution specifically states that the Security Council "[r]ecognizes that hate speech, racism, racial discrimination, xenophobia, related forms of intolerance, gender discrimination, and acts of extremism can contribute to driving the outbreak, escalation and recurrence of conflict, and undermine initiatives to address root causes of conflict and prevent and resolve conflict, as well as reconciliation, reconstruction and peacebuilding efforts."[24] It marks the first time the Security Council has acknowledged racism as a cause of wars and, therefore, as a threat to international peace and security.

Judging Racism at the World Court

The political recognition of the problem of racism by the United Nations did not automatically extend to the realm of legal justice. Acts of racism harm millions of people around the world, and nations are rarely, if ever, held to account for their failure to prohibit and prevent it.

The ICERD treaty envisioned that nations would take their disputes before the International Court of Justice (ICJ). Founded in 1945 as the principal judicial organ of the United Nations, the ICJ was afforded the authority to peacefully resolve disputes between nations on the basis of international law. Over its long history, the ICJ has adjudicated cases involving territorial disputes, diplomatic relations, genocide, and torture, issuing advisory opinions on matters such as the threat or use of nuclear weapons and states' legal obligations concerning climate change.

In recent years, the ICJ has been asked to interpret what is and what is not racial discrimination under the ICERD treaty. As of 2025, there have been five instances in which nations have brought cases against other nations alleging racial discrimination. The first case was brought in 2008 by Georgia against Russia. Then, Ukraine filed a case against Russia in 2017. A year later, Qatar brought a case against the United Arab Emirates in 2018. Two additional cases, which are pending as of 2026, have been brought by Armenia against Azerbaijan and by Azerbaijan against Armenia. The extensive pleadings and the Court's responses—in addition to what the Court has not said—reveal how the Court, individual judges, and nations struggle with differing views about the meaning of racial discrimination and how to define it. Reviewing them together underscores the lack of global consensus about what racism is and when it is illegal under the more narrowly defined ban on racial discrimination in international law.

Georgia v. Russia (2008–2011)

In *Georgia v. Russia*, the Court was asked to make decisions about whether the Russian Federation violated ICERD by engaging in racial discrimination during its military invasion of the South Ossetia and Abkhazia regions of Georgia. The case began in August 2008, when Georgia filed an application with the ICJ against the Russian Federation, alleging that the defendant had violated its obligations under ICERD during its military interventions in South Ossetia and Abkhazia between 1990 and 2008.[25] Specifically, Georgia claimed that the Russian Federation violated Article 2.1.a by "engaging in acts and practices of 'racial discrimination against persons, groups of persons or institutions' and failing 'to ensure that all public authorities and public institutions, national and local, shall act in conformity with this obligation.'"[26] Georgia claimed that the basis for racial discrimination was the number of harms, including "pillage, hostage-taking, beatings and intimidation, denial of the freedom of movement, denial of their right to education in their mother tongue, pressure to obtain Russian citizenship and/or Russian passports, and threats of punitive taxes and expulsions for maintaining Georgian citizen-ship" on the basis of ethnicity of the Georgian, Greek, and Jewish people living in the affected areas.[27] Georgia pleaded to the ICJ that Russia's many failings to comply with ICERD included violating Articles 3, 4, 5, and 6 of the treaty due to Russia's failure to condemn racial segregation, condemn propaganda promoting racial hatred, protect human rights, and provide effective protection.

As the case was pending, the ICJ issued provisional measures calling upon both parties to "refrain from any act of racial discrimination against persons, groups of persons or institutions; abstain from sponsoring, defending or supporting racial discrimination by any persons or organizations."[28] Ultimately, the ICJ never decided this case on the merits, so how it would have dealt with the clear harms that extend beyond discrimination to crimes against groups of people who define themselves by their ethnicity based on culture, language, and ancestry will remain a mystery. Due to complex procedural reasons, the ICJ agreed with Russia's preliminary objection that the Court lacked jurisdiction because Article 22 of ICERD was never met.[29] In practical terms, the Court determined that Georgia had not met its obligation to genuinely attempt to negotiate with the Russian Federation, as required by ICERD, and therefore did not meet the precondition requiring negotiations prior to seeking a remedy at the Court.[30]

This raises important questions about what constitutes "negotiations" with respect to allegations of racial discrimination under international law. Based on prior jurisprudence, "an obligation to negotiate does not imply an obligation to reach an agreement."[31] The parties' fulfillment of this precondition hinges on whether or not their negotiations were meaningful, wherein the ICJ has previously considered the "attitude and views of the Parties on the substantive issues of the question involved."[32] In interpreting the level and kind of negotiation required of Georgia and Russia under Article 22 of the ICERD, the ICJ adopted an ordinary meaning of the treaty language.[33] The Court determined that "the precondition of negotiation is met only when there has been a failure of negotiations, or when negotiations have become futile or deadlocked"[34] and articulated that it treated the matter as a question of fact.[35]

So, what would qualify as substantive negotiation about racial discrimination? In this case, Georgia argued that it tried to negotiate with Russia about racial discrimination when it raised its concerns about Russian forces killing and forcibly displacing over three hundred thousand people of ethnic Georgian background in what Georgia called ethnic cleansing.[36] Russia rebutted that "[a]t no occasion in their bilateral relations did Georgia articulate any claim of racial discrimination by Russia, and Georgia and Russia did not engage in negotiations in respect of any such claim."[37] The Court determined that "although the claims and counter-claims concerning ethnic cleansing may evidence the existence of a dispute as to the interpretation and application of CERD, they do not constitute attempts at negotiation by either party."[38] The Court summarized its finding that Georgia failed to meet negotiation preconditions on the grounds that both parties' communications about issues of ethnic cleansing and extermination "attest to the existence of a dispute between them on a subject-matter capable of falling under CERD. However, they fail to demonstrate an attempt at negotiating these matters."[39] The ICJ determined that these were mandatory preconditions to bringing a case under ICERD before the ICJ.

Not all the judges agreed. Notably, President Owada, Judge Simma, Judge Abraham, Judge Donoghue, and Judge ad hoc Gaja dissented. In their Joint Dissenting Opinion, they argued that the Court should have "found that it had jurisdiction to entertain the Application."[40] They found that the Court's finding that Article 22 of ICERD requires negotiation prior to bringing a case before the ICJ was erroneous and inconsistent with the Court's recent practice.[41] They said "the Court has never conditioned its jurisdiction on the existence of prior negotiations between parties, except on the basis of an express provision to that effect."[42] The judges continued, "[n]o reason can be found for such a surprisingly narrow approach, one at odds with the thrust of the Court's most recent jurisprudence in respect of its consideration of the conditions for jurisdiction and, specifically, at odds with a Judgment as recent—and as clear on this point in its reasoning—as that which the Court handed down on the preliminary objections in the *Croatia* v. *Serbia* case."[43] The Joint Dissenting Opinion further stated "it is surprising to see the Court dismiss the numerous statements in which the Georgian authorities, well before 9 August 2008, accused Russia of encouraging ethnic cleansing or attempting to 'legalize' the results of ethnic cleansing, on the grounds that those statements are unrelated to CERD, or that they do not contain any allegations of racial discrimination aimed at Russia."[44] Such a powerful and joint dissenting opinion signals concern about the ICJ's handling of this case.

Judge Simma pointedly critiqued the Court's judgment as erroneously reasoned. He noted that the judgment "confers legal significance to only two exchanges between Georgia and the Russian Federation, and thus arrives at the conclusion that the dispute arose only between 9 and 12 August 2008," thereby dismissing the rest of Georgia's evidentiary submission.[45] He detailed how the Court missed evidence of racial discrimination, for example, by looking only for the words "racial discrimination" in government communications and not finding them. He further noted that this formalistic approach strayed from past ICJ practice and set a precedent for unwise approaches in the future.

Judge Donoghue also determined in her separate opinion that a nation is not required to notify another nation of its dispute as a prerequisite to seeking dispute settlement at the ICJ, and that this was the consistent practice of the ICJ, and its predecessor, the Permanent Court of International Justice.[46]

The ICJ's handling of its first case regarding racial discrimination and the ICERD treaty raises concerns. In outlawing racial discrimination, the ICERD treaty obligates states to legally ban acts that directly cause racial discrimination and to ensure that the state itself is not engaged in racial discrimination. The Court was asked to determine what kinds of acts constitute racial discrimination. ICERD defines racial discrimination, in part, as a distinction, exclusion, restriction, or preference on the basis of race or ethnicity. Ethnic cleansing has been defined by a UN Commission of Experts as "a purposeful policy designed by one ethnic or religious group to remove by violent and terror-inspiring means the civilian population of another ethnic or religious group from certain geographic areas."[47] Even this general definition constitutes a form of racial discrimination as envisioned by ICERD insofar as it is a form of exclusion on the basis of ethnicity that would violate several of the protected rights enumerated in Article 5.[48]

However, the ICJ did not analyze this question. Instead, it determined it did not have jurisdiction over the case because Georgia had not engaged in the necessary negotiations with Russia before bringing the matter to the Court. Instead of providing clarity about the scope and interpretation of ICERD, the ICJ's first official judicial decision on the matter raised more questions and problematic ones. Is there a legal expectation that a nation under armed attack by a militarily more powerful nation is responsible for telling the aggressor nation to "stop" racial discrimination and human rights violations? Was the Georgian government responsible for formally requesting Russia to remove its peacekeepers, in order to "prove" racial discrimination?[49] Does evidence that two nations have a legal dispute about racial discrimination have to be explicit—for example, documenting it in writing as racial or ethnic discrimination by name?[50]

This case, Russia's conduct, and the ICJ's response underscored the challenges of addressing racism by one state against people in another state under the current interpretation of international law. Within the next decade, four more nations would soon bring claims under ICERD and their concerns about racial discrimination to the ICJ.

Ukraine v. Russian Federation (2017–2024)

In January 2017, Ukraine alleged to the ICJ that the Russian Federation had violated the ICERD treaty (in addition to other claims) with its campaign of cultural erasure of "ethnic Ukrainian and Tatar People in Crimea."[51] In its countermemorial specific to the claim it had violated the ICERD treaty, the Russian Federation took issue with Ukraine's arguments about what constitutes an ethnic group and invoked the negotiation history of the Genocide Convention to argue a distinction between an ethnic group defined as something traditional and stable that a person is born into, and a political group as something a person chooses to join.[52] The Russian Federation further argued, "[T]here is no basis to import political opinions under the terms 'national or ethnic origin'; they are 'obviously outside' the scope of CERD, which 'only deals with racial discrimination.'"[53] They argued that racial discrimination requires the violation of a human right protected under international law.[54]

In its Judgment issued in January 2024, the ICJ found that Russia had violated some, but not all, of its obligations under the ICERD treaty.[55] The Court found the Russia violated Article 2 through its "numerous and pervasive acts of racial discrimination against the Crimean Tatar and Ukrainian communities in Crimea and by engaging in a policy and practice of racial discrimination against those communities."[56] The Russian Federation was also found to have promoted and incited racial discrimination; sponsored, defended, and supported racial discrimination by others; failed to protect or provide access to justice; and failed to combat racial discrimination through effective education, culture, and other efforts.

Here, the ICJ offers more specificity about its understanding of racial discrimination. The Court interprets racial discrimination in the treaty to mean any differentiation of treatment, based on one of the prohibited grounds (race, color, descent, or national or ethnic origin), resulting in an impairment of the recognition, enjoyment, or exercise of human rights and fundamental freedoms arising from its purpose or effect.[57] The ICJ did determine that Crimean Tatars and ethnic Ukrainians in Crimea are both ethnic groups protected by the treaty.[58] Instead of issuing its own independent definition, it relied on Ukraine and Russia's agreement that both are ethnic groups. The ICJ did confirm that political identity or political positions are irrelevant for determining ethnic origin.

The Court deemed it necessary to connect the harm, in this case physical violence, to a form of intent: Did the attackers act because of the victims' ethnic origin? In doing so, it seems the Court attempted to draw a clear line between political identity and ethnic origin identity. This legal reasoning raises pressing questions. What happens when a state targets an ethnic group not merely for its identity but for political behaviors that are stereotypically or systemically attributed to that identity? Does this not support impunity for state violence or repression that falls disproportionately on ethnic groups with politically stigmatized identities? Here, distinguishing political from racial motivation becomes legally and morally fraught.

In this case, the Court concluded that because many kinds of people had been victims of violence, there was no disparate adverse effect on the two ethnic groups in this case—Crimean Tatars and ethnic Ukrainians. The Court further suggested that "any disparate adverse effect on the rights of Crimean Tatars and ethnic Ukrainians can be explained by their political opposition to the conduct of the Russian Federation in Crimea," not other grounds protected by the treaty.[59]

This reasoning raises alarms. Racial discrimination does not happen in a vacuum. It can live alongside other factors. It is entirely possible for a government to target a group of people because of their racial identity and because of their political beliefs. It should concern us if the legal requirement for a finding of discrimination starts to evaluate how many people in a group were harmed or even suggests that the entire group must be harmed for the harm to exist. We are left wondering about the particulars—what is racial discrimination under international law? What kind of evidence would the ICJ find to be convincing?

In this case, the Court did not agree with Ukraine's arguments that police targeted law enforcement measures on Crimean Tatars *because* of their ethnic origin. The Court's articulated standard of proof is "whether there is convincing evidence when considering that allegation made by Ukraine under CERD," with more weight given to single sources, contemporaneous evidence from people with direct knowledge, independent reports, and direct witnesses.[60] Providing such proof is quite difficult for a country under attack.

Similarly, the Court reasoned that Ukraine did not prove that the Russian Federation's measures against the Mejlis and Crimean Tatar leaders were due to their ethnic origin. Instead, it found that the Russian Federation was responding to political opposition and activities it considered extremist or separatist. It agreed that the bans on the Mejlis had disparate impact, but reasoned that Ukraine, yet again, had failed to provide convincing evidence that the basis for the ban was the Mejlis' ethnic origin rather than their political activities.

Here, we return to the meaning of ethnic origin and who gets to decide. How the Mejlis understand their group identity is likely to differ from how the Russian Federation views them. Is there an expectation that a government admits it has a racist reason or ethnic bias behind its actions? And what does that mean absent any universal definition or standard?

This case also highlights the Court's struggles with considering multiple or overlaid causes. Political activity should not be allowed as a pretext for racial discrimination. But the ICJ's reasoning doesn't prohibit a government from targeting a group because of racial characteristics and then attributing their reasons to political characteristics instead.

Even the Russian Federation's ban on ethnic cultural events was not enough to convince the ICJ that the basis was ethnic origin because, in the Court's view, some groups had held successful ethnic cultural events and the Russian Federation's overall approach to public gatherings, regardless of ethnic group, was restrictive. Must racial discrimination must *always* be present in order for it to *ever* be present?

The many powerful separate and dissenting opinions and declarations in this case reveal certain judges' own concerns and perspectives and are worth quoting at length. In her separate opinion, Judge Donoghue, president of the court at the time, disagreed with the majority on the issue of the ban of the Mejlis:

> Even if one accepts the Court's conclusion that the ban on the Mejlis was based on the political activities of the leaders and members of the Mejlis in opposition to the Russian Federation, this conclusion does not foreclose the possibility that the ban was also based on race and had the purpose or the effect of nullifying or impairing the enjoyment or exercise of certain rights and freedoms by person of Crimean Tatar ethnic origin.[61]

She continued:

> It is to be expected that all members of an ethnic minority do not hold identical views on government decisions that affect the ethnic group and that some organizations representing an ethnic group will stridently oppose the authorities in power, while others will adopt a more accommodationist approach toward those authorities. I do not accept the proposition that a ban on one particular organization representing an ethnic group would not amount to racial discrimination so long as other organizations comprised of members of that ethnic group have not been banned.[62]

Judge Sebutinde issued a dissenting opinion:

> [I]t is also not inconceivable that a given measure may have more than one objective. Thus, while it may be true that the law enforcement measures against the Crimean Tatars were based on the political positions and views they espoused, this does not exclude the possibility that the measures also had a discriminatory purpose or effect on the rights of that protected group.[63]
>
> The Court correctly finds that the law enforcement measures undertaken by the Russian Federation in Crimea had a disproportionate effect

upon Crimean Tatars . . . [a]ccordingly, such measures constitute acts of racial discrimination unless they can be credibly justified by reasons unrelated to race, colour, descent or national or ethnic origin." "Such disproportionate targeting of members of a particular ethnic group, with no justified basis, constitutes an act of racial discrimination under Articles 2 and 5 of CERD."[64]

Regarding the argument that the ban against the Mejlis was only politically motivated and therefore the Russian Federation did not violate CERD, Sebutinde concluded, "In my view, the ban constituted an act of racial discrimination."[65]

In his separate opinion, Judge Iwasawa cautions:

> Racial discrimination is one of the most invidious forms of discrimination. A measure based on a prohibited ground listed in Article 1, paragraph 1, of CERD is inherently suspect and must be subjected to the most rigorous scrutiny.[66]
>
> [I]n accordance with the notion of indirect discrimination, equal treatment can also constitute racial discrimination if it has an unjustifiable, disproportionate, prejudicial impact on a protected group under CERD.[67]

Judge Charlesworth's separate opinion articulates the Court's flawed rationale with precision, noting how:

> the Judgment seems to regard the various justifications for differential treatment as mutually exclusive: if differential treatment is "due to . . . political activities," it cannot also be based on grounds of ethnic origin. Yet a common feature of measures that produce a disparate adverse effect on specific groups is that they rely on a variety of justifications. This accords with human experience that almost all actions have multiple motives. So, a finding that differential treatment is based on political grounds does not preclude it also being based on prohibited grounds, such as ethnic origin. In this sense, the Court did not comprehensively examine whether the explanation provided by the Russian Federation relates to on of the prohibited grounds under CERD.[68]

These judicial opinions illuminate the central challenge the ICJ faces in interpreting racial discrimination under ICERD: Acts of repression are rarely motivated by a single cause, and distinguishing political from racial motivations can obscure the lived realities of racism. Several judges urge a broader and more nuanced view, emphasizing that racial discrimination can coexist with other motives and must be evaluated through both intent and impact. The case highlights the Court's reluctance to fully embrace indirect or intersectional understandings of discrimination and human identity, even as multiple judges call for more rigorous scrutiny. Ultimately, these divergent perspectives signal an ongoing struggle to align international legal doctrine with the complexities of racialized harm in practice. This struggle to define and prove racial discrimination under ICERD is not confined to the *Ukraine v. Russia* case. It reemerges in other disputes, where questions of national origin, state conduct, and racialized harm again challenge the Court's interpretive boundaries.

Qatar v. United Arab Emirates (2018–2021)

On June 11, 2018, Qatar brought a case against the United Arab Emirates alleging that the UAE had "enacted and implemented a series of discriminatory measures against Qataris on the basis of their national origin," in violation of the ICERD treaty.[69] As examples, Qatar shared how the UAE had expelled all Qataris from the country without exception, with just two weeks' notice, prohibited Qataris from entering or traveling through the UAE, prohibited speech in support of Qatar, incited hate speech with a media campaign against Qataris, and closed UAE airspace and seaports to Qataris. Qatar referenced a December 2017 report by the Office of the United Nations High Commissioner for Human Rights that documented discrimination and human rights violations of the Qatari people due to the official actions of several countries, including the UAE, Saudi Arabia, Egypt, and Bahrain.

In May 2017, a Qatar News Agency story reported that the Emir of Qatar supported the Islamic Republic of Iran and criticized then US President Donald Trump.[70] Qatar claimed this was a cyberhacking incident, and this claim was widely documented as valid, including by the US Federal Bureau of Investigation. Qatar contended that the UAE and other states used this fabricated story as a pretext for enacting coordinated and discriminatory measures against Qataris.

While the case was pending, the ICJ did instruct the UAE to take provisional measures, which included allowing Qatari students affected by the UAE measure to complete their education there, allowing Qataris access to judicial bodies in the UAE, and allowing reunification of families separated by the UAE measure.

The UAE rejected Qatar's allegations and argued that it severed diplomatic relations with Qatar in June 2017, necessitating the measures it took.[71] It referred to the Riyadh Agreements in 2013, stipulating that Qatar would stop funding terrorism and violent extremist groups. UAE also argued that nationality was not protected by ICERD as they believed the treaty only protected discrimination on the basis of a person's national origin based on "characteristics that are inherent and immutable, namely race, colour, descent, or national or ethnic origin. Nationality, on the other hand, is a legal bond that can change over time."[72] The UAE also argued that national origin is associated with a person's permanent sense of connection to a "particular nation or people" as the treaty says in Article 1.1, but does "not include nationality in the sense of citizenship."[73]

In this case, the Court grappled with the meaning of racial discrimination on the basis of nationality (which is not named in the treaty) as compared to national origin (which is). In the ICJ's order and in various dissenting opinions, the judges disagreed on how to interpret the definition provided in Article 1.1 of ICERD as to the meaning of racial discrimination on the basis of national origin.[74] On February 4, 2021, the ICJ issued a judgment finding that the dispute was outside the scope *ratione materiae*, or subject matter, of ICERD and, therefore, that the ICJ lacked jurisdiction to consider the matter.[75]

The Court's basis for its decision speaks to the core question in this book: Is racism illegal? In this case, the Court examined the meaning of the term "national origin" in the ICERD treaty and considered whether or not that term encompasses current nationality. The Court considered previous legal cases, the practice of the CERD and other human rights bodies, the object and purpose of the treaty, and the historical context in which the treaty was drafted. In paragraph 88 of the Judgment, the

Court declared that the term national origin "does not encompass current nationality."

Eleven judges voted in favor of this Judgment and six voted against, including the president of the Court, Judge Abdulqawi Ahmed Yusuf, who explained his disagreement. His first objection was that the Court undercut Qatar's claims of discrimination by construing those claims as based on nationality and therefore, accurately, concluding that they fell beyond the purview of the treaty. In contrast, Yusuf argued that Qatar was concerned about discrimination that was taking place against people who were Qatari nationals, and *also* because of their national origin. Does the ICJ, with the case, mean to suggest that racial discrimination can be parsed into neat and sometimes exculpatory categories? If the Court finds the discrimination was based on nationality, then is it not based on national origin or anything else?

This contradicts the long-standing approach taken by the CERD and fails to take account of intersectionality in discrimination cases.[76] The CERD General Recommendation No. 30 states that "differential treatment based on citizenship or immigration status will constitute discrimination if the criteria for such differentiation, judged in light of the objectives and purposes of the Convention, are not applied pursuant to a legitimate aim, and are not proportional to the achievement of this aim."[77] The Court's framing of racial discrimination in this case suggests that if the mistreatment was because of nationality, then it could not simultaneously be because of national origin, and hence there was no violation of the treaty. (And, its silence on the matter could imply that mistreatment due to nationality is acceptable.) The Court confirmed that the purpose of the treaty was to "eliminate all forms and manifestations of racial discrimination against human beings on the basis of real or perceived characteristics as of their origin, namely at birth."[78] Yet its own reasoning confounds this conclusion and presumes the inherent separability of nationality as a purely legalistic matter from national origin, ethnicity, color, and race. As we shall see, the definition of nationality as separable and distinct from the identity characteristics included in ICERD continues.

Armenia v. Azerbaijan and *Azerbaijan v. Armenia* (2021–pending as of 2025)

In September 2021, Armenia brought a case against Azerbaijan to the ICJ alleging violations of the ICERD treaty, claiming that Azerbaijan has engaged in racial discrimination for decades against people of Armenian ethnic or national origins, "regardless of nationality" through systemic discrimination, mass killings, torture, formal state policy in schools and government, with Azerbaijan President Ilham Aliyev "leading the way."[79]

Azerbaijan also brought proceedings to the ICJ in September 2021, alleging that Armenia has violated the ICERD treaty by its policy of ethnic cleansing and systemic discrimination against Azerbaijanis during the 1991–1994 war and ensuing thirty-year occupation.[80] They also claim Armenia has violated the ICERD treaty due to widespread hate speech at the highest levels that espouses Azerbaijani inferiority as well as the destruction of cultural heritage sites.

At this writing, both cases are pending before the Court, with additional pleadings due in November 2025. It remains to be seen whether the ICJ will specify what does and does not constitute racial discrimination under the ICERD treaty. But cases such as these, sadly, are widespread in the world. Identity-based armed conflicts have been some of the most intractable in modern history. It is commonplace to dehumanize "the other" and to define otherness along the lines of race or a racialized sense of identity.

*

Is Racism Illegal?

Is racism illegal? The passing of the ICERD treaty at the United Nations in 1965 aimed to create a world free from racial discrimination. Because of these developments, we can affirm that nations have agreed to binding legal rules banning racial discrimination, often with the underlying aim to promote equal treatment under the law. Nations have also affirmed that certain practices are banned by law. Slavery is illegal. Genocide is illegal. Segregation is illegal. Apartheid is illegal. But, there is no legally binding prohibition in international law on racism, by name. International law has yet to explicitly define racism as a violation of human rights under international law. In the end, international law, through the ICERD treaty, only bans racial discrimination.

Under this framework, in simple terms, four basic components are required to find that racial discrimination has occurred. First, an act defined as a distinction, exclusion, restriction, or preference occurs. Second, the act is based on identity factors protected by international law: race, color, descent, and national or ethnic origin. Notably, nationality is not protected. Third, the act causes harm, defined as having a purpose or effect of nullifying or impairing human rights or fundamental freedoms. Fourth, applying heightened scrutiny, there is no legitimate exception or justification for the act.

Let's say you were searched and beaten up by the police in a raid on a community that shared certain identity characteristics, such as appearance, culture, and language. The harms you experienced constitute a violation of your human rights. If the police targeted you because of your human identity—understood as race, color, ethnic origin, and/or national origin—it would be deemed racial discrimination unless they had a legitimate reason. Legitimate purposes for the police to target a person or group of people on this basis might exist for national security or public health purposes, but this would be subject to heightened scrutiny.

As noted earlier, international law recognizes two categories of discrimination: purpose-based discrimination and effect-based discrimination, sometimes called indirect discrimination. An example of purpose-based discrimination is when the police conduct stops and arrests because of their views about a person's racial identity. Effect-based discrimination finds a harm can occur without such racist intention if the actions have a disparate impact on a protected group. As viewed by the ICJ, proving racial discrimination requires convincing evidence that

> a measure, being apparently neutral, produces a disparate adverse effect on the rights of a person or a group distinguished by race, colour, descent, or national or ethnic origin, unless such an effect can be explained in a way that does not relate to the prohibited grounds in Article 1, paragraph 1. Mere collateral or secondary effects on persons who are distinguished by one of the prohibited grounds do not, in and of themselves, constitute racial discrimination within the meaning of the Convention.[81]

A second question concerns how ICERD—and the ICJ's interpretation of it—captures human identity and the concept of race. The ICJ has determined that national and ethnic origin means "a person's bond to a national or ethnic group at birth" and that "[a]ccordingly, the political identity or the political position of a person or a group is not a relevant factor for the determination of their ethnic origin within the meaning of Article 1, paragraph 1, of CERD."[82]

Based on this, no case has meaningfully elaborated on what race is or even attempted to describe how race should be interpreted in a case alleging racial discrimination under international law. Arguments before the Court often presume that ethnicity and national origin must be immutable—traits fixed at birth—while nationality is portrayed as fluid or chosen. Nations defending against claims of racial discrimination launch an array of excuses. A common one is to argue that harms are justified because of political reasons or concerns about national security or terrorism.

The ICJ's current jurisprudence surrounding racial discrimination raises serious concern about its institutional ability to address racism in ways that fully recognize the complexity of human identity in a global sense. The challenge goes beyond the bench to the judges themselves. What fifteen judges perceive as a race or a racial group arguably has an undue impact on the treaty's purpose to eliminate all forms of racial discrimination. To understand what racial discrimination is and, more broadly, what constitutes racism globally today, we have to appreciate human identity in both historical and contemporary contexts where people are experiencing the harms of discrimination, in any form. Sometimes race is a clearly understood identity factor for a group of people; sometimes it is not. Racism is possible in both scenarios, particularly when we understand it as a manifestation of an ideology of racial superiority.

Reviewing these cases and the ICJ's jurisprudence to date revives old questions about race as a category used to define people. Much of the discourse in our modern world about human identity asks if and when people should be able to create our own identities? Should each of us be able to say what we identify as? Should governments create and enforce racial categories? Should courts enforce those categories? Do they go further and assign individuals to these categories? Do individuals get to self-identify race or ethnicity at some point? Our lives are complex, and many of us were moved across national, cultural, and political boundaries before we could speak and before we could form memories. As self-determination becomes more publicly essential in the world—the right to self-identify our gender, our pronouns, our sexual orientation—where is the right to self-identify our race, our ethnicity, our national origin?

*

Racism remains one of the most significant unregulated threats to humanity in the world today. It is a tool of oppression with global reach. It works by dehumanizing individuals and communities not only by denying their inherent equality and dignity, but by doing so on the basis of a constructed category of race, designed for the very purpose of separating humans into a hierarchy meant to permanently elevate some and suppress many. There is something particularly inhumane, morally reprehensible, and egregious about racism. Racism's very nature is insidious. It is often rendered invisible by those who benefit from the social capital, economic power, and political currency that comes from wielding it, even as they use it to maintain their place of power within societal hierarchies.

It has been eighty years since the Charter of the United Nations established the foundational principles and rules by which all nations abide, respecting the human rights and fundamental freedoms of people and the role of nations in upholding international peace and security. Among these is the requirement that all nations respect the principles of equal rights, human rights, and fundamental freedoms for all "without distinction as to race, sex, language, or religion."[83] It has been sixty years since the ICERD treaty was created, and nations committed to the project of eliminating racial discrimination. The ICERD treaty aimed to transform earlier aspirations into binding legal commitments, obligating nations to take specific actions, such as implementing laws that prohibit racial discrimination and eliminating government policies that promote racial superiority. The important work of the CERD and ICJ jurisprudence to address treaty violations in the years since the creation of the ICERD reveals tensions between the theory and practice of law. Many interpretations of racial discrimination and legal enforcement of its violations are incongruent with the realities expressed by people victimized by racism. Nations regulate racial discrimination differently and sometimes not at all. International legal mechanisms lack a unified approach. At the International Court of Justice, individual judges disagree on the nuances of applying the law to particular people in particular cases. Solutions to such challenges require the participation and cooperation of peoples and nations throughout the world.

Back in 2001, nations recognized this at the World Conference against Racism, Racial Discrimination, Xenophobia and Related Intolerance where they called for "a global fight against racism" making it one the first international forums to name and decry racism by name.[84] Held in Durban, South Africa, the resulting Durban Declaration and Programme of Action named racism and called for nations to take measures to protect against it through the use of law, policy, education, and communication technologies. Since then, the global conversation about combating racism has continued to evolve, with UNESCO hosting its 4th Global Forum Against Racism and Discrimination in 2025 calling for a collective international and global human response. As the UN Security Council has finally affirmed, racism is a root cause of wars and conflicts—and a persistent one. Today, there is increased recognition of the need to combat racism at the global level, raising important questions about how to do so effectively.

6

Naming *Global Racism*

When Racism Goes Viral

"I'm not a victim of racism. I am a tormentor of racists."[1] Brazilian footballer Vinícius José Paixão de Oliveira Júnior, better known as Vini Jr., posted these words to X on June 10, 2024. He was responding to a decision from a Spanish court that found three men guilty of a "crime against moral integrity" with "aggravating circumstance of discrimination based on racist motives" for leading racist chants against him during a La Liga game at Valencia's Mestalla Stadium on May 21, 2023.[2] By then, a twenty-four-year-old star for Real Madrid, Vini Jr. had become one of the best players in the world despite facing racist taunts and slurs most everywhere he played.

Football is the world's most popular sport, with an estimated five billion fans, according to the Federation Internationale de Football Association (FIFA), but both its governing bodies and the nations where the sport flourishes have too often looked the other way when racism comes to light, both on and off the pitch. In sentencing these men to eight months in prison, the Spanish court sent a strong message that such taunts went far beyond acceptable norms of fan behavior. Vini Jr. had his own message. In that same X post he wrote, "[M]any people asked me to ignore it, many others said that my fight was in vain and that I should just 'play football.' . . . This first criminal conviction [for racism] in the history of Spain is not for me. It is for all black people."[3] Vini

Global Racism. Anna Spain Bradley, Oxford University Press. © Anna Spain Bradley 2026.
DOI: 10.1093/oso/9780197778388.003.0007

Jr.'s words underscore a profound truth: Racism doesn't just happen; it is caused by people and institutions who must be held to account for the harms they create.

In the weeks that followed, the world of football took notice. A global sport notorious for its pervasive and persistent racism, from racial slurs hurled at players by Italian fans to crowd violence in Serbia, declared it would tolerate racism no more. Responding to the Spanish court's decision, the president of La Liga, Javier Tebas, said, "It sends a clear message to those people who go to a football stadium to insult that La Liga will detect them, denounce them and there will be criminal consequences for them."[4] Meanwhile, in May 2024, FIFA urged all 211 national federations to make racist abuse a disciplinary offense and introduce a global standard gesture—a crossed-hands signal—that players could use to alert referees to incidents of racism. However, only months later, FIFA appeared to have stepped back from its earlier antiracism platform, with a striking absence of antidiscrimination messaging during the 2025 Club World Cup in the United States, despite prior commitments to tackle racist abuse via the revised Disciplinary Code.[5]

Vini Jr.'s racism story shone a spotlight on the systemic racism in football. Of course, racism is also well-documented in rugby, baseball, basketball, and Formula One racing, among other sports. Its prevalence across so many sports and in so many parts of the world has placed racism in sports on the UN's list of contemporary forms of systemic racism. This kind of racism is not confined within certain places or nations. It is global and, at times, it seems to spread like a virus.

Indeed, that was the case in 2019, when a novel coronavirus emerged in Wuhan, China, spreading to Italy and then across the globe. People started to get sick and die. In those early days, doctors were unsure what the disease was or how to treat it. Health officials recommended that people isolate and mask—initially suggesting the use of ineffective cloth masks before ultimately advising respirator masks. By the spring of 2020, much of the world entered lockdown: children were sent home from school, and adults were sent home from work. In those initial two years, at least 14.9 million people lost their lives to what would come to be known as the COVID-19 pandemic.[6]

The pandemic was responsible for more than just disease of the body; it caused another disease, one that W. E. B. Du Bois and Frederick Douglass had warned about decades earlier: racism driven by fearful people. During this time, hate crimes, discrimination, and racist violence targeting people of Asian descent proliferated.[7] In New York City, one man was attacked on the subway by someone who yelled: "You're infected, China boy, you need to get off the train."[8] The hatred was not only toward people perceived to be Chinese. In India and Sri Lanka, for example, Muslim workers faced violence and discrimination, and in Guangzhou, China, government officials targeted people of African descent with forced tests and mandatory isolation. United Nations Secretary-General António Guterres cautioned that "the pandemic continues to unleash a tsunami of hate and xenophobia, scapegoating and scare-mongering" and urged governments to take decisive action to address such racism and to prosecute hate crimes.[9] COVID not only devastated public health; structural racism compounded its inequitable toll on vulnerable communities, captured in the phrase coined by legal scholar Catherine Powell: "the color of COVID."[10]

During the summer of 2024, in the United Kingdom, fear once again fueled widespread racism and xenophobia in a horrific series of events known as the "Southport stabbings." On July 29, close to noon, a seventeen-year-old attacked a Taylor Swift-themed children's dance event in the town of Southport, on the west coast of England. Using a chef's knife, he brutally stabbed fifteen people, mostly children. Three young girls—Bebe King, Alice da Silva Aguiar, and Elsie Dot Stancombe—died.[11] The attacker was arrested at the scene.

As news of the attack spread, so too did anguish, anger, and misinformation. Some were desperate to find a villain to blame, and rumors began to spread that the culprit was dark-skinned and foreign. False claims emerged that the attacker had entered the UK illegally by boat across the English Channel. A wave of racist mob violence followed, with some seven hundred people arrested for rioting, setting fire to mosques and hotels, and violently attacking people in anti-immigrant, anti-Arab, anti-Black, and anti-Muslim assaults.

It turned out, however, that the criminal was a UK citizen and a minor, a seventeen-year-old named Axel Rudakubana. Born in Wales, Rudakubana's parents had immigrated to the UK after the 1994 genocide in Rwanda. One of the chief constables involved in Rudakubana's arrest later revealed that she wanted to release information to the public that he was not Muslim in hopes of quelling mosque attacks, but was told she could not.[12] During the criminal trial and subsequent public inquiry, it came to light that Rudakubana had a history of violent thoughts and attempts, and that he had been under the care of mental health services.[13] He was sentenced to life imprisonment with a minimum term of fifty-two years.

Rudakubana's crimes were horrific and indefensible—acts of unthinkable violence that devastated families and shocked the nation. Yet the wave of racist reprisals they unleashed revealed a deep fault line in society: a reflex of racial animus to conflate the actions of one criminal with entire communities, even with no connection. The speed with which rumor metastasized into mob violence showed how racism can lie dormant, ready to spread when fear and misinformation activate it. International attention followed, and the United Nations CERD called upon the UK government to curb xenophobic rhetoric and racist hate speech, denouncing the "recurring racists acts and violence against ethnic and ethno-religious minorities, migrants, refugees and asylum-seekers by extremist far-right and white supremacist individuals and groups, including the acts committed in late July an early August 2024."[14] But this story also reveals another truth about humanity. Even as they were horrified by Rudakubana's violence, many people rejected the racism that followed. Hailed by the press as "the day Britain fought back," twenty-five thousand people joined antiracism rallies in a public repudiation of racist violence.[15]

*

What's Going On?

These stories and others like them reveal an uncharted feature of racism. Yes, each example is rooted in a particular place and time where people's lives were disrupted, and real harm occurred. But these three cases are not just discrete instances of racism that laws are created to prosecute—like racial discrimination in the form of a nonpromotion in the workplace, or like a hate crime, such as vandalizing a home or shop with racist messages. They are something more—cases where racism spreads through our human ecosystem. They illustrate how, in the modern world, racism in one place can trigger reactions far away. They show that oppression is not merely the product of human actions; it is also rooted in and sustained by human ideologies.

In the first half of this book, we traveled through history and around the world in search of ways to define racism. We have considered racism as a word. We have looked at the types of racism: internalized, interpersonal, institutional, structural, and systemic. We have learned how racism is described by the identities associated with particular groups it harms, including anti-Arab racism, anti-Asian racism, anti-Black racism, anti-Roma racism, and antisemitism. We have also charted racism rooted in ideologies of racial superiority, such as Fascism and ethnonationalism, with Nazi Germany and Imperial Japan as key examples. We have recognized that racism intersects with other forms of oppression, including apartheid, colonialism, genocide, slavery, and xenophobia. What became clear is that racism is more than racial discrimination. It is a word people use to convey deeper pain caused by harms that steal human dignity. Most of all, we have learned that seeing racism in all its forms and describing it conceptually in ways the world agrees upon has proven difficult. The answers are not one, but many.

This journey through racism so far has shown that it is global in scope, causing harm and suffering to millions. Racism is not only a harm among people, inside institutions, or within systems. It can leak beyond and across borders, traversing them, escaping nations and their laws, and eluding accountability mechanisms bound by jurisdictional boundaries.

It is not always contained by country or culture, by border or boundary. So what do we call this aspect of racism that is also something more?

Naming *Global Racism*

I name this phenomenon global racism. Global racism conceptualizes an undefined form of racism operating on a global layer, interacting with the economic, legal, and political structures of world order and with international actors. It recognizes racism's universal availability, often present and always possible wherever people are, including in the digital world. Global racism is both capable of spreading worldwide and is also inconsistent in when and where it flares up. Recall the analogy of racism as weather and global racism as climate. You experience the weather where you are as a local phenomenon—say, a rainy spring day or a midsummer heat wave. But that weather is shaped by global climate you don't see, such as atmospheric conditions and ocean currents that give rise to heat waves and intense storms. We are used to viewing acts of racism as localized and isolated occurrences. They happen here. They happen there. But what if they are connected? What if racism is possible locally because it is sustained globally in our human ecosystem? Global racism frames racism as part of the broader climate of our human ecosystem—perhaps as a superstructure or substructure of ideology that connects people through belief in the inherent racial superiority of some people over others.

Global racism, as a concept, offers a new lens through which to view an old problem. It seeks to capture racism's mobility—how it can spread from one place to another, even when we don't fully understand why or how. It calls attention to racism as both a threat to international peace between nations and a violation of the universal human rights of people. It names a form of mass oppression rooted in struggles for power and dominance, which have brought ruin to humanity before, fueling slavery, the transatlantic slave trade, colonialism, apartheid, segregation, and genocide. Global racism urges us to recognize its role in our human ecosystem, not only taking account of how people behave but what we believe. This concept frames the conditions that provide the climate in which white supremacy and other ideologies of racial superiority proliferate, spotlighting racism's deeper roots. Global racism is not only a problem for some people in some places; it endangers our very humanity. Combating global racism, therefore, is a test of our collective humanity and our worth as a species.

Mapping Global Racism

Maps of the world picture life on Earth as interconnected. They reveal many layers of information. World maps chart the lands and the seas; mark the locations of cities, nations, and political borders; and reveal other notable topographic features. Certain types of information on the world map are universal and immutable. North and South remain the same no matter where you are in the world due to the magnetic poles. Longitude and latitude lines provide a way to harmonize locations. Charted on a sphere, this map is called a globe—the planet Earth represented for all to see and to understand.

Today, technology allows us to digitally map onto our globe layers that were previously invisible. Global weather maps, for example, now chart how ocean currents and jet streams interact with the atmosphere to impact local weather. Satellite-based vegetation maps reveal patterns of deforestation, drought, and regrowth critical to understanding the environment.

If we think of global racism as part of the human ecosystem—shaping local conditions and spawning isolated events while remaining interconnected—then mapping it becomes an essential task. Just as meteorologists layer weather data onto a globe to reveal patterns that no one can see just by standing on the ground, we can chart the forces, flows, and ideologies that allow racism to move, connect, and take root across borders.

As a thought experiment, let's consider mapping racism as a cartographic exercise with three layers. The first layer maps racism as it arises in a particular local context, taking into account social, cultural, and political histories. The second layer maps racism comparatively, examining it across geographic place and over time. Together, these two layers capture the categories of racism already named: internalized, interpersonal, institutional, structural, and systemic. This mapping also accounts for racism identified by the racial group it harms (anti-Asian, anti-Black, anti-Roma, etc.) and racism's intersectionality with other forms of oppression tied to human identity (age, gender, national origin, indigeneity, religion, sexual orientation, etc .). These layers of racism have been well explored by scholars from various disciplines, written about by novelists, spoken about by world leaders, and charted through instruments of international law and world order.

The search for a third layer—global racism—is the focus of the rest of this book. Following the map metaphor, global racism might exist above us, like the Earth's atmosphere, which allows for the exchange and circulation of air molecules, spores, radio waves, and climate regardless of national borders and geopolitical realities. According to this view, global racism is a superstructure.

Alternatively, global racism might manifest in our human ecosystem as a global substructure, like the mycelium that connects and supports mushrooms invisible and hidden deep beneath the forest floor. As a global substructure, racism functions out of sight even as it is, quite literally, foundational.

In either case, the metaphor supports a system in which we can conceive of global racism in the simplest terms as the means by which racism is interconnected and interdependent with human life wherever we are. Global racism can move through human societies much like other globalized phenomena, through the trade of goods, services, and ideas; through physical and virtual technologies; and through the movement of people, politics, and culture. To confront it, we must learn to see it, not only in the places it appears, but in the invisible currents that carry it across the world.

First Layer

Most of us first learned about racism because of something that happened locally—either directly to us or around us. Think of this layer of racism as incidents appearing on our imagined map, a series of dots marking occurrences around the world over time and coded by type. A dot would appear to show, for example, that the antisemitic graffiti "Hass, Juden raus" ("Hate, Jews out") was painted on a public park bench in Austria. Another might represent a woman in South Carolina forced by law to use a water fountain labeled "Colored." We could circle the city in Thailand where a sign outside a public swimming pool notified patrons that the facility was off limits to "Arab people," or mark the Australian town where a Filipino man was called racial slurs at work. Other points might document racism in mass incarceration in Germany, legal barriers to interracial marriage in Brazil, racial stereotypes on Peruvian television, and commercials for skin-whitening "Snowz" medication in Thailand.[16] Our markings would be verifiable through official reports, such as the UN CERD's 2024 report on racism in Belarus, Bosnia and Herzegovina, Iran, Iraq, Pakistan, United Kingdom, and Venezuela noting the "recurring racist acts and violence against ethnic and ethno-religious minorities, migrants, refugees and asylum-seekers by extremist far-right and white supremacist individuals and groups" that took place in the United Kingdom that summer.[17]

What else should be mapped to chart racism in the local context? As we've explored throughout this book, the lack of a global consensus on what racism is or how to define it challenges any effort at mapping. The international legal definition of racial discrimination has notable gaps, and "racial discrimination" falls well short of encompassing the full scope and harms of racism. Nations and people often follow either a broad consensus about racism or the lead of those in power—accepting as racism whatever a powerful person, group, or nation declares it to be—frequently conflating the latter with the former. As a consequence, the most globally accepted definitions or easily acknowledged forms of racism tend to be (1) those that occurred in the past, such as slavery, the transatlantic slave trade, segregation, apartheid, and colonialism; (2) racism against people of African descent, particularly anti-Black racism; and (3) racism that occurs in or is linked to the United States. Also acknowledged as widespread are antisemitism and Islamophobia, though there is some debate about what kind of "ism" these are, since they involve racialized identities combined with other aspects of human identity—in these two cases, religion.[18] The lack of shared definitions means that any local map of racism inevitably reflects not only acts of prejudice and discrimination but also the power structures and cultural biases that determine what the world chooses to see—and what it refuses to name.

Second Layer

This brings us to the second layer of our imagined map. Here we look not only at the dots themselves, but at the connections between them—the relationships between racisms across place and time. What does racism here have to do with racism there? Under what conditions does racism connect, and how does it spread? How do we trace the lines between dots of racism at the first layer, making connections between them at the second? Visually, any answers we find can be drawn as a line between points on the map.

Analysis at this layer is often comparative.[19] Take historian George M. Frederickson's *Racism: A Short History* (2003), which traces the arc of racism from the Middle Ages to the present, highlighting the tension between the idea of equal rights and the reality of unequal societies. Or consider Tanya Maria Golash-Boza's *Race and Racisms* (2015), which compares racism across nations, looking at systemic racism in criminal justice, healthcare, immigration, and more.[20] Judy Root Aulette's *A Global View of Race and Racism* (2017) takes readers on a journey around the world to examine racism by place, type, and theoretical view, finding that "racism can start with what seems to be events and problems that are not part of our world or our responsibility."[21] Alastair Bonnett's *Multiracism* (2022) analyzes the plurality of racism in a multipolar world, finding "racism has a diverse history with multiple roots and routes."[22] Discussing the plight of racially oppressed Yazidis, Uyghurs, Japanese, and Moroccans, he identifies the fatal mix between modernity and racism, which devalues human life and critiques existing "[e]thnic and racial studies . . . [as] dominated by studies of racism in the West."[23] Such a comparative analysis of racism reveals important insights.

Consider, for example, the story of Angela Saini, a British author and journalist born to Indian immigrant parents who moved to the United States in 2023.[24] She describes how racism was worse for her in the UK. In both countries, she is racially categorized as Asian, but her experiences of racism were different in each. She notes that Asians in the United States have the lowest mortality rate of any race, whereas in the UK they have the highest.[25] Saini shared her experiences in her review of Tomiwa Owolade's book, *This Is Not America: Why Black Lives in Britain Matter*. Owolade calls for Black Britons to define their Blackness on their own terms rather than through the lens of Black America.

Both Saini and Owolade align around a view many scholars have confirmed: Racism is context-specific. Racism for you is different from racism for me. Racism here is different from racism there. Racism today is different from racism hundreds of years ago. But does conceptualizing racism as context-specific blind us to the connections across contexts? Books such as Isabel Wilkinson's *Caste: The Origins of Our Discontents* (2020) and David Livingstone Smith's *On Inhumanity: Dehumanization and How to Resist It* (2020) provide a deeper inquiry into these questions, asking us to evaluate the roots of this kind of oppression.

Another aspect of mapping this second layer concerns more theoretical ideas about racism. In the legal field, scholars introduce concepts that illuminate how racism interacts with and is sustained by law.[26] We speak about "intersectionality," coined by Kimberlé Crenshaw, Patricia Williams's *critique of the racial objectivity of law*, Mari Matsuda's *multiple consciousness*, Cheryl Harris's *Whiteness as Property*, Adrien Wing's *Global Critical Race Feminism*, and more.[27] Makau Mutua introduced us to the *savages–victims–saviors metaphor,* revealing the racist colonial vestiges in our human rights approaches today.[28]

International legal scholarship, particularly through Third World approaches to international law, provides an essential lens on racism's transnational and international connections.[29] For example, James Gathii and Ntina Tzouvala articulate racism not only as a cultural or political phenomenon but as a foundational feature of international economic order.[30] This area of legal scholarship has developed a rich account of racism as an organizing idea motivating slavery, colonialism, and empire, and racism's existence throughout the world today.[31]

Scholars from many other fields also advance theoretical discourse about racism. Historians have brought new appreciation for how racism occurring today is linked to the structures of the past. For example, historian Kelly Lytle Hernandez's *Bad Mexicans: Race, Empire, and Revolution in the Borderlands* (2022) reveals the rebellion of the Magonistas against systemic racism by the US government as a catalyst to the 1910 Mexican Revolution. Richard Rothstein's legal history, *The Color of Law: The Forgotten History of How Our Government Segregated America* (2017), reveals how property laws and practices like redlining calcified ideologies of segregation into permanent realities lasting for generations.

There are important studies about racism not in our three-dimensional world but in the digital one. For example, Safiya Noble's *Algorithms of Oppression* (2018) investigates data discrimination in search algorithms. In *Race After Technology* (2019), Ruha Benjamin argues how bias online is by design. Through such analysis, we begin to understand how humans encode racism into digital platforms, search engines, predictive analytics, and artificial intelligence systems.[32] Contributions like these demonstrate that online spaces are not neutral but are instead shaped by the same historical biases, economic incentives, and cultural narratives that shape the offline world. By mapping racism in these emerging domains, we recognize that the structures sustaining it are not limited by geography; they extend into the virtual spaces we inhabit and the technologies that mediate our lives. Most of all, racism is ever-evolving, as are the ways we must understand, confront, and dismantle it.

The second layer of racism reveals its broad reach and underscores our comparative questions. Racism is more than isolated moments on the world map. But what is the connection among them? How do the dots of our first layer connect to the lines of our second layer? Does a connection exist between racism that manifests locally—shaped by place and its social fabric—and racism's ability to manifest globally? These are questions that preoccupy discourse about racism at the second level and begin to move us toward a third layer.

Third Layer—*Global Racism*

Now we reach the as-yet-undefined third layer of our map. At this level, we search for a phenomenon often obscured from direct view, asking what emerges when we zoom all the way out to a truly global perspective. How does racism spread around the world? Is it an inevitable feature of human societies, encoded in human nature? Or can certain conditions weaken it or even dismantle it entirely? What enables it to cross borders, reappear in new contexts, and endure over time? Does a superstructure or substructure of racism operate at the planetary scale, shaping patterns of oppression unconstrained by borders and boundaries?

Global racism names this third layer as a persistent form of oppression. In this layer, we see that racism harms certain groups of people wherever they are. Immediately, we encounter a tension. On the one hand, certain groups of people are the targets of racism everywhere they go. When people cannot escape racism no matter where they travel, they are experiencing global racism—a dynamic that transcends culture and nation, operating on an unmapped global layer. In this way, global racism is inescapable. On the other hand, race itself is not global. Race is a socially constructed category of human identity, often assigned by governments at birth. These assignments are not universal, and there is no menu of racial categories that is recognized worldwide. Some nations define racial groups and count people into them during a census. Other nations claim everyone is of the same race. Still others don't say anything about race, one way or the other. In short, race is not a universally recognized legal category of human identity.

In this sense, racism is a paradoxical local–global phenomenon. Each local manifestation is linked to broader global conditions, but the relationship between the local–global is not fixed. Global racism escapes the local first layer and the transboundary second layer. It is not limited to a particular context of place or time, nor can we always trace how it started in one context and moved to another. Instead, it appears embedded in the human ecosystem itself, sustained by shared ideologies and global systems of power.

*

Theorizing Global Racism

Studying global racism emphasizes the need to look for foundational roots connecting constructed identities, oppressive systems that rank them, and ideologies of superiority that sustain them. Within the conceptual framework of this book, it is useful to distinguish between the basic tenets of race in the global context and those of *Global Racism*. The first set outlines what we know about race as a human category—its lack of biological foundation, its socially constructed nature, and its uneven treatment across nations and cultures. The second set identifies the features of global racism, a form of oppression that transcends borders, undermines human dignity, and threatens world order. Together, these lists provide a foundation for understanding how race operates locally and how racism persists globally.

Five Tenets of Race in the Global Context

1. All humans alive today belong to the same species, *homo sapiens*.
2. There is no biological basis for race.
3. Race is a human-created construct. It is often conceived of as an immutable set of characteristics people are born with, typically based on visible physical traits, like skin color and hair type.
4. Race is an identity assigned at birth by the government in some, but not all, nations.
5. There is no global menu of race. As a construct, it is neither universal nor ubiquitous.

Ten Tenets of *Global Racism*

1. Global racism names a form of racism operating on a global scale that interacts with the human ecosystem and world order.
2. Global racism includes but is broader than racial discrimination.
3. Global racism should be recognized as a violation of universal human rights.
4. Global racism can be perpetrated through international crimes, including genocide, war crimes, and crimes against humanity.
5. Global racism is a threat to international peace and security.
6. Global racism is a form of dehumanization. It works to deny individuals and communities their inherent equality and dignity on the basis of a constructed category designed for the very purpose of separating humans into a hierarchy that elevates some and suppresses many.
7. Global racism is problematized by the lack of any global menu of race. It can be based on the perceived and/or lived experience of the racial identity of people experiencing the harm but is not dependent upon such. The relationship between race and racism is redrawn as neither dependent nor, necessarily, independent.
8. Global racism is fueled by ideologies of racial superiority.
9. Global racism is the thief of humanity.
10. Global racism is a challenge for all peoples and nations of the world.

These tenets clarify the nature of global racism as a form of oppression and provide a conceptual definition that accounts for its global context. As a next step in theorizing global racism, we must look at examples—instances where constructed group identities, ideologies of racial superiority, and cross-border harms converge—that capture the lived realities of how global racism is experienced.

Consider the following nonexhaustive list of examples of racism where each is linked to a constructed group category of human identity based on a concept of human difference according to race. Each example is also linked to ideologies of racial superiority that motivate oppression against the constructed group. It could be the case that a person harmed self-identifies as a member of the group. It may also be the case that they were perceived to be a member of the group. Each example also involves racism not being limited to a single nation that defines race but to a context that is more geographically expansive.

Anti-Asian Racism

Anti-Asian racism harms people on the basis of their real or perceived Asian descent. With an estimated 4.7 billion people, Asia's population accounts for 60 percent of the world's total.[33] The continent spans from Russia to Malaysia and from Turkey to the outer islands of Japan, encompassing a rich array of human genetic, cultural, and linguistic diversity. Yet, the diversity of billions of people has been collapsed into a constructed group labeled "Asian." Experience of racism herein differs from the "Yellow Peril" of the nineteenth century to the "model minority" myth of today. Modern manifestations of anti-Asian racism include hate crimes such as violent assaults and physical harassment as well as various forms of racial discrimination. A common presumption is that anti-Asian racism names harms perpetrated by people who are not identified as Asian. But racism exists within and between various Asian countries and peoples as well.

Anti-Black Racism

Anti-Black racism has been recognized by the UN and many other groups as one form of racism that is global in scope. Anti-Black racism manifests as hate crimes and physical violence, as discrimination in healthcare and policing, and as evidenced by inequitable pay gaps. Moreover, anti-Black racism is well-documented around the world, conflating anyone who is perceived to be Black as belonging to a human group based on a constructed idea that there is a Black race. It is not easily escaped by movement, traveling to a new nation or continent.

Anti-Black racism targets people who are Black. But what does that mean? One approach has been to link Black as a racial construct to the ancestry of a person or to ancestors who came from Africa. However, there are many people in Africa, historically and today, who do not identify as Black. Conflating race and ancestry creates complications. Anti-Black racism is not simply anti-African racism. Nor is it solely based on skin color. Skin color among people deemed Black is varied, ranging from the full spectrum of human shades. When we consider human DNA, two people from Namibia can have more genetic diversity from one another than a person from China and a person from Belgium.

Anti-Indigenous Racism

The United Nations estimates that over five thousand distinct groups, comprising approximately 476 million people across ninety countries, identify as being indigenous in the world today.[34] Due to the formation of nation-states, colonialism, and imperialism, many indigenous peoples have faced widespread genocide, enslavement, forced assimilation, displacement, and cultural erasure. The international community now uses the concept of indigeneity to recognize the precolonial group identities of people who are original to a place and often share a history and ancestry. In 2007, the United Nations adopted the UN Declaration on the Rights of Indigenous Peoples, defining the group as the original inhabitants of a territory, sharing experiences of oppression from colonialism and other causes, and in need of particular human rights protections under international law. However, "indigenous" is also an umbrella term that does not capture the names or chosen group identities of the many distinct peoples who are considered to be indigenous around the world.

Indigeneity is not the same as race, but both are constructed group identities that often fit into the bottom of societal hierarchies that people and governments create. In this way, status as indigenous can be racialized, targeting people on their real or perceived difference from the societally dominant group, ignoring the diversity within indigenous groups. In many cases, a person who identifies as being indigenous may experience racism on the basis of their full identity that includes and extends beyond race.

Consider the Twa, an indigenous hunter–gatherer people from the African Great Lakes Region. Numbering in the tens of thousands today, they are among the oldest continuous populations of Central Africa. They have experienced extreme oppression both under European colonial rule and at the hands of various neighboring groups. During the 1994 Rwandan genocide, Hutu extremists targeted Twa, killing more than a third of the Twa population in Rwanda.[35] Twa have also faced oppression from many other ethnic groups, whether in Uganda, Rwanda, Burundi, or the Democratic Republic of Congo. The oppression stems from both racism rooted in white European ideologies of racial superiority and other ideologies of superiority—ethnic, cultural, political—producing devastating harms.

Indigenous people in Hawaii face oppression rooted in colonial histories and white supremacy as well. In 1921, when the US Congress passed the Hawaiian Homes Commission Act of 1921, "native Hawaiian" became a category defined as a person with a minimum of one-half Hawaiian blood, traced to before 1778. This requirement limited the number of people eligible for land leases and benefits and, over time, reduced the legal recognition of Native Hawaiian identity. At the same time, it upheld a system of land ownership that privileged white settlers and reinforced colonial control of Hawaiian resources through law.[36]

Indigenous people in China have faced significant persecution by the government there. The Chinese government does not recognize indigenous peoples within its territory; instead, it classifies Hui, Mongols, Tibetans, Uyghurs, and Zhuang peoples as ethnic minorities. There is little official recourse for protection against racism. The Uyghurs, for example, are an indigenous people with Turkic ancestry who have historically lived in the Tarim Basin region in Central Asia. Today, China's political border extends across this area, incorporated into the Xinjiang Uyghur Autonomous Region, recognizing Uyghurs as an ethnic minority under Chinese law. In Xinjiang, the largest province in China, Uyghur people were long the majority, constituting at least 90 percent of the total population through the 1950s. Today, Uyghurs make up only 40 percent of the population, reduced by Chinese national policies that supported Han migration into the area and instituted mass surveillance, forced labor, and the internment of over a million Uyghurs and other minorities.[37] The government has sought to justify its persecution of Uyghurs as necessary to protect national security from terrorism or religious extremism.[38]

Anti-Roma Racism

"Roma" is a term used to categorize a number of distinct cultural and ethnic groups, some of which were traditionally nomadic, including Roma, Sinti, Kali, Ashkali, Dom, Lom, Rom, and Traveller populations.[39] By population, Roma are considered to be the most marginalized group in the world. Anti-Roma racism dates back hundreds of years and is geographically widespread, with numerous documented incidents in Europe where Roma are the largest ethnic group, numbering an estimated ten to twelve million people. Roma were victims of the Holocaust, and anti-Roma racism continues today in the form of discrimination in housing, education, healthcare, policing, and employment, as well as segregation, hate speech, physical violence, and societal marginalization.

These broadly diverse people have been treated as a single group and racialized as being inherently inferior. In many cases, Roma and related groups have lived in a nation longer than those discriminating against them yet are treated as foreigners or outsiders. They are often devalued as a whole based on their alleged group traits and lifestyle differences. Some governments and international bodies have sought to define this specific form of racism. For instance, the US State Department's working definition of anti-Roma racism from 2020 includes "glorifying the genocide of the Roma; inciting, justifying, and perpetrating violence against Roma communities, their property, and individual Roma" and more.[40] Here, this global racism targets people on the basis of their real or perceived group identity as Roma, a group that has been constructed, racialized, and applied to people with widely diverse ancestry and cultural traditions.

Antisemitic Racism

Antisemitism is widely recognized as hatred directed toward Jews and may take the form of religious discrimination, racial discrimination, or both. Today, antisemitic racism manifests worldwide through violent crimes, hate speech, denial of the Holocaust, discrimination in education and the workplace, and dehumanization based on Jewish identity. The term "antisemitism" has complex origins. In linguistics, Arabic, Aramaic, and Hebrew are grouped into the Semitic language family, a term applied broadly to many distinct groups that speak these languages. During the nineteenth century, however, proponents of scientific racism constructed a racial category for Jews called the "Semite," which was deemed inferior to the "white race." This ideology of racial superiority underpinned horrific forms of oppression, including pogroms in the Russian Empire and the Holocaust carried out by Nazi Germany.

The persecution of people who are Jewish because they are Jewish is a hallmark of this form of global racism throughout the centuries. Today, antisemitism commonly refers to a range of oppressions on the basis of a person's or group's Jewish identity, which can be intersectional—taking into account religion, ethnicity, ancestry, and nationality. Jews live in many parts of the world, speak different languages, and cannot be easily grouped by nationality or even ethnicity. Many people from around the world identify as Jewish through both religion and ancestry, but not always. A person who converts to Judaism, for example, may not claim ancestry from people who were historically Jewish.

Understanding antisemitic racism as a form of global racism requires recognizing aspects of Jewish identity as a constructed group identity. Antisemitic racism names a form of oppression of people on the basis of their real or perceived group identity. Antisemitic racism is a form of global racism that targets people by grouping them into a constructed racialized category, one that persists across time and place. It is driven by an ideology based in racial hierarchy alongside other aspects of group identity, rooted in religion, culture, and ancestry.

Caste-Based Racism

Caste systems that assign people to intergenerational social hierarchies entrench forms of oppression that manifest as global racism. The Hindu-based caste system that places Dalits at the bottom of society and denies them basic human rights and dignity is the most widely known example. With roots in ancient South Asia, it was codified in Hindu religious texts and later hardened under British colonial rule, which reinforced and institutionalized caste divisions. Yet caste is not limited to Hinduism or to India; it exists in Buddhist, Christian, Muslim, and Sikh communities across South Asia and beyond. As with other examples of global racism, the constructedness of the category matters. Caste fashions group identities and then ranks those groups into societal hierarchies. The construction defies other ways of thinking about human difference. People might share nationality, culture, religion, language, and ethnicity, yet caste divides them into groups assigned at birth, a status passed on to their children, and those differences are ranked hierarchically. This is a clear manifestation of ideologies of superiority based on racialized, constructed group identities.

Other Possibilities

We might consider many other possible manifestations of global racism. For example, mixed-race racism arises globally whenever a person is descended from parents belonging to distinct races, however defined. Antimiscegenation laws, prohibiting interracial marriage, have sought to prevent the birth of mixed-race children—justified through false ideologies of racial superiority that prized "pure blood."

Xenophobic racism is another form of global racism, rooted in xenophobia—described as a fear of outsiders—but expressed through a racialized logic. It is well established that people fear outsiders who look, speak, or live differently from them, while outsiders who share perceived similarities are less often cast as threats.

Taken together, these categories do not function as exhaustive or mutually exclusive. Rather, they illuminate how certain forms of racism recur and reappear across time and place.

Any constructed group identity—Asian, Black, Indigenous, Roma, Jewish, Dalit, or otherwise—becomes racialized through ideologies of superiority that are not confined to a single nation, culture, or legal system. Global racism travels through empire, religion, migration, law, social media, and political rhetoric. Global racism adapts to local conditions while retaining a recognizable global logic—ranking human beings into hierarchies of worth. The purpose of naming these categories, then, is to expose the patterns by which racism spreads, mutates, and sustains itself across borders, revealing global racism as a system rather than a series of injustices experienced in isolation.

*

Consequences

The first half of this book has taken readers on a journey through the history and meaning of racism, revealing it not only as a series of localized events or as a relic of the distant past but as a persistent global phenomenon that resists easy definition and defies effective remedy. Three key lessons emerged. First, racism is a global challenge, possible anywhere and everywhere people are; racism is at once rooted in a particular context yet universally available. Second, nations and people lack a shared consensus about what racism is or how it should be defined. International law offered a starting point, with the 1965 treaty banning racial discrimination. However, the legal definition agreed to does not adequately capture racism or the full extent of its harms. Third, there is no global framework for preventing or combating racism in a harmonized way. In some nations, racism is addressed through domestic law. In others, racism's existence is denied under the claim that every citizen is of the same race. The resulting dissonance disrupts effective remedy.

But racism is not just a problem for some people in some places; it is a challenge for the world. This chapter has named and defined that challenge as global racism, conceptualizing it as a form of racism that moves with impunity, unconstrained by borders or by laws. Introducing global racism as a theory of oppression is a call to understand how distinct manifestations of racism around the world are connected by a common global thread. Whether conceived as a superstructure or substructure, the connectivity of global racism permits the persistent oppression of people and groups, wherever they go in the world, based on created identities often assigned from birth. This manifestation of racism is poorly understood and undertheorized. We lack strong models for explaining how global racism spreads and how it's sustained. We can't yet explain why racism is possible anywhere and everywhere people are, including online.

What we do know is that global racism is a challenge the world cannot afford to ignore. Global racism violates human rights, endangers peace and security between nations, and is a root cause of wars that threaten our very humanity. We've been down this dark tunnel before. To avoid repeating past calamities, we must define who we are as a species by whom we agree not to become. As W. E. B. Du Bois once observed, "We often congratulate ourselves more on getting rid of a problem than solving it. Such an attitude is dangerous. . . . The riddle of the Sphinx may be postponed, it may be evasively answered now; sometime it must be fully answered."[41] Solutions will require global frameworks capable of moving beyond the limits of sovereignty.

The time has come for nations and peoples around the world to recognize and to combat global racism as a challenge for the world. In the four chapters that follow, I advance four discourses vital to dismantling global racism, beginning with acknowledgment of the dangers of ideologies of racial superiority and the leaders who promote them. The second discourse centers on dignity—one of the universal human rights—and explains why it offers a powerful antidote to pernicious ideologies of power. The third discourse examines education, not only in its content but in its methods, as a transformative tool for societal change and explores why education in many places around the world is under attack. Finally, the fourth discourse turns to the principle of *humanitas*: the ideal that by being humane, we become humanity. Whatever else global racism is, it is also something humans have created—and, therefore, something we can end. It is possible to chart a future different from our past.

7

Resisting Ideologies of Racial Superiority

Dangerous Ideologies

In the spring of 2018, Vice Chair of the United Nations Committee on the Elimination of Racial Discrimination (CERD) Gay McDougall called on world leaders to take accountability for racism in their countries by rejecting not only racist acts but also racist ideologies. Addressing the United Nations General Assembly in a statement commemorating the International Day for the Elimination of Racial Discrimination, McDougall decried the "toxic climate created by inflammatory racist hate rhetoric that is being tolerated by political leaders at the highest levels, who have either failed to condemn it or who have adopted it as electoral platforms."[1] Though she singled out no leaders by name, those assembled would have had little trouble identifying the leaders she had in mind—not the least of whom resided just two hundred miles away, in Washington, DC. She continued, "Their failure of leadership has opened the floodgates to the spread of the most damaging ideas of racial superiority and uninhibited expressions of hatred. License has been given to radical white supremacy groups to reassert themselves into the mainstream public discourse." McDougall, who was first appointed as an independent expert at the UN on these matters in 1998, called out the dangers, not only of racist speech but also of "the spread of the most damaging ideas of racial superiority."[2]

Global Racism. Anna Spain Bradley, Oxford University Press. © Anna Spain Bradley 2026.
DOI: 10.1093/oso/9780197778388.003.0008

Five months later, McDougall sounded the alarm on precisely the kind of real-world harms that ideologies of racist superiority can provoke. In her UN role as a Country Rapporteur for China, McDougall reported that the Chinese government had detained more than one million Muslim minorities (specifically, Uyghurs and Kazakhs) in China's northwest province of Xinjiang, turning the Xinjiang Uyghur Autonomous Region into a "massive internment camp . . . a sort of 'no-rights zone.'"[3] The report documented mass deportations and internment where some two million people had been forced into "'re-education camps' for political and cultural indoctrination," noting that the Chinese government was targeting the Uyghur community on the basis of their identity, whether ethnic or religious or both.[4] The effect of these actions has been to legally penalize everyday expression of identity, such as greetings, wearing a beard or headscarf, and observance of religious and cultural practices. China's Permanent Representative to the United Nations in Geneva, Yu Jianhua, responded that China's constitution promoted ethnic equality and prohibited racial discrimination, but that China opposed extremism in all forms, including religious doctrines distorted to "incite hatred, discrimination and violence."[5] Yet this appeal to constitutional principles masked a widening gap between China's stated commitments to equality and the documented realities of its policies in Xinjiang. McDougall's warning was clear. Unchecked promulgation of ideologies of racial superiority by powerful nations is a danger the world cannot afford to ignore.

Challenging ideology is an inherently controversial task. The right to freedom of speech and expression is, after all, a well-established general principle of law. Any suggestion of using law to regulate ideas rather than conduct makes many people uncomfortable. The specter of a "thought police" and the chilling effects such regulation could have on open debate, dissent, and democratic participation make addressing ideology a risky territory. These concerns are not merely theoretical. Indeed, Article 19 of the Universal Declaration of Human Rights affirms the right to freedom of opinion and expression.

However, there is a fundamental difference an individual's own private thoughts or expressions and a national leader's promulgation of dangerous ideologies of racial superiority backed by the vast resources of a nation. As McDougall warns, the danger lies not only in words but in the positionality and power of the speaker. The latter is a grave danger, with roots in some of history's greatest evils, something UNESCO (the United Nations Educational, Scientific and Cultural Organization) warned about in its *1950 Statement on Race.*

This chapter takes up ideologies of racial superiority as the first of four discourses that follow the book's thesis identifying global racism as a challenge for the world. The chapter considers what ideologies are, where ideologies of racial superiority have emerged in the past, and why they continue to hold allure today. The concept of global racism casts a wide net to capture—and to critique—the belief in the inherent superiority of some humans over others based on constructed racial differences. Such beliefs, when consolidated into ideology, fuel global racism's oppressive power and embody the dangers it poses both to peace and to humanity itself.

*

What Is an Ideology?

An ideology is a set of ideas and beliefs that characterize the identity of a person, group, or culture. The formation of a group, within politics or religion or nations themselves, is often founded upon an ideology that organizes meaning, belonging, and purpose. The term derives from the French word *idéologie*, attributed to French philosopher Antoine Destutt de Tracy's 1801 book Elements of Ideology and derived from the Greek word ἰδέα.[6] Originally meaning "the science of ideas," over time, ideology came to designate a coherent system of thought. Whereas an idea is a "formulated thought or opinion," ideology refers to "a systematic body of concepts."[7]

Ideology drives human movements. It has provided the intellectual and moral energy behind many struggles for freedom and justice. Consider, as examples, the American Revolution, the French Revolution, the Haitian Revolution, the abolitionist campaign against slavery, women's suffrage, the environmental movement, and the Civil Rights Movement. Human beliefs and values are deeply embedded in our ideologies about how we understand the world around us and our place in it.

Yet the darker side of history reveals how ideologies have also mobilized widespread violence and oppression. They are often given glorified names to legitimize or to mask their destruction. Manifest Destiny was America's justification for killing or displacing America's indigenous people and enslaving African people for hundreds of years. King Leopold II's brutal exploitation of the Congo Free State was similarly cloaked in the ideology of benevolent philanthropy. At other times, ideologies have been named after dictatorial leaders, as with Stalinism and Maoism. Others take names from political movements, such as Fascism or Nazism. Whether cloaked in the language of liberation or domination, ideologies matter because they organize human thought into collective action, animating history's noblest struggles and enabling its darkest crimes.

Ideologies of Superiority

Throughout the arc of human history, recourse to ideologies of superiority has been consistent. Humans, much like our ancient hominid ancestors, are social beings who survive and sometimes thrive in groups. The first instances of such ideologies far predate the histories that recount them, but we see clear examples of such superiority thinking in early civilizations. In the written records of ancient civilizations, mythologies embed hierarchies of superiority, linking earthly rule with divine sanction. The Sumerian epics tell of divine entities, descendants of the sky-god An, descending from the heavens to govern humankind. In ancient Egypt, the Pharaoh was himself considered a god, the living embodiment of Horus. In ancient China's Zhou dynasty, the emperor ruled by the Mandate of Heaven, styled as the Son of Heaven. As human civilizations evolved, so too did our relationships with the divine and our claims to legitimate rule.

Religious thought today also advances divine rule linked with ideologies of superiority. By the numbers of adherents, there are five major world religions: Christianity, Islam, Hinduism, Buddhism, and Judaism. Each offers a doctrine of faith and a view of the divine and the spiritual realm. Religion provides people access to an afterlife, a faith tradition, and moral codes for discerning right from wrong. Yet religion has also been harnessed to advance ideologies that serve the aims of power, territorial expansion, resource extraction, and social control. In practice, most religions have suppressed the principle of equality, limiting women's rights and frequently endorsing hierarchies of race, caste, or creed. European colonial expansion used Christianity to justify a divine mandate to "civilize" the so-called uncivilized world; Islam has underpinned numerous imperial conquests and the enslavement of nonbelievers; and Hindu established hereditary caste systems. Across many faiths, religious authority has been invoked to legitimize inequality.

One throughline emerges in the passage of rulership from one generation to the next. A justification for such immense authority and power is required. Dynastic succession often rested on bloodlines, with the legitimacy of the new ruler tracing back through divine ancestry. This doctrine of the divine right to rule was later folded into the idea of natural law. Centuries afterward, scientific racism drew on similar logics of blood and lineage, arguing—well before the discovery of DNA—that humanity could be divided into distinct races, some inherently superior to others.

As the example of Pope Urban II's call to the First Crusade illustrates, ideologies of superiority predate the formal creation of race as we understand it today. All that was required was the invention of an "other." One group is inherently superior to the other group based on the distinction of racial difference. The particular meanings of race have changed over the centuries, but the ideology remains rooted in this conviction of superiority.

The process works in three steps: (1) groups are distinguished; (2) their worth is ranked in a hierarchy, with the "superior" at the top and the "inferior" at the bottom; and (3) these categories are presented as immutable. During the First Crusade, Christian and Frankish identity were defined against Muslim and Seljuk identity, with conversion or assimilation rarely able to erase the mark of "inferiority."

Today, race is not globally fixed or even universally recognized, yet for many populations—including those of African descent deemed Black, Roma, and Indigenous Australians—racial inferiority is constructed as permanent, set against whiteness as a standard of superiority.

Ideologies of white supremacy continue to be a problem around the world. In the United States, according to the Southern Poverty Law Center (SPLC), there are some 110 active white nationalist groups in 2024, down from a historic high of 165 in 2023.[8] The Ku Klux Klan—America's oldest hate group—was founded in Tennessee after the Civil War, in 1865, by six Confederate soldiers aiming to thwart Reconstruction and to suppress any gains made by formerly enslaved people. Later iterations of the Klan engaged in lynching campaigns and resisting the Civil Rights Movement. Organized around an ideology of supremacy based on the white race, Protestant Christianity, and nativist sentiment, Klan groups—known for titles like "Grand Wizards" and sections such as the Old Glory Knights and Loyal White Knights—spread slogans such as the 1920s "America for Americans." They were notorious for hate crimes and violence against Black people, Catholics, immigrants, Jewish people, and people identifying as gay or lesbian.

The Southern Poverty Law Center defines white nationalist groups as those having a core goal of creating a white ethnostate and believing that white identity should serve as the organizing principle of Western nations. In recent years, the number of such groups in the United States has fluctuated, often tied to broader shifts in political mobilization and mainstreaming of far-right ideologies. These groups are often linked to transnational far-right networks and authoritarian political movements. Examples include Patriot Front, the National Justice Party, and the so-called Active Clubs, which blend cultural identity forms—such as lifestyle branding, clothing, music, and hypermasculine aesthetics—with extremist ideology.

Another contemporary manifestation of ideologies of racial superiority is neo-Nazis. With origins in Nazism, Fascism, and historical links to World War II, neo-Nazi groups today operate not only in Europe and North America but across the world. As early as the 1930s, Nazi ideologies spread to Asia, giving rise to Imperial Japan's "Asia for Asians," Dutch-Indo Nederlandsche Indische Fascisten Organisatie in Jakarta, and the Partai Fasis Indonesia in Bandung under the leadership of Dr. Raden Pandji, which promoted Javanese supremacy.[9] Over the decades, such ideological influences inspired extremist groups in Asia, including the nationalist Buddhist 969 Movement in Myanmar and the resurgence of Nazi symbols in popular culture in Thailand.[10]

Problematic ideologies of superiority also exist in Africa. In Sudan, for example, there is a long history of ideological thinking that has espoused the superiority of Arabs over indigenous groups and of Muslims over non-Muslims. In Ethiopia, armed conflict has persisted between the Amhara and Oromo, with groups categorized by the federal government in a form of ethnic federalism that has contributed to hardened identity boundaries and conflict. There are many other examples we could analyze. The point is that ideologies of supremacy are even older than the modern concept of race. In our era, race has become a convenient frame through which humanity perpetuates ideological hierarchies. Because race is not a biological truth, it can't be proven or disproven. Instead, race has been constructed by those in power and used as a tool for ranking people into hierarchies.

The persistence of such hierarchies lies not only in the construct of race but also in the human impulse toward superiority. Whether in families, friend groups, communities, cities, or nations, we humans have a persistent habit of defining who we are as individuals in relation to our place in the group. Rankings seem to matter a great deal to many of us. Who is at the top? Who should have the most power? Who gets the best food, land, or other resources? Ideologies of racial superiority simply create a rationale and a justification for how to rank people in a society.

In our deeper past, when most humans were hunter–gatherers, there is evidence that some societies were egalitarian. In these roots, we may find promising insights into alternatives to hierarchy. But most modern human societies have been built around hierarchical structures. Adding in racial superiority has led to broader systems of oppression operating through empire, colonialism, slavery, apartheid, caste, and segregation. These structures operate by racializing human identity and then ranking it, transforming the old temptation to dominate into enduring systems of racial oppression.

Ideological Violence and Genocide

What is the most pernicious ideology of racial superiority you can imagine? For many, the answer is Nazism—both because of its dehumanizing ideology and because the Nazi regime was able to carry out its ideologies on a catastrophic scale. Today, there is a global consensus that Nazism, the ideology of the Nazi regime, is abhorrent and wrong. But such a consensus only crystallized after World War II. Before, and even during, the war, support for Nazism beyond Germany and its ideological relationship to racism tell a far more unsettling story.

Adolf Hitler was deeply interested in and inspired by American policies of segregation, along with the US's effective cultural propagation of white supremacy. When shaping his expansionist ideology of *Lebensraum*, calling for "an enlargement of our people's living space in Europe," Hitler drew inspiration from Hollywood westerns and the policies of westward expansion that they romanticized.[11] In a 1928 speech in Munich, Hitler praised the US model of racial domination, admiring how Americans had "gunned down the millions of redskins to a few hundred thousand, and now keep the modest remnant under observation in a cage."[12] He warned that Germans would be overrun by those he deemed racially inferior masses, elaborating on his views in *Mein Kempf*, where he wrote that

> historical experience offers countless proofs of this. It shows with terrifying clarity that in every mingling of Aryan blood with that of lower peoples the result was the end of the cultured people. North America,

> whose population consists in by far the largest part of Germanic elements who mixed but little with the lower colored peoples, shows a different humanity and culture from Central and South America, where the predominantly Latin immigrants often mixed with the aborigines on a large scale. By this one example, we can clearly and distinctly recognize the effect of racial mixture. The Germanic inhabitant of the American continent, who has remained racially pure and unmixed, rose to be master of the continent; he will remain the master as long as he does not fall a victim to defilement of the blood.[13]

Hitler espoused his ideology of scientific racism, asserting that the dominance and power of a nation were linked to the racial purity of its population and, in particular, its leaders.

Under Hitler's leadership, the Nazi regime turned to America for examples about how to legalize oppression. The infamous Nuremberg Laws of 1935, which legalized the exclusion, persecution, and disenfranchisement of Jews, were directly informed by the US's racial legislation. As legal historian James Q. Whitman documented in *Hitler's American Model* (2017), German jurists studied US segregation statutes, miscegenation bans, and immigration laws when drafting Nazi racial policy.

For example, Justice Minister Franz Gürtner, one of the architects of the Nuremberg Laws, convened meetings in 1934 to review American precedents. It was there that Roland Freisler—later president of the Nazi People's Court—is recorded as saying: "This jurisprudence would suit us perfectly, with a single exception. Over there they have in mind, practically speaking, only coloreds and half-coloreds, which includes mestizos and mulattoes; but the Jews, who are also of interest to us, are not reckoned among the coloreds."[14] The American model of racism, in Freisler's view, omitted attending to the Jewish people, so of concern to the Nazi's aims of racial purification.

Hitler himself also insisted that the Nazis had not invented some of their most notorious practices. In 1941, he claimed, "Concentration camps were not invented in Germany. The English invented them. They use these institutions to break the backbone of other peoples slowly, to wear their national resistance down and to dissolve it, in order to make them accept the British yoke of democracy."[15] He pointed to the British camps in South Africa during the Boer War, as well as to Soviet atrocities like the Katyn Forest Massacre carried out against Poles, to argue that foreign powers had provided precedents.

This exchange of ideological affinities went both ways. Support for Hitler and his Nazi Party was not uncommon in America in the years before Germany lost the war. Far-right groups such as William Dudley Pelley's Silver Legion of America (the "Silver Shirts") called for a Christian government that would exclude Jews and non-whites. The pro-Nazi German American Bund organized mass rallies and established training camps in New York, Wisconsin, and Pennsylvania. Prominent figures, including members of Congress, voiced antisemitic sympathies, while demagogues like Gerald L. K. Smith, who founded the America First Party in 1943, promoted a virulently racist, antisemitic agenda.

Nazism operationalized atrocity on an industrial scale. The Holocaust alone is believed to have ended the lives of at least eleven million people. It is often seen as a historical starting point for the international legal development of the crime of genocide and crimes against humanity. In his book *East West Street*, Phillipe Sands shares the compelling tale of how Raphael Lemkin (1900–1959) and Hersch Lauterpacht (1897–1960), two Jewish men born in Poland who survived the war years, created these central ideas that have defined the field of international criminal law.[16] Both studied law at Jan Kazimierz University in Lwów (then Poland, now Lviv, Ukraine). Lemkin coined the term "genocide" and emphasized the need for legal protection of atrocities targeting a group. Lauterpacht advanced the idea of "crimes against humanity," which emphasized legal protections for atrocities against individuals.

Sands traces Lemkin and Lauterpacht's intellectual connections while noting that the two men may never have met. Sands recalls how Lauterpacht was critical of Lemkin's approach, being against the view of "group identity in the law, whether as victim or perpetrator," believing it would underscore a sense of group identity that reinforced tribalism.[17] Sands shares Lauterpacht's concern, noting "I was instinctively sympathetic to Lauterpacht's view, which was motivated by a desire to reinforce the protection of each individual, irrespective of which group he or she happened to belong to, to limit the potent force of tribalism, not reinforce it. By focusing on the individual, not the group, Lauterpacht wanted to diminish the force of intergroup conflict. It was a rational, enlightened view, and also an idealistic one."[18] Lemkin, however, according to Sands, was invested in ensuring the law tells the truth about why the crimes had been committed—"individuals were targeted because they were members of a particular group, not because of their individual qualities."[19] The tension Sands exposes underscores a persistent challenge that plagues global racism: International law struggles to define and to protect groups in a way that can be applied consistently across the world.

Whether deemed genocide or crimes against humanity, the killing of people on the basis of their identity has proven all too common in modern history. Recall the Ottoman Empire's systemic killing of Armenians through death marches, massacres, and starvation from 1915 to 1923; Stalin's engineered famine in Ukraine, the Holodomor of 1932–1933; the Cambodian genocide by the Khmer Rouge regime, from 1975 to 1979; and the Rwandan genocide of 1994. Many nations have recognized these horrors as acts of genocide. Similar horrors continue today. Consider the plight of people living in Sudan and in Gaza. Anywhere a government or governing power systematically targets a group of civilians because of their group identity, it raises grave concerns, whether or not international law names such atrocities a genocide.

Why is determining a genocide under international law so difficult? At first glance, the task seems simple: when a government targets and massacres a large number of civilians who share the same race or nationality or ethnicity, surely that is genocide. Yet the legal definition set by the 1948 Convention on the Prevention and Punishment of the Crime of Genocide (the "Genocide Convention") imposes a narrower test. The treaty requires not only evidence of widespread killing but also proof of a specific intent: the intent "to destroy, in whole or in part, a national, ethnical, racial or religious group, as such."[20] This threshold of specific intent, *dolus specialis*, is what makes proving genocide uniquely difficult compared to other international crimes, such as war crimes or crimes against humanity.

Consider the Rwandan genocide of 1994. In only a period of about one hundred days, Hutu extremists systematically attacked, sexually assaulted, and killed an estimated one million people. Driven by a stated aim to eliminate the Tutsi people, the perpetrators of the genocide killed many Twa and Hutu people as well.

In 1994, the UN Security Council set up a special court to document and prosecute these international crimes. Named the International Criminal Tribunal for Rwanda, it documented a massive amount of evidence of the horrific crimes that took place during the genocide. The Tribunal had the task of applying the legal standard from 1948, requiring specific intent to destroy a group, to a very different reality in Rwanda some fifty-six years later.

One of the key perpetrators to face trial was Colonel Théoneste Bagosora, a senior Rwandan military officer leading up to and during the genocide. Bagosora was charged with committing genocide, crimes against humanity, and war crimes. The prosecution also sought to prove Bagosora played a role in masterminding the genocide, not just committing it. To do that, they needed to establish evidence of his leadership role and genocidal intent to destroy the Tutsi people. A key piece of evidence was a 1991 report titled *Enemy Commission to Present an Enemy Threat Assessment* commissioned by then Rwandan President Juvénal Habyarimana.[21] Bagosora was the most senior member of the ten-person commission that produced the report.

The Tribunal did not have access to the entire report, but the Prosecution entered into evidence a section titled *Definition and Identification of the Enemy*, which portrayed Tutsis as a group and as a threat to Hutus, deepening the us-versus-them rhetoric.[22] The Trial Chamber reviewed hundreds of pages of additional evidence, covering allegations that Bagosora had created lists naming those to be killed, incited genocidal violence through telegrams and at rallies, been present at the death marches of refugees, and much more. Through the harrowing pages of their judgment, the judges seek to establish the credibility of the evidence, often in the form of survivor testimony.

In the end, the Trial Chamber did not find Bagosora guilty of masterminding the genocide, noting in many instances the lack of evidentiary proof connecting a massacre or mass rape to Bagosora's command. Notwithstanding, in a unanimous judgment dated December 18, 2008, it did find enough evidence to convict Bagosora, alongside others, of the crime of genocide, crimes against humanity, and war crimes.[23] He was sentenced to life imprisonment, where he later died.

There is much to learn from the massive number of records and evidence the Tribunal amassed in the course of its duties, documenting just some of the evils that transpired. Whether deemed credible or merely alleged, there are harrowing details that reveal how genocides are designed rather than merely carried out.

In Rwanda, the long history of colonialism resulted in structural inequities and deep resentments that crystallized into distinct politicized identities and social categories. By the time Bagosora was on the scene, there was consistent evidence of leadership animus characterizing Tutsis as a monolithic enemy to be identified, dehumanized, and eliminated. The resulting Rwandan genocide, like the Holocaust, was built on a foundation of ideological hatred.

A few years before the genocidal violence, a manifesto espousing an ideology of Hutu power was published in a Kigali newspaper in 1990 for all to see, naming its ten commandments.[24] The first commandment said "[e]very Hutu should know that a Tutsi woman . . . works for the interest of her Tutsi ethnic group; the third asserted that "[e]very Hutu should know that every Tutsi is dishonest in business; and the final commandment stated "the Hutu Ideology, must be taught to every Hutu at every level." The manifesto was propaganda that sought to invoke fear among Hutus against Tutsis, relying on a rhetoric that hardened group difference and reduced Rwandans to a logic of "us versus them."

These two histories of genocide, unfolding across different continents and decades, reveal how genocide and ideology are linked. Genocides are a dangerous and extreme expression of ideological violence. Not all ideologies of superiority end in genocide, but every genocide has an ideology of superiority embedded within it.

Ideologies and Their Leaders

It is clear by now that there are important and nuanced links between what people believe and how they behave. Of course, freedom of thought and opinion are key human rights that have great value in the world. But the freedom to promote thoughts that espouse ideologies of racial superiority are dangerous. Such ideologies can grow, giving rise to genocides and to the worst forms of violence in human history. If you believe that the human being you are about to kill is not worthy of life or equality or dignity, you will feel less guilty about taking that life. Herein lurks another danger: the promulgation of such ideologies by leaders who incite large groups of people to follow their lead. Consider, for instance, the statements made by three heads of state in recent years.

On February 21, 2023, President Kais Saied of Tunisia was delivering remarks to the National Security Council when he said that "hordes of irregular migrants from Sub-Saharan Africa" had come to Tunisia, "with all the violence, crime, and unacceptable practices that entails."[25] He called this "unnatural" and a part of a plan to turn Tunisia into "just another African country that doesn't belong to the Arab and Islamic nations anymore." Following his speech, racial violence and hatred against Black people escalated.[26] Angry groups began attacking individuals in the streets, shops, schools, and elsewhere. Many of the victims were later determined to be students, asylum seekers, and migrants from Cameroon, Sierra Leone, Ghana, Nigeria, Guinea, and the Ivory Coast.

At least twenty survivors of these attacks later came forward to Amnesty International and described being attacked by mobs as police just stood by and watched. From February to March 2023, these violent groups targeted at least 840 people for being Black. A twenty-one-year-old construction worker from Sierra Leone named Aziz described the group that attacked him and his wife and recalled their words: "All

Black people must leave . . . We don't want any Black people. Go back to Africa." In another case, Milena, a college student from Burkina Faso, was taken in by police near the supermarket after three Tunisian men had been harassing her. She produced her documents but was handcuffed, assaulted, and detained by police, who claimed, "[Y]ou Blacks create problems."

Tunisia has a law, the Elimination of All Forms of Racial Discrimination Act, that treats racial discrimination as a crime; it went into effect in 2018.[27] Under its own law, the acts described here are illegal. Saied's remarks demonstrate how racialized ideology can rapidly translate into violence within a national context. When such rhetoric is deployed by leaders, its impact can deepen societal fractures into mass harm.

On October 7, 2023, Hamas launched armed attacks against Israel, killing over 1,200 civilians and kidnapping many others as hostages. The victims were primarily nationals of Israel, but also included people from Ireland, Mexico, The Philippines, and other countries.

In response, Israel declared war on Hamas. Speaking on televised news, Israeli Prime Minister Benjamin Netanyahu announced, "We will win because our existence here is at stake" in "a war between forces of light and forces of darkness, between humanity and animalism."[28] Israel's military response was immediate, with then Minister of Defense Yoav Gallant announcing, "I have ordered a complete siege on the Gaza Strip. There will be no electricity, no food, no fuel, everything is closed, . . . we are fighting human animals and we are acting accordingly."[29] These statements by Israel's political and military leadership reveal an animus that extends beyond military targets toward something even more inhumane.

Since that time, Israel's military operations have killed an immense number of civilians trapped inside Gaza and have destroyed housing, infrastructure, and the environment itself. As a result, South Africa brought a case against Israel before the International Court of Justice in 2023, alleging state responsibility for genocide against Palestinians in Gaza. The case, as of this writing, is still pending.[30] The legal challenge will be to prove that Israel's destructive actions in Gaza are linked to the specific intent to destroy Palestinians there because of their group identity, because they are Palestinian.

Netanyahu's speech sheds light on his own intent. His rhetoric sets up a familiar dangerous binary of us-vs-them, framing the war as between two immutable sides: one light and humane and the other dark and animalistic. Netanyahu has referred to animals when speaking about Palestinians before. In 2016, when discussing a proposed security fence around Israel, Netanyahu said, as translated into English, "[i]n our neighbourhood, we need to protect ourselves from wild beasts," and in 2015, he referred to Israeli Arabs as "coming out in droves" to vote in the elections.[31]

As prime minister, Netanyahu's rhetoric and that of his leadership team. Dehumanization by referring to people as animals, insects, or rodents is a key marker of ideologies of superiority that drive genocide and other forms of oppression. Netanyahu's rhetoric and that of other government leaders will play a key role in determining questions about Israel's state responsibility for genocide of Palestinians in Gaza.

If Netanyahu's rhetoric illustrates how dehumanizing language operates in moments of declared war, Donald Trump's hate-filled rhetoric shows how dehumanizing language operates to transform domestic political divides into societal ones. During both of his terms as president of the United States, Trump has repeatedly used racist rhetoric and incited ideologies of racial superiority. His tactics include repetition, amplification, and political reward. In 2018, for example, he referred to Haiti and several African nations as "shithole countries" during a press conference, sparking ire from the leaders of those nations and beyond.[32] In 2024, he once again targeted Haiti, amplifying false reports that Haitian immigrants in the state of Ohio were eating people's pets and has called migrants "animals," "stone-cold killers," and "the enemy from within."[33] A study of twenty of his speeches that year found that Trump's racist and xenophobic rhetoric targeted a wide array of people from marginalized minority groups, immigrants, and migrants.[34]

Trump's racist rhetoric is more than the speech of an individual; it carries the imprimatur of the president of the world's longest, continuous democracy. His dangerous ideologies have created a safe haven for others to follow. After Trump was elected president in 2017, there was a remarkable increase in hate crimes and racial violence.[35] FBI data documented that the rise in hate crimes after his election was the second-largest increase in twenty-five years, surpassed only by the rise in hate crimes after the attacks on September 11, 2001.[36] Most Americans, according to a 2017 Pew Research Poll, believed his election was responsible for worsening racial relations in the United States.[37]

A body of research underscores this data.[38] Trump's dehumanizing and racist rhetoric, combined with his electoral victory, has influenced the attitudes of his supporters. There is an increase in racist ideologies and hate crimes against Black people in particular. When a national leader condones or even applauds racism, that leader becomes a source of ideological inspiration for others to speak and behave the same way.

*

The Dangers of Leadership Rhetoric

Dangerous words by people in power inspire dangerous behavior. But why? Each political leader in Tunisia, Israel, and the United States has distinct reasons behind his rhetoric, yet the use of racist rhetoric to name and to dehumanize others serves the same end: consolidating political power by appealing to the allure of racial superiority. It is a dangerously powerful tool because it conjures a feeling of righteous dominance over an enemy. Throughout history, that enemy has varied—sometimes a rival in war, or an impoverished people seeking resources in your lands to survive, or fear itself. No matter the enemy on the outside, this rhetoric awakens another enemy within, fear.

Fear is our most fantastic enemy. It changes what we think by changing how we think. And when people feel afraid, they behave in ways that they otherwise might not. In global racism, we find the roots of fear. In fear, we find the roots of dehumanization.

This is a serious challenge the world must face, together. To truly combat global racism, we cannot rely solely on international bans against racial discrimination. We must also confront ideologies of racial superiority to prevent global racism from taking root and spreading. This makes some people nervous, on the grounds that such an approach will create a thought police. But ideologies are not the same as ideas. Ideologies of racial superiority are designed to motivate fear.

Herein lies a dangerous conflation. People are designated as threats not on the basis of their actions but on the basis of their group identification. A person's citizenship status, for instance, might become conflated with a racial construct, linking the status of "foreigner" to their dark skin, accent, or appearance. In this manner, an ideological border is drawn between "us" and "them," and beliefs of one group's inherent supremacy over others soon follow.

What may begin as ideas about difference harden into ideologies of superiority, bolstered by the power of those who rule. These ideologies forge the building blocks of oppression: the view that people, although equally human, belong to different groups, often assigned at birth; the view that those groups are not equal; the view that any oppression of the other group is justified by the dominant group's alleged superiority.

History shows how ideology can foment racial violence. Many leaders across time and place have invoked the ideology of racial superiority as a call to unite people around a common cause, allied against another group. Such ideologies have served military ends, making the enemy easier to kill. They have also served political ends, concentrating power and resources through ideological division rooted in racial identity.

At the global level, we find ideological violence where there is war. The study of war reveals how armed conflicts over identity are often the most brutal and the most difficult to bring to a peaceful end.[39] These kinds of wars have a high recurrence rate, with many starting up again within five years. They are also often the sites of ideological violence sponsored or sanctioned by governments.

Since 1945, war between nations has declined. But nations at war against people remains. Civilians in Cambodia, Rwanda, Sudan, and

Gaza have experienced state-sponsored genocide or something that approaches it. Other government-sponsored atrocities have yet to be brought to justice, including North Korea's actions against its own people, China's actions against Uyghurs, Israel's actions against Palestinians and the widespread oppression of Indigenous peoples by governments around the world.

War does not always lead to genocide, but genocide always involves waging war. Key to each genocide are leaders who espouse ideologies of dehumanization through their rhetoric and their power to act upon their words. Today, we are seeing a disturbing revival of leaders endeavoring to unite people behind the platform of global racism, in all of its forms.

Confronting the Allure of Superiority

Ralph Bunche once explained that the deep roots of racism lie in the constructed "sociological being."[40] He observed, "Hitlerism in Germany, for example, has sponsored a vigorous anti-Jewish policy which is directed at driving Jews out of positions desired by 'Aryan' or 'pure' Germans, and dispossessing the Jew of any economic power in Germany." He drew a parallel to the United States and South Africa: "The white population of the South, in its determination to protect its racial supremacy against the threat of the Negro, has presented since the Civil War a solid white front which has ignored class and party lines. A similar situation is found in South Africa when the white population is confronted with its native problem there."[41] Extending this logic, Bunche characterized imperialism as a racist hierarchy of civilized nations versus uncivilized peoples, grounded in a presumed right of domination. He called imperialism "an international expression of capitalism." In Bunche's view, the "sociological being"—a construct that exists only in our minds—is the foundation upon which racism is built.

In this chapter, we have considered how ideologies of superiority connect with and help to construct such beings. Nazism, for example, used existing tropes and prejudices to craft a sociological being: the

"Jude." This figure became the focus of a state-sponsored terror campaign against a multidimensional people with rich, deep, complex histories, stretching from North Africa to the Iberian Peninsula, and across Europe—linked by a faith tradition and a sense of common ancestry. To collapse this history into a trope, Jews had to be reimagined with certain looks, certain last names, and certain ways of living.

During the Rwandan genocide, a sociological being was created around the Hutu. Before colonization, the Hutu, Tutsi, and Twa peoples living in the region shared a common language and culture. Belgian colonial rule divided people into three named groups, each with identity cards, with the Tutsi group favored in the social hierarchy. In 1962, Rwanda gained independence from Belgian rule, and the Hutu majority came into power in the government, with increased dominance and discrimination taking place against the Tutsi and Twa groups. In 1994, a Hutu extremist group committed genocide against the Tutsi people, killing an estimated eight hundred people in just one hundred days. Many Twa were also targeted, as were Hutu who opposed the killings.

Both examples illustrate how widespread ideological violence starts with the construction of a sociological being. The roots of such attacks lie in ideologies that posit a sociological being viewed as inferior—less human, sometimes less than human.

Unfortunately, humans have done a poor job of resisting the allure of superiority, racial or otherwise. From a young age, humans start a journey of self-discovery and identity creation. Early on, children learn to compare themselves to others—who runs fastest or jumps the highest, who's the tallest, the strongest, the most popular. As adults, we perpetuate much of the same, albeit with different names and higher stakes. We look to define ourselves in part by our belonging to groups and by how we compare and relate to others. There is a natural allure to mattering.

This allure can lead to problematic zero-sum thinking, making some people particularly vulnerable to an ideology of superiority. "I am better than you because . . ." or "I matter because I am better than you." Some people, of course, are better at a particular skill than others.

For example, Usain Bolt ran the fastest officially recorded 100-meter time at 9.58 seconds at the 2009 World Championships in Berlin. But racial superiority is different. Here, the claim is that superiority is inherent, rooted in belonging to one race that is by nature superior to others. Justifications for why a particular race is superior have not withstood scrutiny. Yet the global hierarchy based on ideologies of racial superiority remains strong. When asked to justify why one race is superior, the answers themselves reveal the danger. Talk of "bloodlines" and "pure blood" raises the specter of seventeenth-century scientific racism and the pseudoscientific myths that naturalized inequality. DNA evidence has rewritten our scientific understanding of human variation altogether, but the dangerous idea that certain groups are born inherently superior still lingers. Superior at what? To what end? The questions expose the absurdity—and the peril—of racial supremacist ideology.

Assume for the moment that we've lost the battle on the first front—that humans will always be tempted to say, "I am better than you." (It would be great if we could resist this impulse, dismantling various isms altogether, leaving dignity and equality to reign. However, that remains a very long-term evolutionary goal for our species.) But what about the second front? If you believe you are better than someone, you should at least be able to explain why. The idea of merit suggests that superiority can sometimes be objectively measured. Usain Bolt can run faster than you. But other examples of merit-based superiority, such as a promotion at work, are imperfectly subjective and rest on standards shaped by social values and subject to bias.

Claims of superiority based on human identity are another matter. Certain aspects of identity are, indeed, objective: age; hair and eye color; height; weight; and place of birth. Genetics, too, can reveal human adaptation over generations, explaining why some people can sprint fast while others are better at long-distance running. However, none of these facts about identity justify claims of inherent human superiority. Turning descriptive traits into hierarchical categories transforms difference into domination.

Returning to our key inquiry, how can we better understand the persistent allure of ideologies of racial superiority? What foundations makes such ideologies possible? First, such ideologies require denying the basic truth that all humans belong to one species, *Homo sapiens*. Second, they thrive off of hierarchy; the practice of dividing and ranking humanity into separate groups or categories. Third, such ideologies seek to convince us that race is natural and inherent, not created and constructed. Fourth, the allure of ideologies of racial superiority comes from a deep desire to achieve supremacy, to matter more than everyone else. White supremacy, for example, seek to elevate one race about all others.

This understanding centers the racial component. It is important to also recognize the ways that ideologies of superiority can center around other group identities rooted in religion, ethnicity, nationality, and more.

Considering ideologies of superiority in these areas raises important questions. When does being for one group translate into being against another? Does religious pride espousing a sense of superiority give rise to racism? Are forms of ethnonationalism racist? Does national pride beget racism? Analyzing such questions asks us to focus on how ideologies of superiority contribute to global racism even as they are seemingly independent from race. The constructed category of "race" gives way to the complexity of human identity, where place of birth, culture, religion, and more become entangled in the same logic of hierarchy.

Ideology is at the root of global racism. Organizing human life around ideologies rooted in superiority sets humanity up for oppression and suffering. If we believe that we belong to different races, our invented difference becomes humanity's danger. To address global racism, we must fully recognize how dangerous ideologies of superiority are to our humanity.

*

This chapter examined the connections between ideology and global racism, understanding how the former perpetuates the latter. Global racism endures because it is an effective tool for amassing power and wealth. One of the signature ways global racism endures is through ideology. Thus, combating global racism requires combating the ideologies that sustain it. This remains a complicated task. To do so requires rejecting the allure of racial superiority, a price that has been hard for humanity to achieve. Can we relinquish the lust for supremacy or merely replace it with a lust for something else? What will it take to embrace the possibility of true acceptance of others and, most of all, of ourselves?

8

Demanding Dignity

A Declaration of Dignity

In the immediate aftermath of World War II, as the United Nations sought to articulate a new foundation for peace, the drafters of the Universal Declaration of Human Rights (UDHR) placed the concept of dignity at its center. The very first line of the preamble affirms: "Whereas recognition of the inherent dignity and of the equal and inalienable rights of all members of the human family is the foundation of freedom, justice and peace in the world."[1] This was not a casual turn of phrase but a deliberate decision shaped by the drafters' direct experiences of racism, colonialism, and fascism.[2]

René Cassin, the French jurist who survived both world wars and lost family in the Holocaust, is often credited with giving the UDHR its architectural structure. Building on Canadian legal scholar John Humphrey's initial draft and taking into account many proposals by other delegates, Cassin reorganized the text so that dignity stood at the head of both the preamble and Article 1.[3]

His colleagues agreed. Charles Malik of Lebanon, rapporteur of the Commission on Human Rights, championed dignity as "the supreme principle" necessary to counter the racial ideologies that had devastated the world.[4] Hansa Mehta of India pressed the Commission to make its language universally inclusive, changing Article 1 from "All men are born free and equal" to "All human beings are born free and equal in dignity

Global Racism. Anna Spain Bradley, Oxford University Press. © Anna Spain Bradley 2026.
DOI: 10.1093/oso/9780197778388.003.0009

and rights."[5] Together, Cassin, Malik, and Mehta ensured that dignity was not simply a philosophical abstraction but the UDHR's opening premise: a universal quality owed to all humans and now claimed in international law.

This chapter calls for a renewal of the UDHR's promise. Demanding dignity, in more ways in our world, offers a valuable antidote to the allure of ideologies of superiority. Ideologies of racial superiority are dehumanizing—reducing people to categories, stripping away individuality, and justifying hierarchy and exclusion. They are a direct attack on human worth, causing both tangible harms to civil, political, cultural, social, and economic rights and dignity harms—assaults on one's very value as a human being.

Dignity, by contrast, humanizes. It restores recognition of the inherent worth of each person, and, when embedded in law and practice, acts as a safeguard against future dehumanization. Moreover, dignity is not only a personal conviction but also a powerful organizing principle for dismantling racial hierarchy and eradicating global racism. In this way, dignity bridges the movement from individual change to societal transformation, showing how the recognition of human worth at the personal level can scale up to broader reforms in societies and in the world.

There is, however, a catch. As a first principle, dignity must be made universal—applying to all people, in all places, at all times.

What Is Dignity?—A Very Brief History

Dignity is an old idea. What it means has shifted over time. Some of the earliest sources trace their roots to the writings of ancient Greek philosophers, who pondered what it means to be human and how our worth should be measured. This was a violent period of human history, when warfare, slavery, and conquest were part of everyday life. Yet in this context, philosophical reflection on humanity and justice flourished. Though there was no direct translation of the word "dignity" to be found in Ancient Greek, Greek philosophers did develop parallels in their treatment of humanity and the human condition.[6] Ideas such as *axiōma* (that which is worthy), *aretē* (virtue or excellence), and *timē* (honor or respect) reflected concerns with human value, status, and moral worth.[7] These early notions laid an intellectual foundation for later traditions that would more explicitly articulate the concept of human dignity.

In Homer's epics, dignity is closely tied to honor (*timē*) and glory (*kleos*), values that defined the worth of warriors and shaped how society judged a life well lived. Here, dignity was not universal but relational—measured by how one's deeds redounded in the eyes of gods and men.

By the fifth century BCE, Greek thinkers and historians were asking deeper questions about the nature of human value. Herodotus recounts the story of Solon, the Athenian lawgiver, who pondered the worth of two young Athenians, Cleobis and Biton.[8] According to the tale, the youths sacrificed their own lives by pulling their mother's cart to the temple of Delphi when the oxen failed. Solon reflected that in their act of devotion, they had achieved the highest measure of worth, for they died in service of filial loyalty and reverence for the divine. In this story, dignity begins to shift from mere social honor to something rooted in moral choice and self-sacrifice. Worth was no longer only what others bestowed—it could be claimed through virtue, loyalty, and devotion to ideals greater than oneself.

Roman philosophers picked up the threads first woven in Greek thought, developing them further through language and law. The Latin words *dignus* (worthy) and *dignitas* (dignity or worthiness) appear frequently in their writings. The Stoic philosopher Panaetius, in his treatise *On Duties*, had already emphasized virtue, reason, and moral responsibility as central to human worth. Aristotle's influence carried through into the Roman context, though the Romans gave these ideas a more civic and legal inflection.

Cicero, writing *De Officiis* (On Duties) in 44 BCE at the age of sixty-two, gave one of the earliest systematic accounts of dignity.[9] That same year, Julius Caesar was assassinated, and the Roman Republic was struggling to survive—making Cicero's reflections on moral responsibility especially resonant. In *De Officiis*, Cicero, like the Greek philosophers before him, articulated that the very nature of a human exceeds that of "cattle and other beasts." It is our minds—our capacity to learn, to discipline desire with reason, and to orient ourselves toward noble ideals—that distinguishes us.

Dignity for Cicero was not only about external rank or social status—though Roman society often tied *dignitas* to office, reputation, and hierarchy. He also emphasized dignity of character expressed in a life free from fear, anger, envy, and uncontrolled desire. A truly dignified person cultivated virtue regardless of wealth or rank. At the same time, he acknowledged the realities of his society, where enslaved people, foreigners, and non-Romans were relegated to the lowest rungs of the social hierarchy. By expanding the concept of dignity beyond rank, Cicero began to articulate a broader principle. Society itself depended on noble ideals such as justice and the recognition of universal humanity. In passages that foreshadow later traditions, Cicero argued that all who share in soul, speech, and reason should be afforded a certain value. The basis for this value, he suggested, was linked to the soul. If each person carries within them a spark of the divine, then we owe one another treatment that honors the divine in each of us.

Cicero's views on dignity were intertwined with his views on law. In an era when the authority and legitimacy of a ruler had long been linked with the divine, belief in natural law prevailed. Natural law posited that whatever rules humans made to govern themselves must adhere to the superseding laws of nature. Cicero argued that the law governing people—the civil law—must be based on right reason and adhere to natural law.

Dignity is also a moral ideal. In religious thought, dignity is often grounded in humanity's special relationship to the divine. Many world religions variously link moral behavior to the belief that humans—created in the divine image or imbued with divine spirit—must live in ways that rise above base animal existence. To be human is not only to possess reason but to act upon it: to choose good over evil, to honor others, and to reflect divine qualities through right moral conduct. This moral ideal requires not just self-restraint, but also just and respectful treatment of others.

By the late eighteenth century, during the age of revolutions, political thought began to merge with philosophical accounts of dignity. Enlightenment thinkers framed dignity as a foundation for rights owed to man (though at first limited to certain *men*) and as a principle that could constrain the excesses of war.[10] Immanuel Kant articulated dignity as inseparable from the human capacity to make moral choices. Because humans can act through reason and free will, we must be treated as ends in ourselves, never merely as means. For Kant, dignity is indivisible from being human—something we are born with and carry until death—and it serves as a principle upon which the very idea of human rights rests.[11]

Georg Wilhelm Friedrich Hegel extended this idea by emphasizing recognition. Dignity requires not only that one regard oneself as worthy, but that others acknowledge this worth.[12] Human dignity is therefore both inward and relational, embedded in mutual recognition within society. In Hegel's view, freedom and selfhood emerge only through this reciprocal recognition. Without it, dignity is diminished or denied.

This framework would later influence political and social theories that see struggles for rights, from abolition to decolonization, as struggles for recognition. Philosophers in the twentieth century built directly on Hegel. Axel Honneth, for example, argued that social conflicts are fundamentally about achieving recognition of dignity in spheres of love, law, and solidarity.[13] In this sense, Hegel's insight provides a bridge between the abstract principle of dignity and the lived reality of collective struggles against racism and exclusion.

What is the relationship between the principle of equality and that of dignity? The first acknowledges an ideal that all people are equal. The second, by contrast, represents the ideal that all people possess inherent value and therefore deserve to be treated as such. The two concepts overlap but are not identical. Equality is a claim about legal and societal standing, while dignity is a claim about intrinsic human worth.

Scholars have traced how these ideas developed and diverged. Paul Sagar, for example, argues that equality is a "social fiction"—a construct people gradually came to believe, even though it has no natural basis.[14] Teresa Bejan distinguishes between the ancient conception of equality, often tied to civic participation and status, and the modern conception, which claims universality.[15]

Religious traditions also assert dignity as emanating from the divine. Catholic theology teaches that humans have inherent dignity because they are created in the *imago Dei*, the image of God. In Islam, the Qur'an affirms that God has "conferred dignity on the children of Adam," linking dignity to life itself and extending it as a principle of respect for all living beings.[16] Hinduism recognizes dignity through the inherent worth of every being connected through the divine. Across many traditions, the concept of dignity is intertwined with the human condition and what it means to be human. Dignity requires that we be treated with worth, not demeaned or humiliated. As both moral ideal and religious principle, dignity names a standard higher than social status or legal rights: It claims intrinsic value and demands conduct that honors that value in everyone.

Establishing a Human Right to Dignity

Dignity appears in the preamble to the United Nations Charter of 1945. There, the Charter asserts its core purposes: "We the peoples of the United Nations determined to save succeeding generations from the scourge of war, . . . and to reaffirm faith in fundamental human rights, in the *dignity* and worth of the human person, in the equal rights of men and women and of nations large and small." Dignity also appears in the UDHR.[17] The subsequent enumeration of universal human rights in the UDHR proceeds explicitly from the premise that dignity is bound to equal rights. Article 1 states: "All human beings are born free and equal in dignity and rights. They are endowed with reason and conscience and should act towards one another in a spirit of brotherhood." Here, we see a return to Cicero's ancient insight that dignity should not depend upon status or rank but is inherent to the human condition because we are endowed with conscience and reason. The UDHR also articulates that every human is born with dignity, freedom, and equal rights. Both of these foundational sources of international law, which all nations in the world have adopted, establish dignity alongside equality and rights as foundational principles underpinning the rights of nations and of individuals.

The lack of specificity about what dignity actually means in these foundational sources of international law remains the focus of scholarly debate. Is dignity a right in itself? Or is it better understood as the foundation of other rights? What concretely does upholding dignity require of nations and of people? Most fundamentally, what does dignity mean?

Both the Charter and the UDHR were drafted by an array of diplomats from various parts of the world. Perhaps its vague meaning can be owed to cultural differences during this negotiation period, as some have suggested.[18] It was a common practice in international treaties to embed lofty ideals—language that could unite many nations—in the preamble, while leaving the more contentious obligations, such as those concerning religious freedoms or rights affecting the family, underdefined or omitted altogether to avoid disagreements.

The drafting of the UDHR was distinctive in another respect: Several women delegates participated in drafting the text. Angela Jurdak (Lebanon), Fryderyka Kalinowski (Poland), Bodgil Begtrup (Denmark), Minerva Bernardino (Dominican Republic), Laksmi Menon (India) and Hansa Mehta (India), and Evdokia Uralova (Byelorussian Soviet Socialist Republic), all served as delegates the UN Subcommission on the Status of Women, working alongside Chairperson Eleanor Roosevelt (United States).[19] It was Mehta who is credited with changing the phrase "All men" to "All human beings are born free and equal" in Article 1 of the UDHR. With this key edit, the UDHR set up an expectation that human rights applied to all and would not be written in the gendered language of the rights of men who had dominated the independence movements of earlier centuries.[20] Bodil Begtrup sought to have Article 26, enumerating the right to education, state that the right was not for "all men" but for "all," or "everyone." She further proposed that the UDHR explicitly guarantee that universal human rights include minorities, a change that was not adopted. Laksmi Menon pressed the Assembly to declare human rights as "universal" and argued that this required specifying that the UDHR applies to people living under colonial rule.[21]

The diversity of women who contributed to the UDHR's final text is in large part responsible for its bold vision of global inclusiveness. Written at a time when state sovereignty was centered as the foundation for world order and international law within it, the UDHR introduced a new paradigm by which people—all people—were to have a place in world order. They were not just objects of governance, but subjects entitled to rights and protections.

It is worth recalling, however, that the use of dignity in law neither began with the creation of the United Nations nor ended with it. The word "dignity" appeared in English in the seventeenth century. Thomas Hobbes used it in *Leviathan* (1651), situating dignity within discussions of political authority and honor. The 1689 English Bill of Rights recognized "royal dignity" and the 1789 French Declaration of the Rights of Man and of the Citizen established "the dignity of the noble estate."[22] Samuel Johnson's *Dictionary of the English Language* (1755) defined "dignity" in terms of grandeur, rank, and honor. In 1806, Noah Webster published the first American dictionary, in which the entry for dignity read: "dignity, n., grandeur, rank, honor, merit, a post."[23] These definitions reflect the older, status-based meaning of dignity, tied to office and social standing, rather than the later universalist conception of dignity as intrinsic to every human being.

The broader legal usage of dignity, in the sense Cicero had articulated in *dignitas*—as inherent to human beings rather than social position—would not take hold until the twentieth century. Mexico's 1917 Constitution was among the first to reference "the dignity of the person," followed by Ecuador's 1929 Constitution, which explicitly recognized "human dignity."[24] Following the adoption of the UDHR in 1948, several major human rights treaties followed that would also enshrine dignity as a human right, this time in the binding form of international law. The International Convention on the Elimination of All Forms of Racial Discrimination (ICERD) (1965), the International Convention on Economic Social and

Cultural Rights (1966) and the International Convention on Civil and Political Rights (1966) all enshrine dignity within their texts. The latter two covenants both state "[r]ecognizing that these rights derive from the inherent dignity of the human person," further reaffirming dignity's use as a foundation upon which human rights rest and a central rationale for their universality.

The meaning of dignity in international law has continued to confound scholars. Scholars have explored this tension between dignity's centrality and its elusiveness.[25] As Oscar Schachter wrote in 1983, "it has generally been assumed that a violation of human dignity can be recognized even if the abstract term cannot be defined. 'I know it when I see it even if I cannot tell you what it is.'"[26] Despite its vagueness, the right to dignity continues to proliferate. The European Union's Charter of Fundamental Rights opens with Article 1: "Human dignity is inviolable. It must be respected and protected." Article 20 amplifies the claim: "All people are free and equal in their dignity and rights."[27] The Court of Justice of the European Union has interpreted this clause to mean that the dignity of the human person is "not only a fundamental right in itself but constitutes the real basis of fundamental rights."[28] Dignity was confirmed as a fundamental right under the law in the European Union in *Netherlands v. European Parliament* (2001). More recently, in 2023, an Irish court found its own nation in breach of the Charter for failing to uphold the right to dignity in a case involving a man from Afghanistan who traveled to Ireland seeking asylum protections and was not provided with accommodation, food or other basic needs beyond a 28 Euro grocery store voucher.[29]

National constitutions have also enshrined dignity. Legal scholar Erin Daly traces its usage in several constitutions, noting that the word does not appear in the US Constitution but has played a role in judicial opinions that shape the development of American legal thought.[30] Spain's 1978 Constitution makes dignity the foundation of political order and social peace: "The dignity of the person, the inviolable rights which are inherent, the free development of the personality, the respect for the law and for the rights of others are the foundation of political order and social peace."[31] South Africa's 1996 Constitution states in section 10 that "[e]veryone has inherent dignity and the right to have their dignity respected and protected."[32] The 1992 Constitution of the Czech Republic commits its people "to build, safeguard, and develop the Czech Republic in the spirit of the sanctity of human dignity and liberty."[33] As the law of the land, dignity thus becomes a right that courts are obligated to interpret and enforce.

We often see dignity's appearance in the language of law during times of war and great suffering, including times of extreme racism. The lack of dignity in life seems to give rise to reassertions of its importance. Consider the words of one judge, credited with the first usage of racism in a US Supreme Court decision, who also invoked dignity's importance as a first principle of law and of a humane people. Born in Michigan in 1890, Frank Murphy served as the state's thirty-fifth governor before later being appointed to the Supreme Court in 1940 by US President Franklin D. Roosevelt.[34] Sitting on the Court during the entire period the United States was engaged in World War II, Justice Murphy was called upon to decide several historic cases involving racism, civil rights, and civil liberties.

In *Korematsu v. United States* (1944), Murphy dissented from the decision upholding Japanese American internment, warning that

> to infer that examples of individual disloyalty prove group disloyalty and justify discriminatory action against the entire group is to deny that, under our system of law, individual guilt is the sole basis for deprivation of rights. . . . To give constitutional sanction to that inference in this case, . . ., is to adopt one of the cruelest of the rationales used by our enemies to destroy the dignity of the individual and to encourage and open the door to discriminatory actions against other minority groups in the passions of tomorrow.[35]

In *Steele v. Louisville & N.R. Co.* (1944), concerning employment discrimination against Black railroad workers, Murphy wrote in concurrence: "The utter disregard for the dignity and the well-being of colored citizens shown by this record is so pronounced as to demand the invocation of constitutional condemnation."[36] In *United States v. Screws*

(1945), a case involving the killing of a Black man by a Georgia sheriff, Murphy insisted:

> Robert Hall, a Negro citizen, has been deprived of . . . the right to life itself. That right was his because he was an American citizen, because he was a human being. As such, he was entitled to all the respect and fair treatment that befits the dignity of man, a dignity that is recognized and guaranteed by the Constitution.[37]

In *Duncan v. Kahanamoku* (1946), Murphy's concurrence underscored his views:

> Racism has no place whatsoever in our civilization. The Constitution as well as the conscience of mankind disclaims its use for any purpose, military or otherwise. . . . It renders impotent the ideal of the dignity of the human personality, destroying something of what is noble in our way of life. We must therefore reject it completely whenever it arises in the course of a legal proceeding.[38]

Justice Murphy espoused dignity not only as a legal principle but as a human value upon which to resist racism. He applied dignity universally to uphold the rights of people, whether Japanese American, Black American, or anyone else. His judicial opinions illustrate how dignity, though often undefined, operated as a constitutional ideal to resist racial subordination. His approach offers us a lesson for today, to make dignity a touchstone for the very foundation of our human rights. Why is racism wrong, morally and legally? Because dignity demands better of us.

*

Combating Global Racism Through Dignity

Dignity, the foundational norm that establishes the inherent worth of all people, is the key to combating global racism. More than a protection against harm, it is a means of prevention. By grounding law, policy, and culture in the principle of human dignity, we gain not only a defensive shield against racism but also an offensive strategy to stop global racism before it starts.

To understand how dignity can achieve this, let's take a step back. The answer starts with a gap in the current approach to addressing racism, which I've written about in detail before.[39] International law has defined the problem as one of racial discrimination, prohibiting acts of discrimination on the basis of race. This framing establishes not merely a political aspiration but also a binding legal duty on states. They must not discriminate on the basis of race because doing so inhibits certain individual positive rights, namely, equality.

The Commission on Human Rights, which prepared the original draft of the Declaration on the Elimination of Racial Discrimination for the UN General Assembly, justified the Declaration's purpose on the basis of the rights affirmed by the earlier UN Charter and UDHR.[40] The ICERD treaty, which soon followed, requires nations to enact nondiscrimination laws, policies and other measures as a means of protecting the human rights of equality. The rationale is that legally banning racial discrimination upholds nondiscrimination, which upholds equality.[41] This creates a legal definition that frames the harms arising from certain actions or behaviors based on the victim's race.

But, as this book has investigated, this legal view is limiting. Understanding the challenge as one of global racism frames the fuller extent of racism's harms as a form of oppression that works by dehumanizing people on the basis of an assigned group identity that doesn't exist in any scientific or biological way. Its presence is evidenced not only by a discriminatory act but also by harms to dignity. To see global racism in full requires challenging the following assumptions.

First, global racism's harms are not limited to those dependent upon the basis of the victim's race alone. If, for example, the Pamiri, a minority group in Tajikistan, claim that the government is violating their human rights by engaging in racial discrimination, that analysis should not be based on whether or not an international court decides that the Pamiri are a racial group who can therefore experience racial discrimination. A legal regime that addresses only discriminatory acts without acknowledging racism itself remains incomplete.

In his book *Faces at the Bottom of the Well*, Derrick Bell exposed the problem with laws that only prohibit racial discrimination. He said, "[a] preference for whites makes it harder to prove the discrimination outlawed by civil rights laws. This difficulty, when combined with lackluster enforcement, explains why discrimination in employment and in the housing market continues to prevail more than two decades after enactment of the Equal Employment Opportunity Act of 1965 and the Fair Housing Act of 1968."[42] Framing the problem as one of racial discrimination is unduly narrow and misses the root of the problem.[43]

The deeper harm often lies in dignity harms animated by ideologies of racist superiority and hatred. It is the combination of these ideologies with racist acts that so deeply damages dignity and robs us of our humanity. This same combination foments deadly violence, catalyzing war and even genocide. Understanding this helps us acknowledge that racism doesn't even require a racist; it can operate anonymously, embedded in institutions and social systems. Precisely because it harms in so many ways, all around the world, global racism remains among the most dangerous threats to humanity. The universal prevalence of racism challenges the universal ambitions of international human rights law, whose foundational purpose is to affirm that all humans are entitled to basic rights inherent to their very existence. The notion that people can be denied rights or have their rights violated because other people deem themselves racially superior is antithetical to these first principles.

This is why combating global racism requires addressing not only discrete acts and experiences of an isolated victim but also the broader structures of ideology that sustain racist subordination over time. Even under the best of circumstances, banning acts of racial discrimination does little to prevent the large-scale harms of slavery, segregation, apartheid, and genocide that ideologies of superiority have wrought and the international community now decries. To fulfill its promise, international law must move beyond prohibiting discrimination alone.

One of the distinguishing features of global racism is its ability to operate across national borders and legal jurisdictions meant to constrain racial discrimination. It does this, for example, by spreading through ideologies of superiority that become sanctioned by the leaders of countries or powerful groups. But these ideologies are only sustained by masses of believers, everyday people who take up an ideology as their own and act accordingly. Another way to put this is that most people are outwardly proud to declare that they are *not* racist. Instead, they hide their racism behind other ideological purposes, such as patriotism, nationalism, or religious pride.

Creating cultures in society that guard against this kind of ideological proliferation has long been key to stopping the racist views of a few leaders from manifesting as global racism. Dignity offers a counter ideology to ideologies of racial superiority. It offers a way of thinking and being that gives people a constructive, rather than destructive, sense of group identity. Dignity becomes the value we espouse as people who believe that *Homo sapiens* are inherently humane. But for dignity to counter the recourse to superiority complexes built around the construct of race requires a sacrifice. People must forgo a sense of identity that is comparative, rooted in the belief that someone matters because they are better than another kind of person.[44] Gloria Steinem captures the way forward perfectly when she asked us to understand that "we are linked, not ranked."[45]

This is where the human right of dignity offers promise. A world centered on the norm of dignity and an international legal framework that recognizes it sets a higher bar for humanity's behavior. The test becomes whether or not nations, organizations, and people are upholding the inherent worth of every human being. Notably, this test is not tethered to recognizing the harm solely on the basis of a person's race. Dignity harms include global racism, while not being dependent upon race as a construct of human identity. The principle of dignity supports the rationale for universal human rights and pushes back against behaviors and policies that would defy its core meaning. It also recognizes that global racism does more than deny individuals equality; it threatens to steal away our humanity.

*

Dignity as a Universal Value

Dignity is more than a moral idea or even a legal right; it is a fundamental value. Dignity is essential to our most basic human needs. Our bodies require air, water, food, and shelter to survive. But our minds, hearts, and spirits demand something more: recognition and affirmation of our humanity. We need to experience these affirmations often enough to sustain a belief in our inherent worth as human beings.

Unlocking dignity as a powerful antidote to global racism requires recognizing it as both a universal value and a universal human right. The shift requires people, not just nations, to embrace the view that all humans, everywhere, have inherent value and should be treated as such.

Why do values matter? While rights motivate laws, values motivate human behavior. Values are principles or beliefs that fundamentally shape how we understand the world and our place within it. Beliefs drive behavior in ways that law alone cannot, as I have argued before.[46] People may refrain from stealing because it violates a law, and they fear the punishment the law provides if they are caught. But people who choose not to steal because doing so violates their values are guided by a deeper motivation. Values get to the core of our identity, how we see ourselves in the world. Identity, in turn, is a key motivator of our behaviors. In this way, values shape behavior more powerfully than rules enforced by carrots and sticks. When we internalize a value—when it becomes part of our core identity—we align our behavior to remain consistent with it.

Valuing dignity is central to our identity as human beings. We define our humanity by how we treat one another and by the harms we agree not to allow. Dignity, as a value, offers humanity a way to recenter our relationship with global racism. We do not support ideologies of racial superiority, and we build laws and societies and nations that uphold this view, because this is central to our very identity as humans. Dignity, as a value, guides how we live with one another in ways that prevent racism before it takes root.

Prizing dignity as a value as well as a right offers humanity a vital path forward in the fight to combat the dehumanizing dangers of global racism.[47] Protecting the norm of dignity as a foundation for universal human rights requires being proactive. It requires centering dignity as the standard for all human behavior, not as the exception. A dignity-based approach to combating global racism means that you don't have to earn or deserve protection from racism. It is what you are owed as a measure of your inherent worth. Equality demands nondiscrimination, but dignity demands more: actively valuing humanity. The articulation of dignity as both a legal principle and a moral imperative affirms this fundamental truth: Dignity is not only the ground of rights but also the aspirational reach of human potential to live together without racism.

*

Building a Culture of Global Dignity

Building a culture of global dignity requires a reset. As a first principle of international law and a universal human right, dignity is already recognized by nations of the world as inherent and universal. But, in practice, there are far too many flagrant violations of dignity. This book has outlined the many instances of global racism as one category of dignity harms. Global racism, in turn, would not be possible without racist ideologies and racist people, organizations, and nations. Understanding why global racism persists is linked to answering a second set of questions. Why are there so many violations of dignity throughout human history? What makes it difficult to practice dignity in most places most of the time?

First, we need to consider what practicing dignity and building cultures of global dignity require. One of my favorite books offering practical guidance on how to do this is *Dignity: Its Essential Role in Resolving Conflict* (2011) by Donna Hicks.[48] Hicks describes the violation of dignity as a root cause of wars and a barrier to forging lasting peace and proposes ten elements of dignity. Her first element is "Acceptance of Identity. Approach people as being neither inferior nor superior to you." The list goes on to identify inclusion, safety, acknowledgement, recognition, fairness, benefit of the doubt, understanding, independence, and accountability as the other elements.

In every story I have ever heard about racism, including my own, a violation of this first element occurs. Racism creates a lack of dignity by negating the acceptance of a person's identity. How we understand our individual identity is a mix of actual biology and constructed characteristics. Age, for example, is undeniable. But our race is a construct, assigned to us and often used to reinforce hierarchies of harm upon us. Acts of racism are a denial of acceptance of identity and are, therefore, a denial of dignity.

Sadly, this root cause is all too common in the world today. Polarization-based group identity—my kind versus your kind—seems to be on the rise and with it, impulses to dehumanize the other. But recentering human identity, as one species, around the value of dignity offers humanity a better way forward. It is essential both for combating global racism and for forging a peaceful survival in the world to come. Dignity offers us an ideology through which to do so. Its appeal lies in the fact that everyone wants to experience dignity themselves.

What will it take for everyone to behave with dignity toward others? What does adopting the value of dignity as a foundation for world order require? First, it requires individuals to sacrifice the temptation of being "better than" and "superior to" others. This, for some, will be a stretch too far—after all, aren't some aspects of human life ranked? Aren't some people better than others? Yes, there are contexts in which rankings legitimately exist, for example, who can run the fastest or who can do higher math. A complete answer is worthy of its own book. But we should not conflate a ranking with inherent worth. Dignity requires resisting ideologies of superiority based on a constructed identity we call race, a construct that is not biological and that negates the inherent dignity or worth of all human beings.

Valuing dignity in world order also requires societies to meet a higher standard than currently exists. It requires us to design a human ecosystem that has a niche for everyone. Of course, there will be exceptions. A person with a propensity to commit violent crimes, for example, must be prevented from causing further harm. But how might we build a global society that values the inherent worth of every group, not in spite of our differences, but because of them?

Third, it is for those who argue against dignity to bear the burden of justifying their claims. What reason is there for not pursuing dignity as a universal human value? History makes clear to us that some value must order the world. Even those who believe human nature is inherently selfish and violent would argue the same. For, as Thomas Hobbes famously argued in *Leviathan* (1651), without organization in society, "the life of man [is] solitary, poor, nasty, brutish, and short."[49] Our current world order and way of human life are not working, from a universal perspective. It is time for humanity to try something new and adopt the values we need to survive.

Framed this way, the struggle against global racism is, at its core, a struggle to restore, protect, and design human life around dignity. When global racism is manifested throughout history and around the world as a form of dignity stolen or denied, then restoring dignity becomes the foundation for building a future in which global racism is extinct. By promoting human connection, dignity has the capacity to transform communities, repair division, and offer a sense of hope. In the end, dignity is not only for some; it must be for all peoples, within and across all nations. We cannot tell a story of universal dignity and then apply it selectively in world affairs in the service of powerful nations and groups. But practicing dignity as a universal human value will require a collective cultural shift, one that is backed by power. To achieve this, humanity will need to understand and to embrace the true power of education to create transformational cultural change.

9

The Power of Education

Maggy's Story

"Hello," she said to me, "my name is Marguerite Barankitse from Burundi, but you can call me Maggy." It was an uncommonly gloomy day in early May, and I had just sat down at a conference at UCLA, the university where I work in Los Angeles, California, when I met Maggy for the first time. I recognized her immediately as the powerful woman who had spoken on the main stage the evening before and as the first recipient, in 2016, of the Aurora Prize for Awakening Humanity. The room was full of humanitarians, human rights scholars, and advocates from around the world, all participating in a conference hosted by The Promise Institute for Human Rights at UCLA and the Aurora Humanitarian Initiative. That afternoon, I was due to speak on a panel about the right to education, alongside a phenomenal lineup of experts—all women. Our keynote speaker, however, had been unable to make the trip. I asked Maggy if she would be willing to join our panel and share her story, and she graciously agreed.

That afternoon, as Maggy began to speak, the room fell silent. With her permission, I'll share her story with you now. Maggy was born in Burundi in 1957 to a Tutsi family in the remote Ruyigi region of eastern Burundi where she became a schoolteacher. Later, she worked as a secretary to the Catholic bishop. In 1994, a group of armed Tutsi men arrived

Global Racism. Anna Spain Bradley, Oxford University Press. © Anna Spain Bradley 2026.
DOI: 10.1093/oso/9780197778388.003.0010

in Ruyigi and began to attack Hutu families there, including those seeking refuge at the bishop's residence. Maggy pleaded with them to stop—she was Tutsi, too—but they murdered seventeen children she had tried to hide that day, *her* children. They attacked her as well when she refused to tell them where the children were, but left her alive, calling her a "crazy lady." After that, Maggy adopted the name "the Crazy Lady from Burundi" for herself.

"I began with absolutely nothing," Maggy says.

> We were in the middle of a civil war and families were wiped out in my area for ethnic reasons. I managed to rescue some of the children by hiding them in a school nearby. More children started coming and I realized I had a responsibility to care for them. They needed shelter, safety and most of all, love. . . . We took because my children heard on the radio that "shalom" meant peace, and that is our dream. . . . Hate will never have the last word. Not as long as we practice love. . . . I have also learned that the word "impossible" is a lie. Nothing is impossible if you are driven by love and invest yourself fully. Hate will never have the last word. Not as long as we practice love.[1]

Maggy's life is a testament to her ministry of love. After the attacks in 1994, she provided shelter and care for the many children orphaned by the conflict, taking in over twenty thousand children left without a home after the war. She named her community Maison Shalom, or "House of Peace," which became a home to many. Her schools are unlike any other: Tutsi, Hutu, and Twa children learn side by side, because she believes every child is a "child of God."

Maggy's decades of sacrifice and vision have made her a global inspiration and a global leader for the power of peace. She has been awarded prizes and recognized by the government of France, the Council of Europe, UNESCO (United Nations Educational, Scientific and Cultural Organization), the Nobel Women's Initiative, and more. Her story and her example have been applauded by many around the world, including Pope Francis.[2] However, in 2016, she was forced to flee Burundi after being targeted for speaking out against President Pierre Nkurunziza. She now lives in exile in Rwanda, where she continues to support children who are refugees from Burundi, establishing the Community Center Oasis of Peace in Kigali.

Since our first meeting, I have been blessed to spend time with Maggy on several occasions and to keep in touch with her. Her vision of inclusive education, with dignity, for all, offers a powerful example of the point of this chapter.

Education is an effective antidote to oppression, including global racism. Education changes what we think by changing how we think. The key, as Maggy's example illuminates, is to engage in the experience of education with people different from yourself. When ten-year-olds gather to learn and then to play, they resist the framework that society has taught them that they are different because they are Twa, Hutu, and Tutsi. They have direct experience that teaches them that their differences might be about their favorite food or school subject, but not because of some constructed "sociological being" that dictates that certain children are inherently superior and others inferior on the basis of their racial or racialized identities.

Being a professor for over two decades, I have directly experienced the power of education. Not just the fact of it but the method. When people of diverse backgrounds experience inclusive education, they are transformed. Education reduces racial bias. It creates the conditions in which human rights and peace thrive. It is one of humanity's greatest tools for achieving dignity, equality, and progress. Maggy's story, her deep courage and strength, and her unyielding belief in humanity give us a powerful reason to embrace education. Her generosity of love has changed the lives of thousands, including my own, a fact all the more remarkable given the inhumanity she herself has experienced. Maggy dares to hope, not because she denies the existence of evil in the world but precisely because she has faced it. Her life's work shows us that the true power of education is more than a book or a classroom, though it often begins there. It is a chance to believe in the future.

*

The Power of Education

"Education is the most powerful weapon which we can use in order to prepare our youth for their role as leaders of tomorrow."[3] These words came from Nelson Mandela, the South African freedom fighter, on June 23, 1990—just four months after his release following his twenty-seven-year imprisonment. He was in the United States as part of a six-week, eight-country international tour to rally support for South Africa's ongoing antiapartheid struggle. In addition to trips to the White House in Washington, DC, and the United Nations in New York City, Mandela also made a stop at Madison Park High School in Boston's predominantly Black neighborhood of Roxbury.[4] Standing on a makeshift stage in the high school gym in his new gray suit, Mandela commanded the attention and then the admiration of some two thousand teenagers in the audience that day. He said:

> You have filled our hearts with a lot of joy. The warm welcome which you have given us is the source of tremendous strength for us . . . The people of South Africa have always known that amongst you, there are some of our strongest supporters in our struggle . . . We are proud indeed to be able to be here to thank you for that support. We are deeply concerned, both in our country and here, of the very large number of drop-outs by school children. This is a very disturbing situation because the youth of today are the leaders of tomorrow. We know that the reason for our children leaving school and the very elementary standards is because of poverty and frustration. But we would like to advise you to try as much as possible to remain in school. Because education is the most powerful weapon, which we can use in order to prepare our youth for their role as leaders of tomorrow.[5]

The impact of his visit on the community was significant, recorded in interviews published soon after in the *Boston Globe*.[6] One student, a sixteen-year-old named Malissa Willliams, said, "To me he's like a Moses, trying to set his people free." Ego Ezedi, a seventeen-year-old student, reflected:

> Nelson Mandela is an inspiration not only to black people, but for all people. For a man to be imprisoned for 27 years, and then come out and have

> this much of an impact on the world in so few months, make you think what kind of an impact he would have had if he had been free all those years. He comes the closet to what I would consider a living legend.

A sophomore student named George White remarked:

> I think one of the things that's important about Mr. Mandela is how he's been able to pull together people of all colors. I think that's a message young people in this city really need to hear given all the racial tension that exists here. Mr. Mandela doesn't just symbolize the struggle against oppression in South Africa, but the struggle for human rights and for your dignity everywhere.

The centrality of education, the struggle against oppression, the importance of dignity: Mandela's calls to conscience and to action were guiding then; they are guiding now. He wasn't just encouraging young people to stay in school. He wasn't just thanking the students assembled that day and the Black community in America for their courage in helping resist apartheid. Mandela was speaking to the world, claiming education as our most powerful weapon for change. "Weapon" might seem an odd choice of words for someone schooled in Gandhian nonviolence. But a weapon is not only an instrument of war; it is also defined as "a means of gaining an advantage or defending oneself."[7] The education of which Mandela spoke can unite the youth around equality, dignity, and freedom for all. It has the power to help them become the leaders the world needs. But how?

How Education Combats Global Racism

In 1965, the drafters of the International Convention on the Elimination of All Forms of Racial Discrimination (ICERD) treaty envisioned that racial discrimination could be combated through "teaching, education, culture and information" and made it a duty for nations to provide them.[8] In their view, and that which became the ICERD treaty, these arenas were the way to promote "understanding, tolerance and friendship among nations and racial or ethnical groups" as well as promote international peace and security and universal human rights.[9] In 2001, the Durban Declaration further specified that nations are "to ensure that education and training, especially teacher training, promote respect for human rights and the fight against racism, racial discrimination, xenophobia and related intolerance," specifying human rights education as a central tool for addressing these oppressions.[10] Of course, nations have not universally undertaken such educational efforts. Indeed, educating people about race and racism or about the value of human diversity and the need for inclusion is increasingly under attack.

But, because of the success of educational efforts in some places, we know that education can and does help combat racism. In 2020, UNESCO issued a report finding that "[e]ducation systems and educational institutions have an important role and responsibility in addressing and eliminating racism."[11] A 2022 study in southern France of almost three thousand students aged twelve to eighteen found that teaching students about racial discrimination resulted in reduced prejudice.[12] Another 2022 study based in Sweden, noting the turn in Europe from tackling racism to addressing all forms of discrimination in the 2000s, recommended six effective interventions high school teachers could use to specifically combat individual and structural forms of racism.[13] Two 2023 studies focused on educating university students about historical and current forms of anti-Indigenous racism at the University of Manitoba in Canada also demonstrated the positive impact of education in combating racism.[14] Additional studies of proactive education-based interventions in the United States showed positive effects, where white college students reported increased racial awareness after watching a video about racism, and where community members learning about racism for forty hours reported increased knowledge about racism and confidence in discussing it.[15]

These results are not anomalies; they've been confirmed by numerous other studies.[16] People who learn about racism—what it is and how it harms—are more informed. And information changes behaviors—not always, but often. Neuroscience is one area of study that offers valuable insights about why. The field of neuroscience is complex, offering an array of methodologies applicable to the law, which I explored at length in my book *Human Choice in International Law*. Recent breakthroughs in brain imaging technology allow us to better map how brain activity relates to human behavior. A number of studies have shown that when people experience the emotion we call fear, the amygdala—a small, almond-shaped area inside the brain—is activated.

Additional research in behavioral science reveals connections between bias or prejudice and the brain's neural functioning.[17] The amygdala is believed to play a central role in the experience of emotion overall. It also exhibits activity when people describe experiencing both fear and racial bias. In 2000, a widely cited study by Elizabeth Phelps and colleagues evidenced this connection, finding that greater amygdala activation was associated with stronger pro-white/anti-Black bias scores on the Implicit Association Test.[18] These biases, detectable within milliseconds, reveal how quickly the brain categorizes people as "us" and "them." Of course, many caveats apply. Neuroscience doesn't reduce racism to brain activity alone, nor does it excuse bias as somehow hardwired. Nevertheless, evidence of a linkage between fear responses and racial categorization offers a compelling reason to further explore connections between fear and the recourse to racism.

Education is a powerful tool to disrupt existing behavioral and cognitive patterns. But it is not just the mere fact of education. Its power lies in methodology. Education, when experiential, can help retrain these neural responses, reducing reliance on fear of new stimuli and strengthening the brain's capacity for empathy. Like any daily practice, such as brushing your teeth, making a habit of having positive experiences with people whose racial identities you believe to be different from your own reorganizes the neural pathways that produce your behavioral response. Simply put, behavior has the power to change the brain. But here's the key. The educational experience must be designed to promote repeated positive experiences between people who view one another as racially different from themselves.

There is a second reason why education is such a powerful weapon for change. The study of brain development reveals that the human brain grows in stages. During the first year of life, babies are still growing billions of new neurons and forming synapses at an extraordinary pace. The brain continues rapid growth and development until the age of five. From age five through adolescence, the brain is busy developing more complex functions such as language, memory, reasoning, and emotional skills. Our brains are not fully formed until our twenties. What happens to people when they are very young has a deep and lasting impact on their brain's physical and cognitive development, effects that can last a lifetime.

Primary education in many parts of the world begins at age five and lasts through age thirteen, typically kindergarten through the eighth grade. During these formative years, children are expected to learn how to read and write and how to do basic math. But children are also learning as much, if not more, from their environment and the social and cultural cues it provides. The classroom becomes one of the first social laboratories where young people learn who belongs, who is valued, and who is excluded. Classrooms and learning environments that normalize equality and dignity for all from a young age do more than teach tolerance—they shape neural pathways that reinforce empathy, fairness, and the recognition of shared humanity. Such lessons have a lasting impact well beyond childhood.

However, this aspect, inclusive education, is often overlooked. You cannot unlock education's power simply by populating your schools with people from diverse backgrounds, racial and otherwise. The entire school's culture must allow for an immersive experience into a culture of dignity and equality. When students not only see diversity but experience dignity in practice, education becomes transformative, equipping the next generation with the cognitive and moral tools to resist ideologies of racial superiority. This is because education is a place of experience where people join together around a common mission—to learn. Even better, it is a mission to learn together. When this happens among a diverse group of people, the positive experiences of education are bound together with openness to people different from ourselves, in reality and in our neural structures. Education as experience, with these parameters in place, becomes a powerful tool for openness, tolerance, debiasing, and more. It is not the mere fact of education, but the inclusive experience of it that changes people.

The details of educational experience matter. Here, experiential forms of pedagogy are key. Group projects, often dreaded by students at first, are transformed into purposeful exercises in learning how to listen and respond, collaborate, lead and serve, and foster communication skills. Simulations, in which students take on specified roles in exercises meant to reflect real-world situations, teach empathy and compassion and how to rise to the occasion when the world is depending on you through practice and reflection.

Education at its best happens within a diverse and inclusive community. This kind of education can be transformational for societies, promoting human rights, wealth generation, and health. Higher education advances critical thinking, tolerance, and civic participation, while also reducing bias and even lowering risks of extremism and terrorism. Education is also a powerful driver of gender equality and economic growth. Educated women and girls and educated children become aware of their human rights and those of others and demand governments and those in power to uphold them. This is the ultimate power and purpose of the right to education.

These are some of the insights I shared at the UN when I served as Legal Expert in 2021. I was tasked with leading the expert report on prevention. Diplomats asked me, how do we prevent racial discrimination? I asserted then, as I will now, that education is key, especially when delivered in ways that are experiential, participatory, and grounded in subsidiarity—in the needs and the knowledge of local communities. I articulated that it is not the mere fact of education that helps prevent racism, but rather the practice of experiential and inclusive education that cultivates empathy across differences and addresses the root causes of global racism.[19]

*

Upholding the Right to Education

All children around the world are entitled to a free and quality education. It is their human right. This idea, that education should be a right, formally emerged on the international scene in the 1920s. British social reformer Eglantyne Jebb, who founded Save the Children in 1919, had been outraged by the plight of starving children during World War I. She drafted a set of children's rights, including the right to education, which was taken up and adopted by the League of Nations in 1924 as the Geneva Declaration on the Rights of the Child.[20]

In 1948, the right to education was enshrined in Article 26 of the Universal Declaration of Human Rights, which states that "everyone has a right to education." This right has been reaffirmed in Article 13 of the International Covenant on Economic, Social and Cultural Rights (1966) and in the Convention on the Rights of the Child (1989). Regionally, it is protected under instruments such as the African Charter on the Rights and Welfare of the Child (1990) and the Protocol of San Salvador in the Americas (1988).[21] Together, these treaties confirm that every child—regardless of race, gender, or nationality—has the right to free and compulsory primary education, and the progressive realization of secondary and higher education. There is even a proposed fourth optional protocol to the Convention on the Rights of the Child that would expand free education to include at least one year of preprimary and one year of secondary education. As a part of the UN's Sustainable Development Goals, all nations have committed to providing such expanded access.

Historically speaking, the world has made great progress. In 2020, 86.9 percent of all children worldwide received some basic education, a near reversal from two hundred years ago, when 82.8 percent of children did not receive any education.[22] Encouragingly, by 2023, the global gender gap between girls and boys in primary education had nearly closed.[23] Regionally, Central and Southern Asia have seen dramatic gains: the number of out-of-school children has fallen from fifty-three million to about fifteen million over the last two decades.

But challenges remain. According to 2023 data, 272 million young people are not attending school, with upper secondary education seeing the highest nonattendance at 130 million students.[24] UNESCO estimates that only about 58 percent of all young people complete their secondary school education.[25] Reasons for this include poverty, racial and ethnic discrimination, gender discrimination against girls, and armed conflict. The majority of the many millions of children excluded from education today are from marginalized groups.[26]

Demographic data suggests that such disparities in education are likely to deepen. There were approximately 8.14 billion people in the world in 2025, of whom 2.3 billion were children.[27] The global child population is projected to peak in 2050 before declining to 1.9 billion by 2100, even as overall world population is projected to peak in the 2040s. The fastest growth in child populations will occur in African countries such as Angola, Burkina Faso, Burundi, Chad, the Central African Republic, the Democratic Republic of Congo, Mali, Somalia, and Uganda. This growth is driven in part by limited access to family planning, birth control, and overall healthcare for women, especially in rural areas, as well as by declining child mortality.[28]

Even where children are enrolled in school, attendance does not guarantee meaningful education. Many children lack even the most basic literacy. In lower and middle-income countries, half of all ten-year-olds cannot read proficiently.[29] There are also concerns about disparities in learning outcomes.[30] On standardized assessments, an admittedly limited metric that is neither inclusive nor holistic, students in countries such as Australia, the United States, Canada, western Europe, Japan, New Zealand, South Korea, and Vietnam significantly outperform their peers elsewhere in the world. Some of the lowest overall learning outcomes are in Burkina Faso, Gabon, Guinea, Kenya, Namibia, and Senegal.

This overview of the current state of the right to education in the world reveals a pressing tension. Global racism cannot be dismantled without mobilizing education, yet existing and emerging disparities in access and quality of education persist. This gulf between the promise of education as a universal right and education as a lived reality around the world underscores just how much work remains. Education is not simply a service that states provide; it is the foundation of equality, dignity, and peace upon which our collective future rests. Where children are denied education, they are also denied a powerful means of resisting the ideologies of superiority that fuel global racism in the first place.

Increasingly, education is a political act. Viewed as dangerous in the eyes of many, education promotes critical thinking and progressive values. It has the power to inculcate shared histories and construct societal norms. This is why promoting access to education is the dangerous weapon Mandela knew it to be. This is why Maggy's decision to include Twa children in her schools was controversial. Most governments and societies seek to preserve the status quo. Where education disrupts that, it becomes a threat. When a school or place of education does embrace this norm, it often becomes the target of outside hostility from those who view it as a threat to the social order they seek to preserve.

We are witnessing renewed attacks on education by many governments around the world. In Afghanistan, the Taliban have issued seventy decrees limiting the rights of girls and women across society. Over 2.2 million girls are no longer permitted to attend secondary school or higher education.[31] In 2023, the US Supreme Court's decision in *Students for Fair Admissions v. Harvard* ruled that race could no longer be used as a factor for admission to universities, but provided an exception for admissions to military academies. In 2025, the Trump Administration launched an overall attack on higher education, starting with Harvard University, withholding federal research funding to coerce universities to get rid of programs and people who are counter to the Administration's aims, including the widespread dismantling of diversity, equity, and inclusion offices. There have been bans and efforts to curtail classes and programs on critical race theory, on transgender care, and on human rights for Palestinians. Those who dare offer or learn lessons that challenge political, religious, or cultural orthodoxies are targeted. Education is politicized by governments, religions, political parties, and social movements, not in spite of its power but because of it. Yet, combating global racism as a challenge for the world is inseparable from promoting the right to education for all children. Both are rooted in the fundamental pursuit of our common humanity.

10

The Quest for *Humanitas*

To End Racism, Must Race End?

In 2021, just three years before her death at the age of 81, poet and activist Nikki Giovanni gave an interview to the *New York Times* that celebrated her life's work and impact as a poet, writer, educator, and activist. Born three months before my father, in June 1943, Giovanni was a trailblazer in civil rights, women's rights, and much more. In this interview, she issued an eloquent premonition: "[i]f Earth survives—there's a good chance we'll blow ourselves up—gender and race are going to go."[1] To explain her embrace of a raceless future, she recalls a make-believe moment from her childhood growing up in 1940s and 1950s Tennessee and southern Ohio, where her family moved when she was four:

> I thought if I ran into a Martian and the Martian said, "Who are you?" what would my answer be? The only answer could be "I am an Earthling." I realized—and have continued to realize—that it would be illogical if I were to tell the Martian I'm a Black woman. That's because a Martian doesn't know what Black is, and they don't know what a woman is. So we know that race is illogical. It is a construct that is destructive.

In the interview, Giovanni makes plain what she has long explored in her poetry and writing, that race is a dangerous construct that gets in our way of being human. For an author so closely identified throughout her long career with race—her first book was titled *Black Feeling, Black Talk*

Global Racism. Anna Spain Bradley, Oxford University Press. © Anna Spain Bradley 2026.
DOI: 10.1093/oso/9780197778388.003.0011

(1968)—this might seem like a striking statement. Yet for Giovanni, it now seems so elemental.

It is, indeed, elemental. This book has traced some of the many paths that this discourse has traveled over time, place, and discipline. Recall early wisdoms rooted in the Black American intellectual tradition, extending out into the world, as articulated by Frederick Douglass, W. E. B. Du Bois, Ralph Bunche, and an untold number of women who history did not record, all articulating the need to understand race and its role in perpetuating racism. Recall the authors who penned *The Race Question*, with scholars like Ashley Montagu articulating that race was a fallacy, a flawed concept, created by men to justify the evils of the transatlantic slave trade and colonialism, not based on human biology.[2] Recall the long tradition of scholars who have interrogated the fallacy of race and questioned whether abandoning it as a concept might help bring an end to racism.[3] Noting such complexities, Angela Y. Davis, for example, envisioned race as "indispensable but insufficient."[4] Writing in 2023, Subrena E. Smith and David Livingston Smith reengaged with such debates, holding that "[t]o get rid of racism we have to get rid of race," as they believe "[r]ace is and has always been an ideological weapon."[5] Conversations like these about the deconstruction of race, what it is, and where it comes from returns us to critical inquiries in the past that UNESCO's *The Race Question* sought to illuminate. In some form or another, these works ask us to challenge core assumptions about race and about racism.

But I was also struck by Giovanni's words for another reason, so much so that I pulled the *New York Times Magazine* out of the pile and put it on the top of my desk, where it remains to this day. To me, Giovanni's wisdom isn't only about race or gender; it's about humanity. She asks us to sit with the most difficult question of all. What does it mean to be human? To belong to the human species? What categories of identity remain, and which ones must go?

A quarter of the way into the twenty-first century, it seems that we should have accepted our fate as a singular species. With all of our science and history and anthropology and archaeology, we should appreciate the uniqueness of our predicament in time. All other hominids as we know them have gone extinct. We are the only ones left. Most dramatically, we are the only known life of our kind in all the universe. Simply put, we are one human species. The question that follows is this. What does it mean to be a human? What is our human identity, individually and collectively? This, I believe, is a question for the world.

Demographics alone demand it. According to the World Bank, the human population in 2024 reached 8.14 billion.[6] Once upon a time, there were far fewer of us. In 10,000 BC, an estimated one million humans lived on Earth—about the population of present-day Columbus, Ohio, near where I grew up, or of Nairobi, Kenya.[7] This number grew to approximately five million by 5000 BC, and one hundred fifty million by 200 BC. The global population has expanded ever since, sometimes rapidly and sometimes more gradually, depending on complex forces such as climate, habitat, and access to food. By 100 AD, the world's population stood at around 250 million; by 1800 AD, it had reached 813 million. In 1950, the global population had reached 2.5 billion. In the future, the United Nations estimates that the global human population will reach 9.7 billion by 2050, 10.4 billion in the 2080s, and 11.2 billion by 2100.[8] Asia and Africa are at the center of this population surge. By 2100, it is projected that 80 percent of the world's people will live in those regions alone.[9]

How should we identify as individuals in such a globally prolific species? Referring to humans from entire continents with billions of people by one monolithic racial group identity, such as "African" or "Asian," certainly doesn't capture the reality or complexity of identity. Whether conceptualizing race or ethnicity or national origin or nationality, such broad labels fail to capture the political alliances, linguistic differences, cultural ties, and countless other markers of human identity. If race as a category is under scrutiny today, the demographic transformations of tomorrow will render the inadequacy of race as an organizing principle undeniable. But what would a world without race look like? How should humanity organize itself in the world to come? Here, the past reveals wisdom for today.

From Solon to *Humanitas*

When early humans lived hunter–gatherer lifestyles, scientists generally believed that people living in small tribes, often as close relatives, were largely egalitarian, which contributed to the evolution and expansion of our species.[10] Egalitarianism values the well-being of the group through the sharing of resources and equal status. Two groups that still practice aspects of their ancient hunter–gatherer lifestyle—the Hazda in Tanzania and the Kung San in the Kalahari Desert—provide modern-day examples of egalitarian societies. However, human societies became hierarchical and more patriarchal with the transition from hunter–gatherer to agrarian societies. Something about settling in a permanent location and accumulating property and resources fundamentally changed humans' relationship with status, power, resource sharing, and conflict. Population growth combined with limited land and resources led to problems, and ultimately to war.

These were the conditions in the seventh and sixth centuries BC in Ancient Greece during a period that saw the rise of tyrants, men who governed over city-states through absolute power and force, with little to constrain their wants. It was during these times that Solon set forth an example that would inspire generations. Much of what we know of Solon today comes through the writings of Plutarch, some six hundred years after Solon died. Born in Athens around 630 BC, Solon grew up in an era of war and discord.[11] Various city-states went to war for territory and resources, which were increasingly limited as the population expanded. These city-states were governed by aristocratic men with few limits on their power, originating the word "tyrant" that we know today.

Growing up in a noble family in Athens, leading an army there, Solon was named archon (chief magistrate) around 594 BC. To address Athens' many problems, he developed codes—norms that should be followed—and wrote them down for all to see. Solon's laws banned debt slavery, expanded property rights, and permitted commoners alongside aristocrats in the Ekklesia (assembly) and the Heliaia (court). His reforms were later called "seisachtheia," or the "shaking off of burdens."[12]

Solon reportedly chose to leave Greece for ten years after enacting his legal reforms so he would not be pressed into repealing them. Plato later writes that it is during this time, when Solon visited the Temple of Sais in Egypt, that he heard the tale of Atlantis from the priests there. Solon, the great Athenian lawgiver, taught that justice and civic life depended on treating others with fairness and moderation.

Solon's legacy in Ancient Greece predated the Latin concept *humanitas*—human nature, civilization, and kindness—which Cicero expressed as "a kind of fellowship uniting all mankind."[13] But his thinking inspired the concept of a duty to aid one another, bound by natural law and linked to innate inner virtues. Cicero connected this duty to the survival of humankind: "Those who say that we should have regard to our fellow citizens, but not to strangers, destroy the community and the fellowship of the human race."[14] With these origins, the concept of *humanitas* would go on to inspire foundational principles of law and the importance of respecting humanity in social life.

*

From *Humanitas* to Human Rights

Solon's story remains ours today. Since time immemorial, humans have been on a quest for discovery. Often, we must answer "who are we?" before we can determine "who am I?" This is one of the most remarkable aspects of our species: our capacity for self-reflection and group reflection. The history of the idea of *humanitas* helps us see that we have tried to answer this question time and time again. I am worthy because I am human. I am human because I belong to a species that is, on the whole, humane. This is the tale we've told all over the world in great epics and legends of a mythical golden age. Our sense of human worth derives from a vision of ourselves as a humane species.

This rationale was the driving motivation behind the women and men who gathered at the end of World War II to draft the Universal Declaration of Human Rights. They asked, what compelling ingredient could unite people across countries and cultures? What might be the basis for a universal moral code for our species?[15] Having directly experienced the horrors of war, the Declaration's drafters started out prioritizing peace. But peace is an elusive notion not evidenced by the mere absence of war. Instead, peace demands more: a set of positive rights to protect people from violations, including those committed by their nation-state. Indian delegate Lakshmi Menon noted that the Declaration was "born from the need to reaffirm those rights after their violation during the war."[16] Belgian delegate Count Henry Carton de Wiart remarked that "the essential merit of the Declaration was to emphasize the high dignity of the human person after the outrages to which men and women had been exposed during the recent war," with French delegate René Cassin agreeing that the Declaration "was the most vigorous and the most urgently needed of humanity's protest against oppression."[17] The stark absence of respect for basic humanity and decency during the war years heightened the desire to affirm human rights in its aftermath.

The idea of *humanitas* was also a motivator for the drafters of the International Convention on the Elimination of All Forms of Racial Discrimination (ICERD) treaty, who recognized the need to affirm the basic dignity and equality of all people in the face of widespread belief in racial superiority and resulting discrimination in the world. Louis Joseph Alexandre Verret, the representative from Haiti, observed during the drafting of ICERD:

> [W]e have produced a document of which the least that can be said is that it is reasonably reassuring. We applaud it, and . . . to intone in all solemnity the hymn of reconciliation among the races which fantastic theories tend to divide, vaunting the supremacy of some peoples over others regarded as inferior and hence despised and held in servitude, if not indeed destined for utter annihilation.[18]

His reflections highlight the contradiction: In outlawing racial discrimination, the UN nonetheless validated the very concept of race, a construct historically employed to separate and to subordinate.

The idea of *humanitas* over the centuries helped solidify the idea of universal human rights and respect for them under international law.

But *humanitas* has always originated as a value of the people, whether or not it is also upheld as a value of a nation. This is where the limits of law, international or otherwise, become clear. Values are the work of people.

In 1999, Thomas Franck articulated this aspect when he argued that "nationalism is in retreat" and that, in its place, "*individualism*" had emerged.[19] Franck thought that the modern world was "*not* simply a world of sovereign states" and that such "Vattelian . . . assumptions ha[d] become untenable."[20] One manifestation of this is that states cannot be the sole guarantors of rights or the exclusive repositories of duties. To eliminate racism and a host of other ills, people themselves must be directly involved in the work of rights and duties. States must accept new visions of social unity that are inclusive of the complex realities of human identity. Doing so not only helps translate human rights law into human rights behavior but also recenters us in *humanitas*—the recognition that our shared humanity must be the grounding principle in a fractured world.

The Value of a Universal Value

Humanity's path forward is through values. Values matter; what we value matters, but it is that which we value together that matters most. Progress across a diverse human community cannot be achieved without deep commitment to certain shared values that bind us. This becomes even more essential in times of challenge and change. With eight billion people sharing one planet—grappling with the accelerating pace of technological disruption, the destabilizing force of climate change, widening economic inequality, mass migration and displacement, resurgent authoritarianism, and the fraying of trust in democratic institutions—humanity now faces such a moment.

In mathematical terms, we might call this an inflection point: the instant when a curve shifts from concave to convex. Everything around the inflection point changes. In life, as in math, such a change is fundamental: technology is changing, generational preferences are changing, the climate is changing, and even how things change is changing. At such a moment, the point holds the center. As the concave transforms to convex, the cup turns into a cap, and things fall out. Yet a simple shift in perspective can return the cap into a cup, balanced again around its center.

Through the value of *humanitas,* we can stay grounded during this time of change. But we must fight for that value by resisting the temptation toward ideologies of superiority and the allure of racism. We achieve *humanitas* by demanding dignity, universally, as a human right for all. This means valuing all people across borders and boundaries, between cultures and countries. It means affirming life, and freedom and dignity for all—no exceptions. We protect *humanitas* by unlocking the power of diverse and inclusive education, which changes what we think by changing how we think. Finally, we sustain *humanitas* by continuing our species' historical return to the belief that each of our lives has worth because our species is capable of being humane.

*

Fighting for *Humanitas*

The fight against *Global Racism* is, at its core, a fight for *humanitas.* It requires us to confront and resist certain aspects of human nature—namely, the desire for power, the allure of hierarchies, and the seduction of supremacist ideologies. Racism is not simply an attack on individuals; it is a collective threat. When faced with global challenges, such as a pandemic or climate change, racism exposes our greatest weakness. It fractures human solidarity at the very moment we need it most. Without that solidarity, we are unable to mount the collective response required to survive and flourish in the face of common dangers.

Many leaders today who espouse ideologies of superiority wrapped in global racism ignore this historical lesson in favor of their false prophecies. It was not the tyrants who made Ancient Greece great; it was the demos ("the people") and the use of norms and laws to bend power toward democratic ideals. It was not Julius Caesar, or any of the Caesars who followed, who made Rome great; it was Roman ideals rooted in the Republic and the rule of law, not those of powerful men. It is, and always has been, the people who make our species great. Not people as individuals, fighting for their own spoils and power and dominance, but people united in pursuit of a common aim.

Viewed in this light, the fight against racism is a part of a deeper war against oppression itself. To win that war, we must commit to protecting the most vulnerable among us. What harms some of us harms all of us; what diminishes one diminishes us all. As humanity, we become the very thing we consent to tolerate—and therefore, in refusing racism, we commit ourselves to becoming something better than we are today.

If we are to evaluate how to end racism, we must take a hard look at certain truths. One of those is that racism, in all its forms and around the world, is not accidental; it is by design. It persists because it speaks to the raw human desire that many—though not all—humans have for power, a desire often realized by creating hierarchies built on ideologies of supremacy that exist on the biologically false basis of racial difference.

A second truth is that racism is morally, legally, and profoundly wrong. It is a species-wide error we must deeply interrogate. Why do humans, often men in particular, continue to seek power obtained by the explicit or implicit oppression of others? How do current models of human society rely on embedded forms of power, hierarchy, and supremacy? What kinds of restructuring of human life are required to eliminate global racism? Deconstruction and critique are necessary, but they are not enough. If we seek to tackle racism only by deconstructing what it is and why it is wrong, we risk becoming trapped in a negative framework.

This book has asked us also to imagine a positive one. The vision is a world in which dignity is commonplace and racism, alongside other forms of oppression, is rare. A world without racism is a world in which the principle of dignity—that all people have inherent value and should be treated as such—becomes a matter of everyday practice. What will it take to get there from where we stand today? What is to be gained or lost, and by whom? How do we move forward with urgency in a deeply fragmented world? The how and the why of such changes demand rich, complex, and hard conversations.

Achieving this requires a human evolution. We must evolve to fulfill our needs for recognition, belonging, and value, not through power over another but through shared dignity for all. Here, *humanitas* has long been humanity's guiding light in times of chaos. This value, enshrined in law, has helped people and nations build peace.

Recall our history. First, *humanitas* has been a primary tool in constraining war. From Cyrus the Great's Cylinders to the Treaty of Kadesh to the Grotian Moment, law has set forth alternatives to war, means for ending war and norms for how to wage war. Second, *humanitas* arises from moments of great suffering, when enough nations and people in enough places demand its end. The ban on the transatlantic slave trade and, ultimately, on slavery itself offer a vivid example, along with later laws banning genocide, racial discrimination, segregation, and apartheid. To be human, we must not allow such grave inhumanity to exist with impunity.

This is the story of our species we must hold onto in dark times, when it seems many in the world have drifted far from *humanitas*. The long arc of history shows us that oppression does not hold. The allure of *humanitas* is too great. Indeed, it is in humanity's darkest hour that the spark of hope in human connection seems to be reborn, time and time again. After great wars, genocides, and intense periods of suffering, people begin to reach for hope because they know that a world without any is not a world they wish to have.

We already have a path forward. The challenge is to walk it—not alone, but together. The lesson of history is clear. Progress does not come from isolation but from shared effort, from communities large and small recognizing that their fate is bound up with one another. We've learned how this works, found in bonds forged through shared values and a collective of people committed to advancing those values in the world. History repeatedly demonstrates this truth, whether in social movements for justice, coalitions for peace, or collaborations in science and discovery. This is the simple formula that humanity, at its best, offers as a proof of concept. Values connect us, in place and time, to ourselves, to our communities, and to the greater good.

It is time to let our *humanitas* rise once again. In these years and days, we must remember and remind one another of this great lesson of our human history. We can change course if we choose to. Where people are the problem, we are also the solution.

We have the knowledge to uphold these values. Now we must find the integrity, especially when it's hard to do. Integrity is the test of values in practice. This is especially so when silence seems easier than truth. We must have the courage to speak up for those who cannot, to extend healing into the world. Courage is not always loud. More often, it is quiet—found in the small acts of conscience that accumulate into transformation. It is the voice in our hearts that whispers, then shouts: Do what is right.

This book has examined the phenomenon of global racism as a challenge for the world. By doing so, it has also illuminated how combating racism is rooted in a deeper quest to defend our humanity. The quest requires reimagining who we are as a united species. It calls us inward to confront the prejudices within us. It calls us outward to resist the structures of racism in the world around us. It calls us forward, grounded in *humanitas* as the truest source of human value. No one person can change the world, but together we can create a better, more humane future.

Conclusion
The Promise of Us

"Two truths approach each other. One comes from inside, the other from outside, and where they meet we have a chance to catch sight of ourselves."

—Tomas Tranströmer[1]

A promise is a strange idea. It is a commitment to fulfill an obligation. It is a vow we make to one another. It is a pledge we place upon ourselves. This book, *Global Racism: A Challenge for the World*, started as a promise I made to my father. In its original version, the book built upon my earlier work, which articulated racism as a violation of universal human rights that international law has yet to define and ban by name. The project quickly turned to a broader aim, creating a conversation about racism meant for the world. I soon confronted a challenge—the lack of any global consensus about what racism is and the full extent of its harms. This led me to name and to map the concept of global racism as a phenomenon of racism and its varied manifestations that are ubiquitous and universally available, operating in the human ecosystem and interacting with world order.

Naming global racism as a concept creates space for people to connect across continents and cultures in recognizing a shared form of oppression that is the thief of our humanity. It poses a challenge for the world, demanding a united response. This book has certainly not covered all that is possible to cover on a topic that spans the entirety of humanity,

Global Racism. Anna Spain Bradley, Oxford University Press. © Anna Spain Bradley 2026.
DOI: 10.1093/oso/9780197778388.003.0012

geography, and eras of human history. What is has aimed to do is to take the broad view: to place the study of global racism on the agenda for our time. My concluding message in this book is this: understanding global racism is inextricable from the age-old quest to understand our humanity, defined as that which makes us a human species.

At once, the answer is damning. Global racism continues to harm millions of people around the world, wildly violating human rights and causing economic, health, cultural, and dignity harms in its wake. At its worst extreme, global racism is at the root of slavery, apartheid, segregation, genocide, and other *jus cogens* that are universally condemned and banned through international law. Global racism is particularly stubborn. It is a problem both old and new, with ever-evolving manifestations. Its existence remains a cornerstone of modernity. Global racism is also evasive, mutating and reappearing throughout the human ecosystem through ideologies of superiority and in new ways we are only beginning to fully understand.

However, the study of global racism also illuminates the case for optimism. The reason for hope is us, as humanity. Even in our worst moments as a species, people seek a return to that which makes us humane. Today, the world enjoys an era more peaceful, prosperous, and full of human rights than at any other period in modern history. Of course, this is not the reality for many people in many places, and these gains are not equitably or equally distributed. But our past provides proof of concept that it is possible through dignity and *humanitas*, and through the human rights and laws we build around them, to construct a better world. In these moments of progress, however fragile, we can celebrate the victory of our species.

One book cannot put an end to global racism. Only people can do that, working for a common cause. Yet books, and the conversations they spark, can seed connections among peoples and nurture experiences of shared humanity. This book teaches us something about our shared humanity. In times of great suffering, people come together to say never again. From the Treaty of Kadesh to the Cylinder of Cyrus to Solon's Laws to Roman *humanitas* to the Universal Declaration of Human

Rights, after times of great oppression and suffering, our ancestors have worked to construct a better humanity. *Global Racism: A Challenge for the World* invites us to try to do the same, once again. It invites us to live fully in our humanity as people, as nations, and as one interconnected species. Most of all, it reminds us that the arc of human history bends, however imperfectly, toward the promise of us.

Acknowledgments

There are many people, including family, friends, and colleagues, I wish to thank for their contributions, critiques, inspiration, and overall support for this book. To start, the origins of this book evolved out of an earlier publication, *Human Rights Racism* (2019), and I reiterate my deep appreciation to all those I thanked before for their contributions to that project. It was on the strength of that law review article that Oxford University approached me about writing this book. I am grateful for the support and great patience of the OUP editorial team, including Merel Alstein, who first saw the promise of this book, Robert Cavooris, Rebecca Lewis, and Jacqueline Ridberg Larabee, as well as their colleagues at NewGen who provided excellent editorial support. Thank you to the two anonymous manuscript readers who saw the promise of this book project and challenged me to make it stronger with their critiques. I am also grateful for the efforts of developmental editor Pamela Haag, who helped me shape this book for a general audience.

A number of my colleagues in academia provided important interventions and helpful insights on drafts of this book along the way, helping me to think more deeply and write more clearly. I am particularly grateful to several colleagues who took extra time to provide in-depth feedback on earlier drafts: Ariela Gross, Gay McDougall, Saira Mohamed, Matiangai Sirleaf, and Ntina Tzouvala. Thank you to everyone who provided valuable feedback when I presented this work at conferences, workshops, and symposia at the American Society of International Law, American University Washington College of Law, Arizona State Sandra Day O'Conner College of Law, Association of American Law Schools, UCLA Department of Neurology, UCLA Department of

Political Science, UCLA International Institute, UCLA School of Law, University of Connecticut School of Law, University of Essex Human Rights Center, University of Wisconsin Law School, Washington and Lee, and Yale Law School.

I am grateful to a number of people for research support, including my UCLA Law Library colleagues Eli Edwards, Shangching Huitzacua, and Gabe Juarez for patience and creativity in obtaining obscure sources and ancient texts. A special thanks to my excellent team of UCLA law student research assistants. Minerva Ruda worked as my research assistant on this project for two years, providing thoughtful contributions along the way. Edna Bella Salčin and Kasper Jastrzebski joined near the end of the project and injected enthusiasm and diligence to the crucial tasks of citation and fact checking.

This book was greatly inspired by people I met during my leadership experiences serving as UCLA's Vice Chancellor for Equity, Diversity and Inclusion and as Legal Expert to the United Nations Ad Hoc Committee on the Elaboration of Contemporary Standards. To those who shared their painful experiences of racism and oppression with me, thank you from the bottom of my heart. By doing so, you helped me appreciate the complexities and urgency of this book.

Special thanks to the following friends and colleagues who've been a source of deep inspiration to me as a human rights advocate and as a writer. To Marguerite Barankitse, thank you for your kindness, friendship, courage, and continued force for love and peace in our world. To Gay McDougall, thank you for promoting equality and human rights through your decades-long tireless leadership at the United Nations and for your support of this project. Phillipe Sands, thank you for your support and for being a leading voice on the importance of international law and justice in the world. There are many other colleagues and friends at UCLA who I am indebted to but very special thanks are owed to Jared Diamond whose many books have inspired me to think bigger, bolder, and for a public audience; Andrea Ghez whose brilliance through unyielding curiosity has inspired me to keep investigating hard questions; and Kelly Lytle Hernández whose courageous passion to work toward a more just world has inspired me to keep going, especially when it is hard.

Most of all, I thank my family. Ava, your courage in the service of justice inspires me every day. Amaya, your indefatigable commitment to joy, humor, and wisdom is my guiding light. The grace in which you've both handled your own experiences with racism and indignities in life and your commitment to what is good, fair, and just in the world inspire me every day. May your future, and that of all your generation, sees less global racism and more *humanitas*. To my husband, Dr. Adam Bradley, thank you for all the encouragement and support you've given me over the years spent on this project. This book would not have been possible without your brilliant edits and endless patience as I talked over the idea for the thousandth time. To my sister Dr. Sarah Spain Shelton, who has remained my biggest cheerleader in life, thank you for always believing in me. Most of all, this book is dedicated to my mom and dad, who have now passed away, Mary Foody Spain and William G. Spain; your lives and testament to the power of love despite racism live on every page.

Notes

PREFACE

1. Ralph J. Bunche, United Nations Mediator in the Middle East, "The Human Factor in the Development of International Understanding: United Nations Intervention in Palestine," lecture at Colgate University, May 20, 1949, 19. Transcript available at UCLA Special Collections.
2. Derrick A. Bell, *Faces at the Bottom of the Well* (Basic Books, 1992), 5, "Black people are the magical faces at the bottom of society's well. Even the poorest whites, those who must live their lives only a few levels above, gain their self-esteem by gazing down on us."
3. Big Bill Broonzy, Memphis Slim, and Sonny Boy Williamson, "Black, Brown and White," on *Trouble in Mind*, recorded by Alan Lomax, 1947, https://www.youtube.com/watch?v=koc1coZsTLA.
4. John F. Kennedy Jr., Statement by the President Upon Signing Order Establishing the Peace Corps, March 1, 1961. Public papers of the Presidents of the United States: John F. Kennedy, containing the public messages, speeches, and statements of the President, 1961. Washington, D.C.: U.S. G.P.O., 1962.
5. Anna Spain Bradley, "International Law's Racism Problem," *Opinio Juris*, April 9, 2019.
6. Anna Spain Bradley "Human Rights Racism," *Harvard Human Rights Journal* 32, no. 1 (2019).
7. U.N. Human Rights Council, The Ad Hoc Committee on the Elaboration of Complementary Standards, Mandate, *International Convention on the Elimination of All Forms of Racial Discrimination*, adopted Dec. 21, 1965, 660 U.N.T.S. 195, 94-1120 T.I.A.S.

INTRODUCTION

1. W. E. B. Du Bois, *The Problem of the Color Line at the Turn of the Twentieth Century: The Essential Early Essays*, ed. Nahum Dimitri Chandler

(Fordham University Press, 2015); *see also* W. E. B. Du Bois, *The Souls of Black Folk* (A. C. McClurg, 1903), 1, "[T]he problem of the Twentieth Century is the problem of the color line."

2. Frederick Douglas, "The Color Line," *The North American Review* 132 (1881): 567–77.
3. W. E. B. Du Bois, *Color and Democracy: Colonies and Peace* (Kraus International, 1945).
4. Ralph J. Bunche, *A World View of Race* (Associated Publishers, 1936), 42; *see generally* Kal Raustiala, *The Absolutely Indispensable Man: Ralph Bunche, the United Nations, and the Fight to End Empire* (Oxford University Press, 2023)
5. Anna Spain Bradley, *Human Choice in International Law* (Cambridge University Press, 2021).
6. This book extends arguments and research I previously published, including in "Human Rights Racism," *Harvard Human Rights Journal* 32 (2019): 1, and *Human Choice in International Law* (Oxford University Press, 2021).
7. This book relies on research and inspiration from many sources. Two books served as particular inspiration for this project: Henry Richardson III, *The Origins of African American Interests in International Law* (Carolina Academic Press, 2008) and Patrick Thornberry, *The International Convention on the Elimination of All Forms of Racial Discrimination* (Oxford University Press, 2016). For recent books on global aspects of racism from various academic disciplines, *see generally* Judy Root Aulette, *A Global View of Race and Racism* (Oxford University Press, 2017); Ludovica Lorusso and Rasmus Grønfeldt Winther, *Remapping Race in a Global Context* (Routledge, 2021); Alastair Bonnett, *Multiracism: Rethinking Racism in a Global Context* (Polity, 2022); Tanya Maria Golash-Boza, *Race and Racism: A Critical Approach*, 3rd ed. (Oxford University Press, 2022); Marzia Milazzo, *Colorblind Tools: Global Technologies of Racial Power* (Northwestern University Press, 2022); William Schabas, *The International Legal Order's Colour Line* (Oxford University Press, 2023). For an overview of TWAIL scholarship, *see generally* Makau Mutua, "What Is TWAIL?," in *Proceedings of the 94th Annual Meeting of the American Society of International Law* (2000): 31–40; Antony Anghie and B. S. Chimni, "Third World Approaches to International Law and individual Responsibility in Internal Conflict," *Chinese Journal of International Law* 2 (2003): 77–103; B. S. Chimni, "Third World Approaches to International Law: A Manifesto," *International Community Law Review* 8 (2006): 3–27; James T. Gathii, "TWAIL: A

Brief History of Its Origins, Its Decentralized Network and a Tentative Bibliography," *Trade Law and Development* 3 (2011): 26–48. For an overview of critical race theory scholarship, *see generally* Derrick Bell, *Faces at the Bottom of the Well: The Permanence of Racism* (Basic Books, 1993); Kimberlé Crenshaw et al., *Critical Race Theory: The Key Writings That Formed the Movement* (New Press, 1996); Kimberlé W. Crenshaw, "Mapping the Margins: Intersectionality, Identity Politics, and Violence Against Women of Color," *Stanford Law Review* 43 (1991): 1241; Patricia J. Williams, *The Alchemy of Race and Rights* (Harvard University Press, 1991); Mari Matsuda, "When the First Quail Calls: Multiple Consciousness as Jurisprudential Method," *Women's Rights Law Reporter* 14 (1992): 297–300; Mari Matsuda, "Looking to the Bottom: Critical Legal Studies and Reparations," *Harvard Civil Rights-Civil Liberties Law Review* 22 (1982): 323–99; Cheryl I. Harris, "Whiteness as Property," *Harvard Law Review* 106 (1993): 1707; Adrien Wing, *Global Critical Race Feminism: An International Reader* (New York University Press, 2002); Adrien Wing, *Critical Race Feminism: A Reader*, 2nd ed. (New York University Press, 2003). For books that have shaped public discourse on racism *see* Michelle Alexander, *The New Jim Crow: Mass Incarceration in the Age of Colorblindness* (New Press, 2010); Robin DiAngelo, *White Fragility* (Beacon Press, 2018); Richard Rothstein, *The Color of Law* (Perfection Learning Corporation, 2019); Ibram X. Kendi, *How to Be an Antiracist* (One World, 2019); and Isabelle Wilkerson, *Caste: The Origins of Our Discontents* (Random House, 2020).

CHAPTER I

1. UNESCO, *The Race Question* (1950), 2. *See, e.g.*, Johann Friedrich Blumenbach, *On the Natural Varieties of Mankind* 3rd ed. (1795), reported in Johann Friedrich Blumenbach, *The Anthropological Treatises of Johann Friedrich Blumenbach* (Thomas Bendyshe ed. & trans., 1865), 145 (creating a five-part division of human races: Caucasian, Mongolian, Malay, Ethiopian, and American); As an example, see the Nuremberg Race Laws of 1935, *Source Book on European Governments: Switzerland, France, Italy, Germany and the Soviet Union* (William Rappard et al., eds., 1937), 77–83.
2. *Id.*
3. "Declaration of the Three Powers (Tehran Conference)," *Foreign Relations of the United States: The Conferences at Cairo and Tehran, 1943* (U.S. Government Printing Office, 1961), Document 411, 602–3.

4. Mohandas K. Gandhi to President Roosevelt, July 1, 1942, in *Foreign Relations of the United States, 1942*, vol. 1.
5. Constitution of the United Nations Educational, Scientific and Cultural Organization, Preamble (Adopted in London, November 16, 1945).
6. *Id.* at 3.
7. "Racial discrimination is one of the most common grounds for discrimination worldwide." *The Sustainable Development Goals Report 2023: Special Edition, United Nations Department of Economic and Social Affairs, Statistics Division*, July 10, 2023, https://unstats.un.org/sdgs/report/2023/.
8. "UNESCO launches the Global Alliance on Racism and Discriminations After the 4th Edition of the Global Forum," UNESCO, January 16, 2025.
9. "Reduced Inequalities," *Sustainable Development Goals Report 2023*.
10. UNICEF, "Racism and Discrimination Against Children Rife in Countries Worldwide," press release, November 17, 2022, https://perma.cc/M4SP-UF78.
11. "Discrimination Is Getting Worse Globally," *World Justice Project*, March 21, 2023. *See also* "WJP Rule of Law Index," World Justice Project, accessed August 5, 2025.
12. "China: Combat Anti-Black Racism on Social Media," *Human Rights Watch*, August 16, 2023
13. Dylan Schexnaydre, Factsheet: Sinicization of Religion: China's Coercive Religious Policy, U.S. Commission on Int'l Religious Freedom (2024).
14. U.N. Office of the High Commissioner for Human Rights, "Committee on the Elimination of Racial Discrimination Reviews the Report of China," press release, August 13, 2018.
15. Daniel Boffey, "'Pervasive and 'Relentless' Racism on the Rise in Europe, Survey Finds," *The Guardian*, October 25, 2023.
16. European Union Agency for Fundamental Rights, "Muslims in Europe Face Ever More Racism and Discrimination," press release, October 24, 2024.
17. "Number of police recorded racial hate crimes in England and Wales from 2011-12 to 2023-24," *Statista Research Department*, October 10, 2024.
18. Amanda Audi, "Brazil's Racial Makeup Shifted in a Unique Way," *The Brazilian Report*, January 9, 2024, reporting from primary source in Portuguese, "Censo 2022," *Agencia Ibge Noticias*, December 22, 2023.
19. "Percentage Distribution of Wealth in Brazil in 2021, by Wealth Percentile," *Statista*; *see generally* "Report on Brazil 2023," *Amnesty International*; Pedro Fandiño et al., "A Genesis of Poverty and Inequality in Brazil," *World Bank* (2022).

20. "Who Experiences Racism?" *Australian Human Rights Commission. See also* "Mental Health Impacts of Racial Discrimination in Victorian Aboriginal Communities: The Localities Embracing and Accepting Diversity Survey," *VicHealth* (2012).
21. "Tackling Racism in Australia," *Australian Human Rights Commission* (2014), 32.
22. *The Immigration Restriction Act 1901*; *The Racial Discrimination Act 1975*; *see generally* "White Australia Policy," *National Museum of Australia*, May 16, 2023, https://www.nma.gov.au/defining-moments/resources/white-australia-policy.
23. Kiana Cox and Khadijah Edwards, "Black Americans Have a Clear Vision for Reducing Racism but Little Hope It Will Happen," *Pew Research Center*, August 30, 2022.
24. "Police Shooting Database 2015-2024," *The Washington Post*, online database. Between 2014 and 2016, for example, Eric Garner, Michael Brown, Tamir Rice, Alton Sterling, Laquan McDonald, Freddie Gray, Sandra Bland, and Philando Castile were among the disproportionate number of African Americans killed by police or who died in police custody. *See, e.g.*, Jasmine C. Lee and Haeyoun Park, "15 Black Lives Ended with Confrontations with Police. 3 Officers Convicted," *The New York Times*, October 5, 2018. Alvin Chang, "There Are Huge Racial Disparities in How US Police Use Force," *vox*, November 14, 2018 (reporting that black people make up 62.7 percent of all the unarmed people killed by police based on available FBI data).
25. "The Fight Against Voter Suppression," ACLU, accessed August 5, 2025. Maham Javaid, "Biden Condemns Neo-Nazi March in Streets of Ohio's Capital," *The Washington Post*, November 18, 2024.
26. Act of Sept. 14, 2017, Pub. L. No. 115-58, 131 Stat. 1150 (joint resolution of Congress acknowledging the "growing prevalence" of "hate groups that espouse racism, extremism, xenophobia, anti-Semitism, and White supremacy").
27. "Racial Discrimination in Contemporary America," *The White House*, July 3, 2024.
28. Laura Silver, "More People Globally See Racial, Ethnic Discrimination as a Serious Problem in the U.S. than in Their Own Society," *Pew Research Center*, November 2, 2021.
29. Eugene M. Avrutin, *Racism in Modern Russia: From the Romanovs to Putin* (Bloomsbury Academic, 2022).
30. *See generally* Rabiat Akande, "An Imperial History of Race-Religion in International Law," *American Journal of International Law* 118, no. 1

(January 2024): 1–33; Daniel Abusuampeh, "Racism Across the World: Tribalism in Africa," University of Pittsburgh Center on Race & Social Problems, accessed August 4, 2025.

CHAPTER 2

1. "Racism," Fact Sheet, *Oxford English Dictionary* ("OED's earliest evidence for racism is from 1903, in Proceedings 20th Ann. Meeting Lake Mohonk Conf. Friends of Indian 1902"). Lake Mohonk Conference of Friends of the Indian, Proceedings of the 20th Annual Meeting of the Lake Mohonk Conference of Friends of the Indian, 17th–20th (1899–1902), at https://hdl.handle.net/2027/hvd.32044041993536.
2. Lake Mohonk Conference of Friends of the Indian, 134 (p. 542 on the electronic version). *See* Gene Demby, "The Ugly, Fascinating History of the Word 'Racism,'" *NPR*, January 6, 2014.
3. Larry E. Burgess, "We'll Discuss It at Mohonk," *Quaker History* 60, no. 1 (1971): 14–28.
4. *Webster's Collegiate Dictionary* (1947) contains a definition of "racialism" as "racial prejudice, race hatred," but not "racism." By 1974, racism was defined in *Webster's Collegiate Dictionary*. Racism was used in the UNESCO (United Nations Educational, Scientific and Cultural Organization) Constitution, Preamble (1945), and in UNESCO, *The Race Question* (1950).
5. *Dictionary.com*, s.v. "Racism"; *Merriam-Webster*, s.v. "Racism."
6. *Cambridge Dictionary*, s.v. "Racism, English-Chinese"; *Nkọwa okwu*, s.v. "Racism"; *Cambridge Dictionary*, s.v. "Racism, English-Hindi"; *Cambridge Dictionary*, s.v. "Racism, English-Spanish."
7. *See generally* George M. Fredrickson, *Racism: A Short History* (Princeton Classics, 2002); Ali Rattansi, *Racism: A Very Short Introduction* (Oxford University Press, 2007); *Theories of Race and Racism: A Reader* (Les Back and John Solomos eds., Routledge, 2009).
8. U.S. Census Bureau, *U.S. Census Form Sample 2020* (2020); Nicole Chavez, "US Government Changing How It Asks About People's Race and Ethnicity," *CNN*, March 28, 2024.
9. The most recent census in Zambia was conducted online for the first time. Central Statistics Office, "Census of Population and Housing 2000" (2000), as reported by International Household Survey Network (Feb. 19, 2014).
10. Fiji Bureau of Statistics, "Population 2017 Census: Population by Major Ethnicity Groups" (2017), https://experience.arcgis.com/experience/

fd6bb849099f46869125089fd13579ec/page/Population-by-Major-Ethnicity-Groups.

11. A similar challenge faces the lack of definition of xenophobia. *See, e.g.*, Report of the Ad Hoc Committee, *Elaboration of Complementary Standards on Its Ninth Session*, 30 U.N. Doc. A/HRC/37/76 (Feb. 9, 2018) ("Ms. Achiume described the phenomenon of xenophobia as illegitimate anti-foreigner acts or attitudes, and further elaborated that xenophobia was compounded by foreignness (on account of their nationality or national origin) and other intersectional social categories including race, ethnicity, religion, class and gender. She added that racism and xenophobia were overlapping when race is often an explicit or implicit basis for xenophobic discrimination and anxiety. At the same time, she stated that there existed a distinction between the two when race is not always salient in the construction of foreignness where migrants are concerned, including when non-citizenship can amplify the negative impact of racism, and addressing racism alone may not appropriately address the circumstances of non-citizens experiencing racial discrimination."). *See also* Human Rights Council, "Report of the Special Rapporteur on Contemporary Forms of Racism, Racial Discrimination, Xenophobia and Related Intolerance," paras. 36–67, U.N. Doc. A/HRC/32/50 (May 13, 2016).
12. US Department of Justice, "White Supremacist Gangs," *Police: Law Enforcement. Magazine* 16, no. 10 (2002); US Federal Bureau of Investigation, "Gangs/Extremist Groups"; "White Supremacist Propaganda Incidents Soar to Record High in 2023," *ADL*, March 26, 2024. For recent data, see "Hate Map," SPLC, accessed August 5, 2025.
13. SPLC, "White Nationalist."
14. "The Global Rise of White Supremacist Terrorism," *Brookings*, June 10, 2022.
15. U.N. Committee on the Elimination of Racial Discrimination, "UN Committee on the Elimination of Racial Discrimination Publishes Findings on Albania, Mexico, Qatar, Moldova and San Marino," press release, April 29, 2024.
16. U.N. Committee on the Elimination of Racial Discrimination, "Concluding Observations on the Combined Thirteenth and Fourteenth Periodic Reports of Albania," CERD/C/ALB/CO/13-14, May 23, 2024.
17. European Roma Rights Centre, *Written Comments of The European Roma Rights Centre Concerning Albania* (2024).
18. "Ash and Tai's story," Victorian Equal Opportunity & Human Rights Commission, accessed August 5, 2025.

19. Paul Mozar, One Month, 500,000 Face Scans: How China is Using A.I. to Profile a Minority, *New York Times* (April 14, 2019). Vincent Wong, "Racial Capitalism with Chinese Characteristics," *African Journal of International Economic Law* 3, no. 1 (2022): 7–39.; Alastair Bonnett, "Asia Has Its Own Strands of Racism. It's Time to Take Them Seriously," *The Diplomat*, June 9, 2022; "Break Their Lineage, Break Their Roots' China's Crimes Against Humanity Targeting Uyghurs and Other Turkish Muslims," *Human Rights Watch*, April 19, 2021. Paul Mozur, "One Month, 500,000 Face Scans: How China Is Using A.I. to Profile a Minority," *Seattle Times*, April 14, 2019. Vincent Wong, "Racial Capitalization with Chinese Characteristics: Analyzing the Political Economy of Racialized Dispossession and Exploitation in Xinjiang," *Afronomics Law* 3 (2022).
20. "Denmark Faces EU Court Questions on Housing Policy, Racism," *Reuters*, September 30, 2024. "EU Top Court to Review Denmark's 'Racially Discriminatory' 'Ghetto Package,'" *Open Society Justice Initiative*, June 17, 2024. "Tenants of Mjølnerparken v. Danish Ministry of Transport and Housing," Open Society Justice Initiative, accessed August 5, 2025.
21. "EU Court Says Denmark's Ethnic-Based 'Ghetto Law' May Be Discriminatory," *Reuters*, December 18, 2025.
22. Arnold Davis v. Guam, et al., District Court of Guam Civil Case No. 11-00035 (2017); Davis v. Guam, 932 F.3d 822 (9th Cir. 2019); "Challenge to CHamoru Self-Determination: Davis v. Guam," Guampedia, accessed August 5, 2025.
23. Office of the Governor of Guam/Ufisinan I Maga'Haga Communications Department, "Acting Governor Responds to Attorney General's Opinion Regarding a Political Status Plebiscite," press release, May 17, 2024.
24. Kelly Ng, "Japan: Foreign-Born Residents Sue Government for Alleged Racial Profiling, *BBC News*, January 29, 2024. Aniket Singh Chauhan, "Indians in Japan: Work, Life, and Racism," *The Diplomat*, April 10, 2024.
25. The Editors, "Your Stories of Racism," *The Atlantic*, July 13, 2015.
26. Denise Mota, "Racist Slur Used in Uruguay Football Match Ignites National Debate," *The Guardian*, June 3, 2024. "Racist Slur Probe Dropped Against Uruguay Club Football Coach," *RFI*, June 18, 2024.
27. Sterling A. Brown, "Out of Their Mouths 'From Massachusetts to Mississippi,'" The Library of America, Reporting Civil Rights Part I, American Journalism 1941-1963 (2003), 29. Statement by "white liberal."
28. Equal Justice Initiative, *Lynching in America: Confronting the Legacy of Racial Terror*, 3rd ed. (2017).

29. James H. Cone, *The Cross and the Lynching Tree* (Orbis Books, 2011)
30. Benjamin Harris and Sydney Schreiner Wertz, "Racial Differences in Economic Security & the Racial Wealth Gap." U.S. Department of the Treasury, September 15, 2022.
31. Regina S. Baker and Fenaba R. Addo, "Barriers to Racial Wealth Equality," *American Bar Association*, January 6, 2023.

CHAPTER 3

1. Fulcher of Chartres, Recueil de Historiens de Croisades, Historiens Occidentaux, III. 322–24). Translated as "Pope Urban II's Speech at Clermont," *A Source Book for Mediæval History: Selected Documents Illustrating the History of Europe in the Middle Age*, trans. Oliver J. Thatcher and Edgar Holmes McNeal (Charles Scribner's Sons, 1905), 516–17.
2. *See, e.g.*, s. Langdon and Alan Gardiner, "The Treaty of Alliance Between Hattusili, King of the Hittites, and the Pharaoh Ramesses II of Egypt," *Journal of Egyptian Archaeology* 6 (1920): 179–205; Aristide Theodorides, "The Concept of Law in Ancient Egypt," in *The Legacy of Egypt*, ed. J. R. Harris (Clarendon Press, 1971), 291; J. G. Manning, "The Representation of Justice in Ancient Egypt," *Yale Journal of Law & the Humanities* 24, no. 1 (2012): 111–47.
3. The term "philanthropy" is the English translation of Greek word meaning "loving people," Merriam-Webster Dictionary, accessed August 5, 2025; *see* Marty Sulek, "On the Classical Meaning of Philanthropy," *Nonprofit and Voluntary Sector Quarterly* 39, no. 3 (2010): 385–408, noting the limited usage of the word in surviving texts and complexities regarding its translation.
4. Adolf Berger, "Encyclopedic Dictionary of Roman Law," *Transactions of the American Philosophical Society* 43 (1953): 333, 489.
5. Cicero, *ad Quintum fratem* I.I.27, trans. in Greg Woolf, *Becoming Roman: The Origins of Provincial Civilization in Gaul* (Cambridge University Press 1998), 68.
6. *Confucius, The Analects*, trans. Raymond Dawson (Oxford University Press 1993). *See* Daniel Gardner, *Confuscianism: A Very Short Introduction* (Oxford University Press, 2014), 23–24.
7. Hugo Grotius, *De Jur Bello ac Pacis* (1625). Hugo Grotius, *De Jure Belli ac Pacis Libri Tres* (Francis W. Kelsey trans., Oxford University Press, 1925), bk. I, ch. I, §1, 35 ("The disputes arising from those who are held together by no common bond of civil laws to decide their dissensions, who formed

no national community or the numerous unconnected communities . . . all bear a relation to the circumstances of war and peace.").

8. Kelsey. *See generally* Martin van Gelderen, "The Challenges of Colonialism: Grotius and Vitoria on Natural Law and International Law," *Grotiana* (1993): 3–31, 14; "The Grotian Moment," in *International Law: A Contemporary Perspective*, ed. Richard Falk et al. (1985), 7–10, 7.
9. Kelsey, Prolegomena, para. 28.
10. Oona A. Hathaway and Scott Shapiro, *The Internationalists: How A Radical Plan to Outlaw War Remade the World* (Simon & Schuster, 2018), 8–9, 11.
11. Hathaway and Shapiro, 10–13, 13 ("To substantiate these accusations, Grotius cited a letter found by Van Heemskerck's men aboard a captured Portuguese frigate. The dispatch described a Dutch expedition to the Chinese town of Macao in September 1601. . . . The Portuguese threw the captives in a cave and tortured them. The letter reported that seventeen were hanged on the orders of the Portuguese magistrate.")
12. Hathaway and Shapiro, *The Internationalists*, 6–11.
13. It is not known from where those enslaved aboard the ship were taken. *See, e.g.*, Peter Borschberg, "The Seizure of the St. Catarina Revisited: The Portuguese Empire in Asia, VOC Politics and the Origins of the Dutch-Johor Alliance (1602–c.1616)," *Journal Southeast Asian Studies* 33(2002): 31–43 ("Second, the presence of women and possibly children can also be taken as evidence that the Portuguese were actively involved in shipping human cargo out of China."); Hathaway and Shapiro, *The Internationalists*, 3.
14. *See* Boutros Boutros-Ghali, "The Role of International Law in the Twenty-First Century: A Grotian Moment," *Fordham International Law Journal* 18 (1995): 1609; Richard Truck, *The Rights of War and Peace: Political Thought and the International Order from Grotius to Kant* (Oxford University Press, 1999); B. S. Chimni, "The Eighth Annual Grotius Lecture: A Just World Under Law: A View from the South," *American University International Law Review* 22 (2007): 199–202; Michael P. Scharf, "Seizing the 'Grotian Moment': Accelerated Formation of Customary International Law in Times of Change," *Cornell International Law Journal* 43 (2010): 439.
15. Treaty of Westphalia, *Peace Treaty Between the Holy Roman Emperor and the King of France and their respective Allies*, art. 1 (English translation).
16. Hersch Lauterpacht, *The Function of Law in the International Community* (1933), 154 (noting "A wrong done to the individual is a wrong done to his State.").

17. Hugh Thomas, *The Slave Trade: The Story of the Atlantic Slave Trade 1440-1870* (Simon & Schuster, 1997), 58.
18. Thomas, *The Slave Trade*, 124, 125.
19. *Id.* at 126. *See* Fernando De Oliveira, *Arte da Guerra no mar* (Coimbra, 1555).
20. Thomas, *The Slave Trade*, 126.
21. *Id.* at 147. *See also* Martin de Ledesma, *Commentaria in Quartum Sententiarum* (Coimbra, 1560); Francisco de la Cruz. Inquisición, Actas II–2 (eds. Vidal Abril Castelló & Miguel J. Abril Stoffels, CSIC, 1997).
22. "First Enslaved Africans Arrive in Jamestown, Setting the Stage for Slavery in North America," *History.com: This Day in History*, August 13, 2019.
23. *Id.*
24. Laws of Virginia, Act XII (December 1662), establishing the legal principles of partus sequitur ventrem. *See generally* William Waller Hening, ed., *The Statutes at Large; Being a Collection of All the Laws of Virginia*, vol. 2 (R. & W. & G. Bartow, 1823), 170, 260.
25. *See generally* Thomas, *The Slave Trade*.
26. *The Declaration of Independence* (United States, 1776); *Declaration of the Rights of Man and of the Citizen* (France, 1789).
27. *See generally* "The Haitian Revolution," *Encyclopedia Britannica*, accessed August 6, 2025; David P. Geggus, *The Haitian Revolution: A Documentary History*, (Hackett, 2014); Elizabeth Beckett, "Warrior Women: Heroines of the French Revolution," *French Library*, March 8, 2022.
28. Kim Ives, "Haiti: Independence Debt, Reparations for Slavery and Colonialism, and International 'Aid,'" *Centre for Research on Globalization*, May 10, 2013. For the history of the Haitian Revolution, *see generally* C. L. R. James, *The Black Jacobins: Toussaint L'Ouverture and the San Domingo Revolution* (Vintage Books, 1989).
29. Sabelo J. Ndlovu-Gatsheni, "Nelson Mandela and the Decolonial Paradigm of Peace," in *The Routledge History of World Peace Since 1750*, ed. Christian Philip Peterson et al. (Routledge, 2019), 155–56 ("The foundation for these decolonial struggles is the Haitian Revolution of 1804 which was spearheaded by the enslaved black people and produced the first black republic of Haiti.").
30. *See generally* Jenny S. Martinez, *The Slave Trade and the Origins of International Human Rights Law* (Oxford University Press, 2012) (demonstrating how tribunals set up in Cuba, Brazil, and Sierra Leone during the transatlantic slave trade formed the first international adjudicative bodies designed to hear human rights cases).

31. An Act for the Abolition of the Slave Trade, 47 Geo. 3 Sess. 1 c. 36 (May 1, 1807) (U.K.); An Act Prohibiting Importation of Slaves, ch. 22, 2 Stat. 426 (enacted March 2, 1807) (U.S.).
32. Thomas Jefferson, "Sixth Annual Message to Congress to U.S. Congress," December 2, 1806, in *A Compilation of the Messages and Papers of the Presidents, 1789–1897*, vol. 1, ed. James D. Richardson (Government Printing Office, 1896): 408–18 ("I congratulate you, fellow-citizens, on the approach of the period at which you may interpose your authority constitutionally, to withdraw the citizens of the United States from all further participation in those violations of human rights which have been so long continued on the unoffending inhabitants of Africa, and which the morality, the reputation, and the best interests of our country, have long been eager to proscribe.").
33. *See generally* Jenny S. Martinez, *The Slave Trade and the Origins of International Human Rights Law* (Oxford University Press, 2012).
34. Act of 1819, *To Protect the Commerce of the United States, and to Punish the Crime of Piracy*, Pub. L. No. 15-77, §§ 1–6, 3 Stat. 510, 509–14 (1819).
35. Act of 1820, *To Continue in Force "An Act to Protect the Commerce of the United States, and Punish the Crime of Piracy," and Also to Make Further Provision for Punishing the Crime of Piracy*, Pub. L. No. 16-113, § 5, 3 Stat. 600, 600–1 (1820).
36. Thomas, *The Slave Trade*, 763.
37. "Important Trial—The African Slave Trade: Trial of Capt. James Smith for Piracy," *The New York Times*, November 7, 1854; "The Slave Trade—An Important Trial," *The New York Times*, November 10, 1854; *United States v. James Smith*, U.S. National Archives, September 30, 1854; Thomas, *The Slave Trade*, 763.
38. Thomas, *The Slave Trade*, 763. The law was tested during the 1854 trial of James Smith, who was convicted of bringing hundreds of enslaved people from Angola to Trinidad.
39. Abraham Lincoln, "Respite of Execution for Nathanaiel Gordon," Washington D.C., February 4, 1862, Transcript published by *Gilder Lehrman Institute of American History*; See also Lincoln on the Execution of a Slave Trader, 1862," *Gilder Lehrman Institute of American History* (1862).
40. U.S. Constitution, amend. 13, § 1 ("Neither slavery nor involuntary servitude, except as a punishment for crime whereof the party shall have been duly convicted, shall exist within the United States, or any place subject to their jurisdiction."). The Civil Rights Act of 1866 followed providing citizenship rights and equal protection rights to African Americans.

41. *See, e.g.*, United States v. Rhodes, 27 F. Cas. 785 (C.C.D. Ky. 1866); Blyew v. United States, 80 U.S. 581 (1871); Civil Rights Cases, 109 U.S. 3 (1883); Plessy v. Ferguson, 163 U.S. 537 (1896); and Hodges v. United States, 203 U.S. 1 (1906).
42. Plessy v. Ferguson, 163 U.S. 537 (1896).
43. Slavery Convention, September 25, 1926, 60 U.N.T.S. 253.
44. M. Cherif Bassiouni, "International Crimes: *Jus Cogens* and *Obligatio Erga Omnes*," *Law & Contemporary Problems* 59, no 4 (1996): 68.
45. James Brown Scott, ed., *The Hague Conventions and Declarations of 1899 and 1907* (Oxford University Press, 1918) [hereinafter *Declarations*]; Convention for the Pacific Settlement of International Disputes, July 29, 1899, 32 Stat. 1779, art. 1; Ruth Mackenzie et al., *The Manual on International Courts and Tribunals* (Butterworths, 2010) (noting that the Convention "marked a turning point in favour of international adjudication before standing bodies" and describing the formation of the PCA as the first standing body for international adjudication).
46. *Declarations* (The original conference came about when Russia circulated a proposal for initiating such a peace conference, stating "[t]he maintenance of general peace and a possible reduction of the excessive armaments which weigh upon all nations present themselves, in the existing condition of the whole world, as the ideal toward which the endeavors of all Governments should be directed . . . . The preservation of peace has been put forward as the object of international policy.").
47. Convention for the Pacific Settlement of International Disputes, July 29, 1899, 32 Stat 1779, (entered into force September 4, 1990) art. 1; *see* Philippe Sands, "Introduction," in Ruth Mackenzie et al., *The Manual on International Courts and Tribunals* (Butterworths, 2010), ix: "The 1899 Convention marked a turning point in favour of international adjudication before standing bodies."
48. S. Doc. No. 444, at 62 (1909), in *Declarations*, xxvii–xxx (Statement by US Secretary of State, Elihu Root, to US Congress in letter of transmittal, 60th Cong., 1st Sess.).
49. Woodrow Wilson, *War Messages*, 65th Cong., 1st Sess. (Government Printing Office, 1917).
50. "President Woodrow Wilson's 14 Points, 1918," *National Archives.*
51. Adolf Hitler, *Mein Kampf* (Verlag Frz. Eher Nachf, G.M.B.H., 1927) trans. Ralph Manheim (Mariner Books, 1999), Preface.
52. Hitler, *Mein Kampf*, 679.
53. *Id.*, Conclusion.

54. Charter of the International Military Tribunal for the Far East, (Jan. 19, 1946), Treaties and International Acts Series No. 1589. *See* Daqing Yang, "Nanjing Massacre," in Oxford Research Encyclopedia of Asian History (Aug. 27, 2020).
55. Universal Declaration of Human Rights, G.A. Res. 217 A (III), U.N. GAOR, 3d Sess., Res. 218A (Dec. 10, 1948) (forty-eight votes in favor, eight abstentions, two did not vote, zero no votes).
56. *See generally* Ruth B. Russell and Jeannette E. Muther, *A History of the United Nations Charter: The Role of the United States 1940-1945* (Brookings Institution, 1958).
57. *Id.* at 812.
58. *Id.* at 815–16.
59. *Id.* at 823 n. 27.
60. *Id.* at 531–48. *See also* "The Tehran Conference, 1943," *Office of the Historian*, US Department of State.
61. *See generally* Susan Butler, *Roosevelt and Stalin: Portrait of a Partnership* (Alfred A. Knopf, 2015).
62. *Id.* at 251 citing Robert A. Divine, *Second Chance: The Triumph of Internationalism in American During World War II* (Atheneum Press, 1967), 25.
63. *Id. See generally* Henry J. Richardson III, "Dr. Martin Luther King, Jr. as an International Human Rights Leader," 471 *Villanova Law Review* 52 (2007): 473–75 (recalling the efforts of W. E. B. Du Bois, the NAACP, Thurgood Marshall, Dr. Martin Luther King Jr., and other civil rights leaders in shaping international human rights and the creation of the United Nations); Carol Anderson, *Eyes off the Prize: The United Nations and the African-American Struggle for Human Rights, 1944–1955* (Cambridge University Press, 2003), 108.
64. W. E. B. Du Bois and the NAACP, *A Statement on the Denial of Human Rights Minorities in the Case of Citizens of Negro Descent in the United States of America and an Appeal to the United Nations for Redress* (Oct. 23, 1947).
65. United Nations Charter (June 26, 1945). *See also* Statute of International Court of Justice, art. 38, June 26, 1945, 59 Stat. 1031; Vienna Convention on the Law of Treaties, May 23, 1969, 1155 U.N.T.S. 331.
66. UN Charter art. 1; Bernard Boxill, "The Duty to Seek Peace," *Journal of Social Philosophy and Policy* 27 (2010); *see* Christopher Greenwood, "The United Nations as a Guarantor of International Peace and Security: Past, Present and Future—A United Kingdom View," *The United Nations at the Age of Fifty 60–61*, ed. Christian Tomuschat (1995) (observing

restrictions on use of force as the means by which the UN Charter supports peace).

67. UN Charter art. 1(3).
68. *Id.*, arts. 2(3), 2(4) (calling all members to settle disputes peacefully and to refrain from the use of force), 33 (providing the available peacemaking mechanisms), 37 (requiring parties to a dispute to refer the matter to the UN Security Council if peacemaking mechanisms fail).
69. *Id.*, arts. 24 ("In order to ensure prompt and effective action by the United Nations, its Members confer on the Security Council primary responsibility for the maintenance of international peace and security, and agree that in carrying out its duties under this responsibility the Security Council acts on their behalf."), 39 ("The Security Council shall determine the existence of any threat to the peace, breach of the peace, or act of aggression and shall make recommendations, or decide what measures shall be taken in accordance with Articles 41 and 42, to maintain or restore international peace and security."); UN Charter art. 26 ("In order to promote the establishment and maintenance of international peace and security with the least diversion for armaments of the world's human and economic resources, the Security Council shall be responsible for formulating, with the assistance of the Military Staff Committee referred to in Article 47, plans to be submitted to the Members of the United Nations for the establishment of a system for the regulation of armaments."); Chapter VI and VII authorize the Security Council to respond to threats to peace and security through diplomatic and coercive means.
70. G.A. Res. 290 (IV), U.N. GAOR, 4th Sess., Supp. No. 3, U.N. Doc. A/1775 (Dec. 1, 1949); *See also* G.A. Res. 377 (V), U.N. GAOR, 5th Sess., Supp. No. 20, U.N. Doc. A/1775 (Nov. 3, 1950) ("Uniting for Peace").
71. Alexander Orakhelashvili, *Collective Security* (Oxford University Press, 2011), 281–335 (describing the framework for peace operations at the UN).
72. *Id.* at 19 (describing the framework for peace operations at the UN).
73. Report on High-level Panel on Threats, Challenges and Change, *A More Secure World: Our Shared Responsibility* (United Nations, 2004), (discussing the need for a new and more comprehensive definition of collective security).
74. Theodor Meron, "The Meaning and Reach of the International Convention on the Elimination of All Forms of Racial Discrimination," *American Journal of International Law* 79 (1985): 283–317.
75. "1960: The year of independence," *France 24* (Feb. 14, 2010).

76. W. E. B. Du Bois, *The Problem of the Color Line at the Turn of the Twentieth Century: The Essential Early Essays*, ed. Nahum Dimitri Chandler (Fordham University Press, 2015).

CHAPTER 4

1. Patrick Thornberry, *The International Convention on the Elimination of All Forms of Racial Discrimination: A Commentary* (Oxford University Press, 2016), 2. ICERD was adopted on December 21, 1965, and entered into force on January 4, 1969. It was adopted with 106 votes in favor, none against, and one abstention by Mexico. U.N. GOAR, 20th Sess., 1406th plen. mtg. at 60 U.N. Doc. A/PV.1406 (Dec. 21, 1965).
2. U.N. Charter pmbl. (1945).
3. U.N. Charter arts. 1(3), 13(1)(b), 55(c), 76(c).
4. "Timeline of Independence," Brooklyn Museum, https://www.brooklynmuseum.org/resources/africa-timeline, accessed August 5, 2025.
5. The UN Security Council (UNSC) adopted a resolution calling for a voluntary embargo for South Africa. *See* S.C. Res. 182 (Dec. 4, 1963).
6. Thornberry, *The International Convention on the Elimination of All Forms of Racial Discrimination*, 71–72.
7. G.A. Res. 1904 (XVIII), art. 1, U.N. GAOR, 18th Sess., Supp. No. 15, U.N. Doc. A/RES/1904 (XVIII) (Nov. 20, 1963) (stating that "[d]iscrimination between human beings on the ground of race, colour or ethnic origin is an offence to human dignity and shall be condemned as a denial of the principles of the Charter of the United Nations, as a violation of the human rights and fundamental freedoms proclaimed in the Universal Declaration of Human Rights, as an obstacle to friendly and peaceful relations among nations and as a fact capable of disturbing peace and security among peoples."), https://docs.un.org/en/A/RES/1904%20(XVIII).
8. "1965 Selma to Montgomery March Fast Facts," *CNN*, February 28, 2018.
9. "A Significant Ruling," *Chicago Daily Defender*, July 7, 1964, p. 11. "A National Victory," *The New York Times*, July 3, 1964.
10. John F. Kennedy, "Radio and Television Report to the American People on Civil Rights," John F. Kennedy Presidential Library and Museum (June 11, 1963).
11. Gerhard Peters and John T. Woolley, "Statement by the Presidential Following on Senate Passage of the Civil Rights Bill," *The American Presidency Project*, June 19, 1964.

12. "Essay: The Other South," *Time Magazine*, May 7, 1965. *See also* "Area Reaction to Rights Law: Maryland Has Own Regulations but U.S. Act Covers Loopholes," *The Washington Post, Times Herald*, July 3, 1964, p. 10; David Nevin, "Day of Accusation in Mississippi," *Life*, December 1964, 36–37.
13. Art Carter, "'64 Review of Top News in Pictures—Civil Rights Top News of 1964," *Afro-American*, January 9, 1965, p. 12.
14. Martin Luther King, Jr., "Letter from a Birmingham Jail," *Negro History Bulletin* 27 (1964). Martin Luther King Jr., "I Have a Dream" (speech, March on Washington for Jobs and Freedom, Washington, DC, August 28, 1963), reprinted in *A Testament of Hope: The Essential Writings of Martin Luther King Jr.*, ed. James M. Washington (Harper & Row, 1986), 218–19. Martin Luther King, Jr., "Preamble, in Letter From a Birmingham Jail," *Negro History Bulletin* 27 (1964).
15. The Nobel Prize, "Facts: Martin Luther King Jr."; Henry J. Richardson III, "Two Treaties, and Global Influences of the American Civil Rights Movements, Through the Black International Tradition," *Virginia Journal of Social Policy & the Law* 18 (2010): 59–64.
16. *See generally* Thomas F. Jackson, *From Civil Rights to Human Rights: Martin Luther King, Jr., and the Struggle for Economic Justice* (University of Pennsylvania Press, 2007).
17. *Malcom X: The Last Speeches*, 173 (Bruce Perry ed., Pathfinder, 1989); Malcolm X, "Not just an American problem, but a world problem," Speech, Corn Hill Methodist Church, February 16, 1965.
18. International Convention on the Elimination of All Forms of Racial Discrimination (ICERD), opened for signature Dec. 21, 1965, 660 U.N.T.S. 195 (entered into force Jan. 4, 1969); Patrick Thornberry, *The International Convention on the Elimination of All Forms of Racial Discrimination: A Commentary* (Oxford University Press, 2016); David Keane and Annapurna Waughray, *50 Years of the International Convention on the Elimination of All Forms of Racial Discrimination: A Living Instrument* (Manchester University Press, 2017).
19. International Convention on the Elimination of All Forms of Racial Discrimination, adopted Dec. 21, 1965, G.A. Res. 2106 (XX), 660 U.N.T.S. 195; at the UN, there are 193 member states and 2 non-member observer states, Vatican City and Palestine.
20. International Convention on the Elimination of All Forms of Racial Discrimination, adopted Dec. 21, 1965, G.A. Res. 2106 (XX), 660 U.N.T.S. 195.

21. Thornberry, *The International Convention on the Elimination of All Forms of Racial Discrimination*, 2.
22. U.N. GAOR, 20th Sess., 1406th plen. mtg., ¶¶ 109–10, U.N. Doc. A/PV.1406 (Dec. 21, 1965).
23. ICERD. For a comprehensive treatment of the treaty, see Thornberry, *The International Convention on the Elimination of All Forms of Racial Discrimination*.
24. International Convention on the Elimination of All Forms of Racial Discrimination, art. 1(1), adopted Dec. 21, 1965, G.A. Res. 2106 (XX), 660 U.N.T.S. 195.
25. *Id.*, art. 1(2).
26. *Id.*, art. 1(3).
27. *Id.*, art. 1(4).
28. See, e.g., 39 U.N. GAOR Supp. No. 18, ¶ 284, U.N. Doc. A/39/18 (1984) ("protection of the one group might be considered discrimination against others").
29. 31 U.N. GAOR Supp. No. 18 Un Doc. A/31/18 (1976).
30. Theodor Meron, "The Meaning and Reach of the International Convention on the Elimination of All Forms of Racial Discrimination," *American Journal of International Law* 79 (1985): 283–97. Article 4 seems to extend beyond Article 1. Meron thought so as well on the reasoning that Article 4 "explicitly mandates legislative action to implement its provisions." CERD has enacted this legal obligation by requiring states report on their duty to legislate as a matter of being party to the treaty, not if or when circumstances dictate.
31. Thornberry, *The International Convention on the Elimination of All Forms of Racial Discrimination* 98, 104, 443. 32 U.N. GAOR Supp. (No. 18), ¶ 87, U.N. Doc. A/32/18 (1977). The Government of the Federal Republic of Germany, "after careful consideration, reached the conclusion that dissemination of opinions of racial superiority should be punishable if it was intended to create racial discrimination or hatred."
32. *Id.*
33. ICERD, Preamble. *See also* Thornberry, *The International Convention on the Elimination of All Forms of Racial Discrimination*, 74.
34. Thornberry, *The International Convention on the Elimination of All Forms of Racial Discrimination*, 74–75, noting which representatives proposed specific names and kinds of racism.
35. *Id.*
36. *Id.*

37. *Id.* at 74 n. 20 (citing U.N. GAOR, 20th Sess., 3d Comm., 1300th mtg., ¶ 6), U.N. Doc. A/C.3/SR.1300 (Oct. 12, 1965)).
38. *Id.* at 74–75.
39. *Id.* (citing U.N. GAOR, 20th Sess., 3d Comm., 1301st mtg., ¶ 38, U.N. Doc. A/C.3/SR.1301 (Oct. 12, 1965)).
40. *Id.* at 1 (citing U.N. GAOR, 20th Sess., 1406th plen. mtg., U.N. Doc. A/PV.1406 (Dec. 21, 1965)).
41. *Id.* at 5. (citing U.N. GAOR, 20th Sess., 1406th plen. mtg., ¶¶ 79–87, U.N. Doc. A/PV.1406 (Dec. 21, 1965)).
42. *Id.* at 74 ("This was despite an earlier decision to include references to segregation and apartheid in Article 3 of the Convention, an inconsistency that troubled some delegates." Greece and Hungary proposed a draft resolution A/C.3/L.1244 that the Convention not include any specific references regarding racial discrimination, which was adopted by eighty-two to twelve with ten abstentions.).
43. International Convention on the Elimination of All Forms of Racial Discrimination art. 3, adopted Dec. 21, 1965, G.A. Res. 2106 (XX), 660 U.N.T.S. 195 ("States Parties particularly condemn racial segregation and apartheid and undertake to prevent, prohibit and eradicate all practices of this nature in territories under their jurisdiction.").
44. *Id.* at 74.
45. United Nations Declaration on the Elimination of All Forms of Racial Discrimination, Preamble.
46. Thornberry, *The International Convention on the Elimination of All Forms of Racial Discrimination*, 79.
47. David Keane, *Caste-Based Discrimination in International Human Rights Law* (Ashgate, 2007), 176–77.
48. *Id.*
49. Thornberry, *The International Convention on the Elimination of All Forms of Racial Discrimination*, 3.
50. *Id.* at 29 (noting the same conditions for the creation of the Declaration: "The Declaration is hesitant on the ubiquity of racial discrimination, referring to its 'manifestations' 'in certain areas of the world', some of which are imposed by certain governments by means of legislative, administrative, or other measures, in the form, *inter alia*, of apartheid, segregation, and separation, as well as by the promotion and dissemination of doctrines of racial superiority and expansionism.").
51. Universal Declaration of Human Rights art. 1, G.A. Res. 217A (III), U.N. Doc. A/810, at 71 (Dec. 10, 1948).

52. *See, e.g.*, Civil Rights Congress (U.S.), We Charge Genocide: The Historic Petition to the United Nations for Relief from a Crime of the United States Government Against the Negro People, International Publishers (1951). U.N. Human Rights Council, Reps. Submitted by States Parties under Article 9 of the Convention: Third Periodic Reports, United States of America, CERD/C/351/Add.1 (2000) (ICERD was not ratified by the U.S. Senate until 1994. In its initial report to ICERD, the U.S. noted "even though U.S. law is in conformity with the obligations assumed by the United States under the treaty, American society has not yet fully achieved the Convention's goals.").
53. Thornberry, *The International Convention on the Elimination of All Forms of Racial Discrimination*, 104, 114.
54. Washington v. Davis, 426 U.S. 229 (1976). *See also* Griggs v. Duke Power Co., 401 U.S. 424, 432 (1971), where the Supreme Court stated and emphasized "Congress directed the thrust of the Act to the *consequences* of employment practices, not simply the motivation."
55. International Convention on the Elimination of All Forms of Racial Discrimination, art. 4, adopted Dec. 21, 1965, G.A. Res. 2106 (XX), 660 U.N.T.S. 195.
56. Thornberry, *The International Convention on the Elimination of All Forms of Racial Discrimination*, 73.
57. UNESCO, *The Race Question* (1950), 1.
58. Population Registration Act, No. 30 (1950) (S. Afr.).
59. International Status of South West Africa (Advisory Opinion) [1950] I.C.J. Rep. 128 (July 11).
60. International Status of South West Africa (Advisory Opinion) [1950] I.C.J. Rep. 128, 143 (July 11). *See also* David Weissbrodt and Georgina Mahoney, "International Legal Action Against Apartheid," *Law and Inequality* 4, no. 3 (October 1986), 485–508.
61. South West Africa (Ethiopia v. South Africa; Liberia v. South Africa), Judgment, 1966 I.C.J. 6; *cf.* U.N. Charter art. 77 (stating that the trusteeship system applies to territories under mandate).
62. Legal Consequences for States of the Continued Presence of South Africa in Namibia (Advisory Opinion), 1971 I.C.J. 16 (June 21).
63. Legal Consequences for States of the Continued Presence of South Africa in Namibia (Advisory Opinion), 1971 I.C.J. 16, 62. Declaration of President Sir Muhammad Zafrulla Khan ("The policy of *apartheid* was initiated by Prime Minister Malan and was then vigorously put into effect by his successors, Strijdom and Verwoerd. It has been continuously proclaimed that the purpose and object of the policy are the maintenance

of White domination.") *See* David Weissbrodt and Georgina Mahoney, "International Legal Action Against Apartheid," *Law and Inequality* 4, no. 3 (Oct. 1986): 485–508.

64. "The End of Apartheid," U.S. Department of State Archive (2009).
65. Rome Statute of the International Criminal Court art. 7, July 17, 1998, 2187 U.N.T.S. 3 (defining apartheid as an inhumane crime "committed in the context of an institutionalized regime of systematic oppression and domination by one racial group over any other racial group or groups and committed with the intention of maintaining that regime.").
66. International Convention on the Suppression and Punishment of the Crime of Apartheid art. 2, Nov. 30, 1973, 1015 U.N.T.S. 243 (defining the crime of apartheid).
67. U.N. Office of the High Commissioner for Human Rights, "Committee on the Elimination of Racial Discrimination Concludes Its Ninety-Seventh Session," press release, December 14, 2018.
68. Comm. on the Elimination of Racial Discrimination, *United Nations Human Rights Treaty Bodies* (2019).
69. U.N. Comm. on the Elimination of Racial Discrimination, *General Recommendation No. 35: Combating Racist Hate Speech*, ¶ 12, CERD/C/GC/35 (Sept. 26, 2013).
70. *For general background see* Eleanor Albert and Andrew Chatzky, "The Rohingya Crisis," *Council on Foreign Relations* (Jan. 23, 2020, updated).
71. *Selected Decisions of the Comm. on the Elimination of Racial Discrimination* (vol. 1, U.N. Hum. Rights Office High Comm'r, 2012).
72. *Id.*
73. *Id.* at 204.
74. *Id.*

CHAPTER 5

1. Sam Blake, "Why the George Floyd Protests Feel Different—Lots and Lots of Mobile Video," *dot.LA*, June 12, 2020.
2. United Nations, "Experts Condemn Modern-Day Racial Terror Lynchings in U.S. and Call for Systemic Reform and Justice," press release, June 5, 2020.
3. U.N. Committee on the Elimination of Racial Discrimination, *Prevention of Racial Discrimination, Including Early Warning and Urgent Action Procedures-Statement 1: United States of America* (2020). *See* U.N. Office of the High Commissioner for Human Rights, *Statement on the Protests Against Systemic Racism in the United States*, U.N. Statement, June 5,

2020 (issued by the independent experts of the UN Office of the High Commissioner).

4. *See, e.g.*, U.N. Office of the High Commissioner for Human Rights (@ UNHumanRights), Twitter post, March 21, 2019, "Racism is the opposite of everything we stand for." #fightracism.
5. U.N. Office of the High Commissioner for Human Rights, #FightRacism campaign page. Just after the horrific attacks on Al Noor and Linwood mosques in Christchurch, New Zealand, on March 15, 2019, the UN Office of the High Commissioner for Human Rights made a statement on March 21, 2019, saying "[r]acism is the opposite of everything we stand for" and, in the days prior, the UN started posting on Twitter with the hashtag #fightracism.
6. U.N. Human Rights Council, Rep. of the Human Rights Council on its 43rd Sess., at 13 (June 17, 2020); E. Tendayi Achiume, "Black Lives Matter and the UN Human Rights System: Reflections on the Human Rights Council Urgent Debate," *EJIL Talk*! (Dec. 15, 2020), https://perma.cc/57L5-KD5W.
7. United Nations, "U.N. Human Rights Chief Urges Immediate, Transformative Action to Uproot Systemic Racism," press release, June 28, 2021. *See* U.N. High Commissioner for Human Rights Michelle Bachelet, "Video Statement for the 2019 International Day for the Elimination of Racial Discrimination," video statement, June 28, 2021.
8. *Permanent Forum on People of African Descent*, U.N. Office of the High Commissioner for Human Rights.
9. For an overview of developments from 1997 to 2022, *see* Rosana Garciandia and Philippa Webb, "The UN's Work on Racial Discrimination: Achievements and Challenges," *Max Planck Yearbook for U.N. Law* 25, no. 1 (2022).
10. Ad Hoc Comm. on the Elaboration of Complementary Standards, *U.N. Hum. Rights Office of the High Commissioner* (2019).
11. Anna Spain Bradley, expert testimony, in UN Human Rights Council, *Report of the Ad Hoc Committee on the Elaboration of Complementary Standards on Its Eleventh Session*, September 12–October 7, 2022, Agenda Item 9, pp. 36–38, ¶¶ 118–137.
12. U.N. Hum. Rights Council, *Rep. of the Ad Hoc Comm. on the Elaboration of Complementary Standards on Its Ninth Session*, ¶ 20, U.N. Doc. A/HRC/37/76 (Feb. 9, 2018).
13. U.N. Doc. A/HRC/37/76 ¶ 23 (Feb. 9, 2018) ("The European Union was of the view that the development of comprehensive anti-discrimination

legislation was relevant and it stated that it would continue to engage in the promotion of equality and non-discrimination.").

14. U.N. Hum. Rights Council, *Rep. of the Ad Hoc Comm. on the Elaboration of Complementary Standards on Its Ninth Session*, 43, U.N. Doc. A/HRC/37/76 23–24 (2018).
15. U.N. Doc. A/HRC/37/76 ¶ 15 (Feb. 9, 2018).
16. U.N. Hum. Rights Council, *Rep. of the Ad Hoc Comm. on the Elaboration of Complementary Standards on Its Ninth Session*, 43, U.N. Doc. A/HRC/37/76 24–25 (2018).
17. U.N. Hum. Rights Council, *Rep. of the Ad Hoc Comm. on the Elaboration of Complementary Standards on Its Ninth Session*, U.N. Doc. A/HRC/37/76 ¶ 18 (2018).
18. U.N. Doc. A/HRC/37/76 ¶ 37 (Feb. 9, 2018).
19. U.N. Hum. Rights Council, *Rep. of the Ad Hoc Comm. on the Elaboration of Complementary Standards on Its Ninth Session*, 42, U.N. Doc. A/HRC/37/76 (2018) (on "Structural Xenophobia Discrimination Against Refugees").
20. U.N. Hum. Rights Council, *Rep. of the Ad Hoc Comm. on the Elaboration of Complementary Standards on Its Ninth Session*, 43, U.N. Doc. A/HRC/37/76 (2018).
21. U.N. Human Rights Office of the High Commissioner, *Report to the Ad Hoc Committee on the Elaboration of Complementary Standards to the International Convention on the Elimination of All Forms of Racial Discrimination on the Intersessional Legal Expert Consultation Considering the Elements of a Draft Additional Protocol to the Convention Prepared by the Ad Hoc Committee at Its Tenth Session* ¶ 24. Anna Spain Bradley, expert testimony, ¶¶ 118–37.
22. U.N. Human Rights Council, *Ad Hoc Committee on the Elaboration of Complementary Standards*, Programme of Work 2024.
23. U.N. Doc. A/HRC/37/76 ¶ 59 (Feb. 9, 2018) ("The representative of the European Union said that she had not yet received comments from all members of her regional group on the Chairperson's text. Nevertheless, certain points must be clarified regarding the 2008 European Union Framework Decision on combating certain forms and expressions of racism and xenophobia by means of criminal law. In particular, she said that the Framework Decision did not define the term "xenophobia" per se but criminalizes certain acts that respond to certain criteria, which notably have to be crimes punishable by law. Hence, the Framework Decision criminalized hate speech but not xenophobic fears and attitudes.").

24. U.N.S.C. S/RES/2686, ¶ 1, (June 14, 2023). *See also* United Nations, "Unanimously Adopting Resolution 2686 (2023), Security Council Urges International and National Action to Prevent Incitement, Condemn Hate Speech, Racism, Acts of Extremism," press release, June 14, 2023. Controversy surrounding resolution for the UAE's frame of "human fraternity" seen by some critiques as a push to reframe universal human rights to empower state sovereignty over cultural and religion moving away from existing universal human rights framework. UK interest may be to protect religious freedom as political priority of then ruling Conservative Party. *See* Saskia Brechenmacher, "New UN Security Council Resolution on "Human Fraternity" Raises Human Rights Concerns," *Just Security* (June 23, 2023).
25. Application of the International Convention on the Elimination of All Forms of Racial Discrimination (Georgia v. Russian Federation), Application Instituting Proceedings, 2008 I.C.J. ¶ 1 (Aug. 12).
26. *Id.* at ¶ 82.a.
27. *Id.* at ¶ 81.d.
28. Application of the International Convention on the Elimination of All Forms of Racial Discrimination (Georgia v. Russian Federation), Provisional Measures, Order, 2008 I.C.J. ¶ 149 (Oct. 15).
29. *Id.* at ¶ 144 ("Whereas States parties to CERD 'condemn racial discrimination and undertake to pursue by all appropriate means and without delay a policy of eliminating racial discrimination in all its forms'; whereas in the view of the Court, in the circumstances brought to its attention in which there is a serious risk of acts of racial discrimination being committed, Georgia and the Russian Federation, whether or not any such acts in the past may be legally attributable to them, are under a clear obligation to do all in their power to ensure that any such acts are not committed in the future." The Court ordered provisional measures but found the case could not proceed to the merits for Georgia's lack of engaging in negotiation prior to bringing its case before the Court.).
30. Application of the International Convention on the Elimination of All Forms of Racial Discrimination (Georgia v. Russian Federation): Overview of the Case, I.C.J.
31. Railway Traffic Between Lithuania and Poland, Advisory Opinion, 1931 P.C.I.J. (ser. A/B) No. 42, ¶ 31 (Oct. 15). *See also* North Sea Continental Shelf Cases (Ger./Den.; Ger./Neth.), Reports, 1969 I.C.J. 3.

32. South West Africa Cases (Eth. v. S. Afr.; Liber. v. S. Afr.), Preliminary Objections, 1962 I.C.J. 212. *See also* South West Africa Cases (Eth. v. S. Afr.; Liber. v. S. Afr.), Judgment, 1962 I.C.J. 319, 346 (Dec. 21).
33. Georgia v. Russian Federation, Judgment on Preliminary Objections, I.C.J. Rep. 2011, ¶¶ 123–41 (Apr. 1, 2011). *See also* ICERD, art. 22 ("Any dispute between two or more States Parties with respect to the interpretation or application of this Convention, which is not settled by negotiation or by the procedures expressly provided for in this Convention, shall, at the request of any of the parties to the dispute, be referred to the International Court of Justice for decision, unless the disputants agree to another mode of settlement.").
34. Georgia v. Russian Federation, at ¶ 159 (citing Mavrommatis Palestine Concessions (Greece v. Britain), Judgment, 1924 P.C.I.J. 13; South West Africa (Eth. v. S. Afr.; Liber. v. S. Afr.), Preliminary Objections, Judgment, 1962 I.C.J. 345; United States Diplomatic and Consular Staff in Tehran (U.S. v. Iran), Judgment, 1980 I.C.J. 27; Applicability of the Obligation to Arbitrate Under Section 21 of the United Nations Headquarters Agreement of 26 June 1947, Advisory Opinion, 1988 I.C.J. 33; Questions of Interpretation and Application of the 1971 Montreal Convention arising from the Aerial Incident at Lockerbie (Libya v. U.S.), Preliminary Objections, Judgment, 1998 I.C.J. 122).
35. Application of the Int'l Convention on the Elimination of All Forms of Racial Discrimination (Georgia v. Russia), Preliminary Objections, Judgment, 2011 I.C.J. 70, 129–30, ¶¶ 160–62 (Apr. 1) ("In the present case, the Court is therefore assessing whether Georgia genuinely attempted to engage in negotiations with the Russian Federation, with a view to resolving their dispute concerning the Russian Federation's compliance with its substantive obligations under CERD. Should it find that Georgia genuinely attempted to engage in such negotiations with the Russian Federation, the Court would examine whether Georgia pursued these negotiations as far as possible with a view to settling the dispute. To make this determination, the Court would ascertain whether the negotiations failed, became futile, or reached a deadlock before Georgia submitted its claim to the Court.")
36. Georgia v. Russian Federation, Provisional Measures, ¶ 27.
37. Georgia v. Russian Federation, Judgment on Preliminary Objections, ¶ 166. *Id.* at Provisional Measures 97. The Court determined earlier in its Judgment at ¶ 97 that "On 19 April 2008 the Georgian Foreign Ministry in a press statement referred to the *de facto* annexation of Georgia's integral parts . . . and neglect of human rights of an absolute majority of

the regions' population—victims of ethnic cleansing. The statement is primarily about the status of the two regions and Russian Federation policies and practices relevant to those regions and makes no claim against the Russian Federation about racial discrimination." ("The Court considers that the reference to ethnic cleansing may again be read as relating to the events of the early 1990s. This reference is to be understood in the context of the principal theme of the press release, that is, the concern of Georgia in relation to the status of Abkhazia and the territorial integrity of Georgia. In light of the record it remains unclear whether the press release came to the attention of the Russian Federation. In any case, the press release raised the issue of the proper fulfilment of the mandate of the CIS peacekeeping force, and not the Russian Federation's compliance with its obligations under CERD.").

38. Georgia v. Russian Federation, Judgment on Preliminary Objections, ¶ 178.
39. *Id.* at ¶ 181.
40. Joint Dissenting Opinion of President Owada, Judge Simma, Judge Abraham, Judge Donoghue & Judge ad hoc Gaja, ¶ 2.
41. *Id.* at ¶ 16.
42. *Id.* at ¶¶ 24, 25. ("It omits to quote the dictum, in our view much more important, in the Judgment handed down by this Court in 1998 in the case concerning Land and Maritime Boundary between Cameroon and Nigeria (Cameroon v. Nigeria): 'Neither in the Charter nor otherwise in inter- national law is any general rule to be found to the effect that the exhaustion of diplomatic negotiations constitutes a precondition for a matter to be referred to the Court.' Land and Maritime Boundary between Cameroon and Nigeria (Cameroon v. Nigeria), Preliminary Objections, Judgment, 1998 I.C.J. Reports 303. It is clear that while diplomatic negotiations concerning a dispute may be helpful before judicial proceedings are brought, particularly in clarifying the terms of the dispute and delimiting its subject-matter, they as a general rule are not a mandatory precondition to be satisfied in order for the Court to be able to exercise jurisdiction. There is such a requirement only if, and to the extent that, it is embodied in the clause or declaration on which the jurisdiction of the Court is founded.").
43. *Id.* at ¶ 37.
44. *Id.* at ¶ 80.
45. Georgia v. Russian Federation, Separate Opinion of Judge Simma, ¶ 3.
46. Georgia v. Russian Federation, Separate Opinion of Judge Donoghue.
47. U.N. Secretary-General, Letter dated May 27, 1994, from the Secretary-General addressed to the President of the Security Council, U.N. Doc. S/1994/674 (May 27, 1994). ¶ 130.

48. ICERD, art. 5.
49. Georgia v. Russian Federation, Separate Opinion of Judge Simma, ¶ 4.
50. Georgia v. Russian Federation, Separate Opinion of Judge Donoghue 18 ("Georgia's Permanent Representative to the United Nations transmitted to the General Assembly a 2006 resolution of the Georgian Parliament describing 'attempts to legalize the results of ethnic cleansing' as a part of the 'reality brought about as a result of peacekeeping operations' (para. 86), but the Judgement dismisses the value of the transmitted resolution because Georgia failed to refer in its transmittal letter to agenda items covering ethnic discrimination (para. 89).").
51. Application of the Int'l Convention for the Suppression of the Financing of Terrorism and of the International Convention on the Elimination of All Forms of Racial Discrimination (Ukraine v. Russian Federation), Application Instituting Proceedings, 2017 I.C.J. 1 (Jan. 16).
52. Application of the Int'l Convention for the Suppression of the Financing of Terrorism and of the International Convention on the Elimination of All Forms of Racial Discrimination (Ukraine v. Russia Federation), Countermemorial on the Case, 2021 I.C.J. 1 (Aug. 9).
53. *Id.*, wherein the Russian Federation cites N. Lerner, *The UN Convention on the Elimination of All Forms of Racial Discrimination* (Brill/Nijhoff, 2015), ¶ 36.
54. Application of the Int'l Convention for the Suppression of the Financing of Terrorism and of the International Convention on the Elimination of All Forms of Racial Discrimination (Ukraine v. Russian Federation), Judgment, 2024 I.C.J. 1, ¶ 190 (Jan. 31).
55. *Id.*
56. *Id.* at 27(f).
57. *Id.* at 194 (ICJ references its earlier Application of the ICERD (Qatar v. United Arab Emirates), Preliminary Objections, Judgment, 2021 I.C.J. 108–9 ¶ 112).
58. Application of the Int'l Convention for the Suppression of the Financing of Terrorism and of the International Convention on the Elimination of All Forms of Racial Discrimination (Ukraine v. Russian Federation), Judgment, 2019 I.C.J. 558, 595 ¶ 95 (Nov. 8).
59. Application of the Int'l Convention for the Suppression of the Financing of Terrorism and of the International Convention on the Elimination of All Forms of Racial Discrimination (Ukraine v. Russian Federation), Judgment, 2024 I.C.J. 1, 74, ¶ 217 (Jan 31).
60. *Id.* at 63, ¶ 170.

61. Ukraine v. Russian Federation, Separate Opinion of President Donoghue, ¶ 14.
62. *Id.* at ¶ 24.
63. Ukraine v. Russian Federation, Dissenting Opinion of Judge Sebutinde, ¶ 22.
64. *Id.* at ¶¶ 23–24.
65. *Id.* at ¶ 25.
66. Ukraine v. Russian Federation, Separate Opinion of Judge Iwasawa, ¶ 12.
67. *Id.* at ¶ 21.
68. Ukraine v. Russian Federation, Separate Opinion of Judge Charlesworth, ¶ 32.
69. Application of the International Convention on the Elimination of All Forms of Racial Discrimination (Qatar v. U.A.E), Application Instituting Proceedings, 2018 I.C.J. (Jun. 11) ¶¶ 2–3.
70. Reported in English by Karen DeYoung and Ellen Nakashima, "UAE Orchestrated Hacking of Qatari Government Sites, Sparking Regional Upheaval, According to U.S. Intelligence Officials," *The Washington Post*, July 16, 2017.
71. Application of the International Convention on the Elimination of All Forms of Racial Discrimination (Qatar v. U.A.E.), Preliminary Objections, 2019 I.C.J. 1 (April 29).
72. Qatar v. U.A.E., Judgment, 2021 I.C.J. 71, 97, ¶ 79 (Feb. 4).
73. *Id.*
74. Qatar v. U.A.E, Order, 2018 I.C.J. Jul. 23, ¶ 27 ("In the Court's view, the acts referred to by Qatar, in particular the statement of 5 June 2017—which allegedly targeted Qataris on the basis of their national origin—whereby the UAE announced that Qataris were to leave its territory within 14 days and that they would be prevented from entry, and the alleged restrictions that ensued, including upon their right to marriage and choice of spouse, to education as well as to medical care and to equal treatment before tribunals, are capable of falling within the scope of CERD *ratione materiae*. The Court considers that, while the Parties differ on the question whether the expression 'national . . . origin' mentioned in Article 1, paragraph 1, of CERD, encompasses discrimination based on the 'present nationality' of the individual, the Court need not decide at this stage of the proceedings, in view of what is stated above, which of these diverging interpretations of the Convention is the correct one."); *id.*, Joint Declaration of Judges Tomka, Gaja, and Gevorgian, at ¶ 4 ("When the Convention considers 'national origin' as one of the prohibited bases for discrimination, it does

not refer to nationality. In our view, the two terms are not identical and should not be understood as synonymous."); *id.*, Dissenting Opinion of Judge Crawford, at ¶ 1 ("Qatar's request for provisional measures faces two principal difficulties, one legal, the other evidential. The legal difficulty is that Article 1 of the International Convention on the Elimination of All Forms of Racial Discrimination (CERD) distinguishes on its face between discrimination on grounds of national origin (equated to racial discrimination and prohibited per se) and differentiation on grounds of nationality (not prohibited as such)."; *id.*, Dissenting Opinion of Judge Salam, at ¶ 3 ("The aim of CERD is thus to bring an end, in the decolonization and post-decolonization period, to all manifestations and governmental policies of discrimination based on racial superiority or hatred; it does not concern questions relating to nationality.").

75. Qatar v. U.A.E., Preliminary Objections, Judgment, 2021 I.C.J. ¶ 1 (Feb. 4).
76. William Thomas Worster, "The Divergence Between the ICJ and the Committee on the Elimination of Racial Discrimination Regarding Nationality-Based Discrimination," *ASIL Insights* 26, no. 13 (2022) (analyzing the ICJ's divergence from the CERD's General Recommendation 30 that contemporary forms of racism and human rights violations can include xenophobia against people who are non-nationals or who are migrating, seeking refuge, and seeking asylum and noting how CERD looked at two parts of the treaty, whereas the ICJ relied only on one).
77. CERD Comm., General Recommendation 30 on Discrimination against Non-Citizens, U.N. Doc. CERD/C/64/Misc.11/rev.3 ¶ 4 (2004).
78. Qatar v. U.A.E., Preliminary Objections, Judgment, 2021 I.C.J. ¶¶ 1, 86 (Feb. 4).
79. Application of the International Convention on the Elimination of All Forms of Racial Discrimination (Armenia v. Azerbaijan), Request for Provisional Measures, 2021 I.C.J. 1, 6, ¶ 3 (Sept. 16).
80. Application of the International Convention on the Elimination of All Forms of Racial Discrimination (Azerbaijan v. Armenia), Request for Provisional Measures, 2021 I.C.J. 1 (Sept. 16).
81. Ukraine v. Russian Federation, Judgment, 2021 I.C.J. ¶¶ 1, 196 (Jan. 31).
82. *Id.* at ¶ 200.
83. UN Charter, arts. 1.2, 1.3 (1945).
84. World Conference Against Racism, *Racial Discrimination, Xenophobia and Related Intolerance, Declaration and Programme of Action, United Nations Department of Public Information* (2002), p. 13.

CHAPTER 6

1. Guillermo Rai and Mario Cortegana, "Vinicius Jr: Three People Sentenced to Eight Months in Prison for Racially Abusing Real Madrid Forward," *The Athletic*, June 10, 2024.
2. As specified under Spain's Código Penal, Art. 173.1 (1995). Reported by Nota De Prensa, LALIGA Land First Conviction in Spain for Racist Abuse at a Football Match (Oct. 6, 2024).
3. Vinícius Júnior (@vinijr), "Many asked me to ignore it, many others said that my fight was in vain and that I should just 'play soccer' . . . ," *X* (formerly Twitter), June 10, 2024, translated from Portuguese, https://x.com/vinijr/status/1800224417651568979.
4. Rai and Cortegana, "Vinicius Jr."
5. Colin Millar and Adam Crafton, "FIFA Dropping Anti-Racism Messages a 'Human Rights Risk' for 2026 World Cup, Say Rights Groups," *The Athletic*, July 4, 2025.
6. "14.9 Million Excess Deaths Associated with the COVID-19 Pandemic in 2020 and 2021," United Nations Department of Economic and Social Affairs, accessed August 18, 2025.
7. *See, e.g.*, "In Pandemics, More Than Viruses Spread," UCLA Fielding School of Public Health, accessed August 18, 2025.
8. ""Covid-19 Fueling Anti-Asian Racism and Xenophobia Worldwide," *Human Rights Watch*, May 12, 2020.
9. António Guterres, "We Must Act Now to Strengthen the Immunity of Our Societies Against the Virus of Hate," *United Nations Covid 19 Response*, May 8, 2020.
10. Catherine Powell, Color of Covid: The Racial Justice Paradox of Our New Stay-At-Home Economy, *CNN Op-ed*, April 18, 2020 (updated), https://www.cnn.com/2020/04/10/opinions/covid-19-people-of-color-labor-market-disparities-powell. See also Catherine Powell, "Color of Covid and Gender of Covid: Essential Workers, Not Disposable People," *Yale Journal of Law & Feminism 33* (2021): 1.
11. ""UK Teenager Jailed for Minimum of 52 Years for Southport Girls' Murders," *CNN World*, January 23, 2025.
12. Dominic Casciani and Emily Holt, "Police Chief 'Told Not to Reveal Rudakubana's Faith,'" *BBC News*, February 25, 2025, https://perma.cc/83AM-T7DS.
13. Josh Halliday, "Axel Rudakubana: From 'Unassuming' Schoolboy to Southport Killer," *The Guardian*, January 25, 2025.

14. U.N. Office of the High Commissioner for Human Rights, "U.N. Committee on the Elimination of Racial Discrimination Publishes Findings on Belarus, Bosnia and Herzegovina, Iran, Iraq, Pakistan, United Kingdom and Venezuela," press release, August 23, 2024; Alma Teffera, "After Riots, UN Calls on UK to Tackle Systemic Racism, Colonial Legacies," *Human Rights Watch*, September 4, 2024.
15. Joe Middleton, "The Day Britain Fought Back: Public Praised for Anti-Racism Gatherings That Shut Down Far-Right Riots," *The Independent*, August 8, 2024; "Fueled by Disinformation, Far-Right Protesters Spark New Clashes with UK Police in Wake of Knife Attack," *France 24*, August 4, 2024; Mallory Moench, "Thousands of Anti-Racism Protestors Rally Across UK," *BBC News*, August 10, 2024; Kate Holton et al., "Anti-Racism Protests Sweep Britain After Far-Right Riots," *Reuters*, August 8, 2024.
16. Tanya Maria Golash-Boza, *Race and Racism: A Critical Approach*, 3rd ed. (Oxford University Press, 2022), 176.
17. U.N. Office of the High Commissioner for Human Rights, press release, "UN Committee on the Elimination of Racial Discrimination publishes findings on Belarus, Bosnia and Herzegovina, Iran, Iraq, Pakistan, United Kingdom, and Venezuela," August 23, 2024.
18. *See generally* Chris C. Allen, *Reconfiguring Islamophobia: A Radical Rethinking of a Contested Concept* (Palgrave Pivot, 2020).
19. Kamari Maxine Clarke and Deborah A. Thomas, eds., *Globalization and Race: Transformation in the Cultural Production of Blackness* (Duke University Press, 2006); Kevin Reilly et al., *Racism: A Global Reader* (Routledge, 2002); A. Sivanandan, "The Contours of Global Racism," Address at *Crossing Borders: The Legacy of the Commonwealth Immigrants Act of 1962*, November 2002; Pinar Batur-Vanderlippe and Joe Feagin, *The Global Color Line: Racial and Ethnic Inequality and Struggle from a Global Perspective* (Emerald Publishing, 1999).
20. Tanya Maria Golash-Boza, "Thinking Globally," in *Race and Racisms*, ed. Tanya Maria Golash-Boza (Oxford University Press, 2022).
21. Judy Root Aulette, *A Global View of Race and Racism* (Oxford University Press, 2017), 146.
22. Alastair Bonnett, *Multiracism: Rethinking Racism in a Global Context* (Polity Press, 2022).
23. *Id.* at 1.
24. Angela Saini, *Superior: The Return of Race Science* (Beacon Press, 2019); Angela Saini, *The Patriarchs: The Origins of Inequality* (Beacon Press, 2023).

25. Angela Saini, "Review: Britain's Racism Isn't America's: The United Kingdom Needs to Examine Its Own Bigotries," *Foreign Policy*, July 30, 2023; Tomiwa Owolade, *This Is Not America: Why Black Lives in Britain Matter* (Atlantic Books, 2023).
26. *See generally* Kimberlé Crenshaw et al., *Critical Race Theory: The Key Writings That Formed the Movement* (The New Press, 1996); Makau Mutua, "What Is TWAIL?," Proceedings of the 94th Annual Meeting of the American Society of International Law (2000): 31–40; Antony Anghie and B. S. Chimni, "Third World Approaches to International Law and Individual Responsibility in Internal Conflict," *Chinese Journal of International Law 2* (2003): 77–103; B. S. Chimni, "Third World Approaches to International Law: A Manifesto," *International Community Law Review* 8 (2006): 3–27; James T. Gathii, "TWAIL: A Brief History of Its Origins, Its Decentralized Network and a Tentative Bibliography," *Trade Law and Development 3* (2011): 26–48. For detailed offerings of scholars at the intersection of TWAIL and CRS, *see* "Critical Perspectives on Race and Human Rights," 2019 Symposium, UCLA Promise Institute for Human Rights.
27. Kimberlé W. Crenshaw, "Demarginalizing the Intersection of Race and Sex: A Black Feminist Critique of Antidiscrimination Doctrine, Feminist Theory and Antiracist Politics," *University of Chicago Legal Forum* 139 (1989); Kimberlé W. Crenshaw, "Mapping the Margins: Intersectionality, Identity Politics, and Violence Against Women of Color," *Stanford Law Review* 43 (1991): 1241 Patricia J. Williams, *The Alchemy of Race and Rights* (Harvard University Press, 1991); Mari Matsuda, "When the First Quail Calls: Multiple Consciousness as Jurisprudential Method," *Women's Rights Law Reporter* 14 (1992): 297–300; Mari Matsuda, "Looking to the Bottom: Critical Legal Studies and Reparations," *Harvard Civil Rights-Civil Liberties Law Review* 22 (1982): 323–99; Cheryl I. Harris, "Whiteness as Property," *Harvard Law Review* 106 (1993): 1707; Adrien Wing, *Critical Race Feminism: A Reader*, 2nd ed. (New York University Press, 2003); Adrien Wing, *Global Critical Race Feminism: An International Reader* (New York University Press, 2002). *See also* David Theo Goldberg, *The Racial State* (Wiley-Blackwell, 2002); David Theo Goldberg, *The Threat of Race: Reflections on Racial Neoliberalism* (Wiley-Blackwell, 2008), 21–23.
28. "Savages, Victims, and Saviors: The Metaphor of Human Rights," *Harvard International Law Journal* 42 (2001): 201. *See also* Makau Mutua, *Human Rights: A Political and Cultural Critique* (University of Pennsylvania Press, 2002).

29. *See, e.g.*, Patryk I. Labuda, "Concept Note," *In Search of Second World Approaches to International Law (SWAIL) Programme* (Central European University, February 21–22, 2025); Ntina Tzouvala, *Capitalism as Civilisation: A History of International Law* (Cambridge University Press, 2020); Natsu Taylor Saito, *Settler Colonialism, Race, and the Law: Why Structured Racism Persists* (New York University Press, 2020); Tara Van Ho, "Angels, Virgins, Demons, Whores: Moving Towards an Antiracist Praxis by Confronting Modern Investment Law Scholarship," *The Journal of World Investment & Trade* 23 (2022), 347–87; William Mpofu, "Xenophobia as Racism: The Colonial Underside of Nationalism in South Africa," *International Journal of Critical Diversity Studies* 3 (2020): 33–52; Sundhya Pahuja, *Decolonising International Law: Development, Economic Growth and the Politics of Universality* (Cambridge University Press, 2011).
30. James Thuo Gathii and Ntina Tzouvala, "Racial Capitalism and International Economic Law: Introduction," *Journal of International Economic Law* 25 (2022): 199–206.
31. Many works have examined racism on a global scale and across different societies and historical contexts, including Michael Banton, *International Action Against Racial Discrimination* (Oxford University Press, 1996); Michael Banton, *The International Politics of Race* (Polity Press, 2002); Herbert Hunter and Sameer Y. Abraham, *Race, Class, and the World System: The Sociology of Oliver C. Cox* (Monthly Review Press, 1987); Gargi Bhattacharyya et al., *Race and Power, Global Racism in the Twenty First Century* (Routledge, 2002), investigates "race in global terms" arguing the "forces of globalization inhibit older cultures of racial division to benefit the privileged economically"; Alexander Anievas et al., *Race and Racism in International Relations: Confronting the Global Colour Line* (Routledge, 2014).
32. Safiya Noble, *Algorithms of Oppression* (New York University Press, 2018); Ruha Benjamin, *Race After Technology* (Polity Press, 2019).
33. United Nations, Department of Economic and Social Affairs, Population Division, Estimated Mid-Year Population by Major Area and Regions 2022 and 2023 (2024), accessed August 28, 2025.
34. Fight Racism, *Indigenous Peoples*, United Nations, accessed August 19, 2025.
35. Minority Rights Group, Twa in Rwanda (October 2022), accessed October 16, 2025.
36. *See* J. Kehaulani Kauanui, *Hawaiian Blood: Colonialism and the Politics of Sovereignty and Indigeneity* (Duke University Press, 2008).

37. Minority Rights Group, Uyghurs in China (July 2023), accessed October 16, 2025.
38. "The Colourful Propaganda of Xinjiang," *BBC News*, January 12, 2015.
39. "Roma Equality, Inclusion and Participation in the EU," European Commission, accessed August 19, 2025; *see generally* "Background: Who Are the Roma?," United Nations, accessed August 19, 2025.
40. "The Working Definition of Anti-Roma Racism," U.S. Department of State, October 8, 2020.
41. W. E. B. DuBois, *The Problem of the Color Line at the Turn of the Twentieth Century: The Essential Early Essays*, ed. Nahum Dimitri Chandler (Fordham University Press, 2014).

CHAPTER 7

1. Gay McDougall, "Statement of Ms. Gay McDougall" Commemorative Plenary Meeting, 72nd session of the General Assembly, United Nations Headquarters, New York, March 20, 2018.
2. United Nations, "Racial Equality 'Is Under Attack', Experts Warn General Assembly, Urging States to Mark International Day by Stamping Out Discrimination, Intolerance," Meetings Coverage, General Assembly 72nd session, 79th meeting, March 20, 2018.
3. U.N. Committee on the Elimination of Racial Discrimination, "U.N. CERD Reviews the Report of China," press release (August 13, 2018).
4. *Id. See also* "One Million Muslim Uighurs Held In Secret China Camps: UN Panel," *Al Jazeera* (August 10, 2018), accessed October 16, 2025.
5. *Id.*
6. Antoine Louis Claude Destutt de Tracy, *Éléments d'idéologie* (Courcier, 1804) 1801–15, vols 4–5.
7. Merriam-Webster, s.v. "idea," and s.v. "ideology," accessed August 21, 2025.
8. "White Nationalist," *Southern Poverty Law Center*, accessed August 21, 2025. *See* Cassie Miller and Hannah Gais, "The White Power Movement Hits the Streets," *Southern Poverty Law Center*, June 4, 2024.
9. Munira Mustaffa, "Right-Wing Extremism Has Deep Roots in Southeast Asia," *GNET*, July 14, 2021.
10. Conflict in Myanmar Case Study, Harvard Divinity School (2018).
11. Hitler, *Mein Kampf*, 653. *See also* James Q. Whitman, *Hitler's American Model: The United States and the Making of Nazi Race Law* (Princeton University Press, 2017), 9; *see generally* Carroll P. Kakel III, *American West and the Nazi East: A Comparative and Interpretive Perspective* (Palgrave Macmillan, 2011); Bradley W. Hart, *Hitler's American Friends* (Griffin,

2018); Alex Ross, "How American Racism Influenced Hitler," *The New Yorker*, April 23, 2018.

12. Whitman, *Hitler's American Model*, 9–10. *See* Adolf Hitler, *Reden, Schriften, Anordnungen*, speech at Oldenberg, October 18, 1928, reprinted in *Reden, Schriften, Anordnungen: Februar 1925 bis Januar 1993*, ed. Institut für Zeitgeschichte (K.G. Saur Verlag & Co. 1992).
13. Hitler, *Mein Kampf*, 286.
14. Roland Freisler, June 5, 1934, translated in Whitman, "Introduction."
15. Adolf Hitler, speech at Sportspalast, Berlin (January 30, 1941), in Max Domarus, *The Complete Hitler: Speeches and Proclamations, 1932-1945* (Mary Fran Golbert, trans. Bolchazy-Carducci, 1990), 2360.
16. Phillipe Sands, *East West Street: On the Origins of Genocide and Crimes Against Humanity* (Alfred A. Knopf, 2016)
17. *Id.* at 281.
18. *Id. See also* Stephen Moss, "Interview with Phillipe Sands: 'Alarm bells are ringing in this country,'" *The Guardian*, November 16, 2016, accessed October 16, 2016.
19. Sands, *East West Street,* 281.
20. Convention on the Prevention and Punishment of the Crime of Genocide, Dec. 9, 1948, 78 U.N.T.S. 277.
21. The Prosecutor v. Théoneste Bagosora et al., Judgment and Sentence, Case No. ICTR-98-41-T ¶¶ 198–199, p. 46 (Dec. 18, 2008). See Thierry Cruvellier, "Justice Info Publishes the Report Supposedly Behind the Genocide Plot in Rwanda, Bagosora Report," JusticeInfo.net, September 25, 2023. Report of The Commission (French).
22. The Prosecutor v. Théoneste Bagosora et. al, Judgment and Sentence, ¶ 202, pp. 47–48.
23. *Id.*, ¶ 2368, at 594.
24. "The Hutu Ten Commandments," Kigali, 1990, accessed August 21, 2025.
25. "President Kais Saied Chairs a Meeting of the National Security Council," *Carthage*, February 21, 2023. "Tunisia: President's Racist Speech Incites a Wave of Violence Against Black Africans," Amnesty International, March 1, 2023.
26. "Tunisia: Wave of Attacks on Black African Migrants Has Been Fueled by President's Racism," Amnesty International, March 10, 2023.
27. Sharan Grewal, "In Another First, Tunisia Criminalizes Racism," *Brookings*, October 15, 2023.
28. Carrie Keller-Lynn, "Netanyahu to Knesset: Fight with 'Nazi' Hamas Is War Between Light and Darkness," *The Times of Israel* (October 16,

2023). *See* Shannon Vavra, "Netanyahu Evokes Religious Prophecy in Israel-Gaza War Speech," *Yahoo News*, October 25, 2023. "Excerpt from PM Netanyahu's Remarks at the Opening of the Knesset's Winter Assembly," Gov.il, October 16, 2023; Tamara Tamimi and Daniela Suarez Vergas, "Propaganda vs. Truth: Israeli Propaganda and Palestinian Demonisation," *E-International Relations*, February 13, 2024.

29. "'We Are Fighting Human Animals' said Israeli Defence Minister Yoav Gallant," posted October 10, 2023, by No Comment TV, *YouTube*, 0:20, https://www.youtube.com/watch?v=ZbPdR3E4hCk. Mick Krever et al., "Israel's Far-Right Wants to Move Palestinians out of Gaza. Its Ideas Are Gaining Attention," *CNN*, January 17, 2024; Ashraf Khalil, "Harsh Israeli Rhetoric Against Palestinians Becomes Central to South Africa's Genocide Case," *AP News*, January 18, 2024.

30. In 2024, the International Criminal Court issued arrest warrants for Netanyahu and Gallant for charges of war crimes and crimes against humanity. The ICC charged three Hamas leaders as well, Mohammed Deif, Ismail Haniyeh, and Yahya Sinwar, who have since been killed. United Nations, News (November 23, 2024).

31. Peter Beaumont, "Netanyahu Plans Fence Around Israel to Protect It from 'Wild Beasts,' *The Guardian*, February 10, 2016.

32. Ali Vitali et al., "Trump Referred to Haiti and African Nations as 'Shithole' Countries," *NBC News* (January 11, 2018), accessed October 17, 2025; Tom Embury-Dennis, "UN Calls Donald Trump's s***Hole Immigrants Comments 'Racist,'" *The Independent* (January 12, 2018) ("'If confirmed these are shocking and shameful comments from the President of the United States,' spokesperson Rupert Coleville said. 'There is no other word you can use but 'racist'.'"); Katherine Faulders, "White House Appears Unfazed by Trump's 's—-hole countries' Comment," *ABC News* (January 11, 2018); "African Ambassadors to the UN Condemn Trump over 'Shithole' Comment," *GHANAWEB* (January 14, 2018).

33. Myah Ward, "We Watched 20 Trump Rallies. His Racist, Anti-Immigrant Messaging Is Getting Darker," *Politico*, October 12, 2024.

34. *Id.*

35. Vanessa Williamson and Isabella Gelfand, "Trump and Racism: What Do the Data Say?," *Brookings*, August 14, 2019; Griffin Edwards and Stephen Rushin, "The Effect of Trump's Election on Hate Crimes," *SSRN Electronic Journal* (January 14, 2018).

36. FBI, Hate Crime in the United States Incident Analysis (August 15, 2025).

37. "Most Americans Say Trump's Election Has Led to Worse Race Relations in the U.S.," *Pew Research Center* (December 19, 2017), accessed October 17, 2025.

38. Ashley Jardina and Spencer Piston, "Trickle-Down Racism: Trump's Effect on Whites' Racist Dehumanizing Attitudes," *Current Research in Ecological and Social Psychology* 5 (2023) ("Reported hate crimes against Black people surged following Trump's election.").
39. *See generally* Siri Aas Rustad, "Conflict Trends: A Global Overview, 1946-2024," PRIO Paper, Peace Research Institute Oslo, 2023; Merdith Reid Sarkees and Frank Wayman, *Resort to War: 1816-2007 (Correlates of War)* (CQ Pres, 2010).
40. Ralph Bunche, *A World View of Race*, 13–14.
41. *Id.* at 19.

CHAPTER 8

1. Universal Declaration of Human Rights, G.A. Res. 217 A (III), U.N. GAOR, 3d Sess., Res. 218A (Dec. 10, 1948).
2. *See* John P. Humphrey, *Human Rights and the United Nations: A Great Adventure* (Transnational, 1984) (recalling the history of the creation of human rights bodies and instruments at the UN and his own personal recollections of such as principal author of the first draft of the Universal Declaration of Human Rights).
3. Johannes Morsink, *The Universal Declaration of Human Rights: Origins, Drafting, and Intent* (University of Pennsylvania Press, 1999), 36–37, 244–45. See Chapter 8 for an account of the drafting of the preamble and Article 1.
4. Morsink, *Universal Declaration of Human Rights*, 281–328 (discussing the negotiation history behind the preamble and Article 1).
5. Mary Ann Glendon, *A World Made New: Eleanor Roosevelt and the Universal Declaration of Human Rights* (Random House, 2001), 78; U.N. GAOR, 3d Sess., 3d Comm., 85th mtg., U.N. Doc. A/C.3/SR.85 (1948).
6. Patrice Rankine, "Dignity in Homer and Classical Greece," in *Dignity: A History*, ed. Remy Debes (Oxford University Press, 2017).
7. *See generally* Aristotle, *Nicomachean Ethics*, trans. Terence Irwin (Hackett, 1999) (Aristotle defines aretē (virtue/excellence) as a state concerned with choice, related to human flourishing in Book II, chs. 5–6); Homer, *Iliad*, trans. Richmond Lattimore (University of Chicago Press, 2011) (the epic consistently links timē (honor) to social recognition and human worth, especially in Achilles' conflict with Agamemnon in Book I); Plato, "Apology," in *Plato: Complete Works*, ed. John M. Cooper (Hackett, 1997) (Socrates ties axiōma (what is worthy) and moral excellence to the examined life and to human value (29d–30b)); Jean-Pierre Vernant, *The*

Origins of Greek Thought (Cornell University Press, 1982) (discusses how concepts like timē and aretē structured early Greek concerns with status, honor, and social order, which later underpinned ideas of moral worth); Martha C. Nussbaum, *The Fragility of Goodness: Luck and Ethics in Greek Tragedy and Philosophy* (Cambridge University Press, 1986) (explores how Greek ethical thought connected aretē and recognition of human worth to broader ideas of dignity).

8. Herodotus, *Histories*, trans. A. D. Godley (Harvard University Press, 1920), 1.31.
9. Cicero, *De Officiis*, trans. Andrew P. Peabody (Little, Brown, and Co., 1887), I, ¶ 30.
10. *See, e.g.*, The Declaration of Independence (United States, 1776); Déclaration des Droits de l'Homme et du Citoyen de 1789 (Fr. 1789); Thomas Paine, *The Rights of Man* (J. S. Jordan, 1791).
11. Immanuel Kant, *Groundwork of the Metaphysics of Morals*, trans. Mary Gregor (Cambridge University Press, 1998); Immanuel Kant, *The Metaphysics of Morals*, trans. Mary Gregor (Cambridge University Press, 1996).
12. Georg Wilhelm Friedrich Hegel, *Phenomenology of Spirit*, trans. A. V. Miller (Oxford University Press, 1977): 178–96.
13. Axel Honneth, *The Struggle for Recognition: The Moral Grammar of Social Conflicts*, trans. Joel Anderson (MIT Press, 1996); Axel Honneth, *Freedom's Right: The Social Foundations of Democratic Life*, trans. Joseph Ganahl (Columbia University Press, 2014).
14. Paul Sagar, *Basic Equality* (Princeton University Press, 2024), 12–15.
15. Teresa M. Bejan, "Acknowledging Equality," 7th Annual Balzan-Skinner Lecture, University of Cambridge, April 22, 2016.
16. *The Qur'an*, trans. M. A. S. Abdel Halleem (Oxford University Press, 2008), 17,70.
17. Universal Declaration of Human Rights, G.A. Res. 217 A (III), U.N. GAOR, 3d Sess., Res. 218A (Dec. 10, 1948).
18. *See* Conor O'Mahoney, "There Is No Such Thing as a Right to Dignity," *International Journal of Constitutional Law* 10, no. 2 (2012): 551–57 (discussing scholarly interpretation of the meaning of dignity in these early sources of international law); Christopher McCrudden, "Human Dignity and Judicial Interpretation of Human Rights," *European Journal of International Law* 19 (2008): 655–724.
19. "Women Who Shaped the Universal Declaration," United Nations. *See also* Rebecca Adami, *Women and the Universal Declaration of Human Rights* (Routledge, 2018).

20. Morsink, *The Universal Declaration of Human Rights*, 36–39.
21. "Women Who Shaped the Universal Declaration," United Nations (referencing Rebecca Adami, *Women and the Universal Declaration of Human Rights* (Routledge, 2018).
22. Bill of Rights 1689, 1 Will. & Mar. Sess. 2. c. 2, (Eng. 1689); Déclaration des Droits de l'Homme et du Citoyen de 1789 (Fr. 1789).
23. Noah Webster, *A Compendious Dictionary of the English Language* (Sidney's Press, 1806), 85.
24. Constitución Política de los Estados Unidos Mexicanos [C.P.], art. 3, cl. 1, Diario Oficial de la Federación [D.O.], 5 de febrero de 1917 (Mex. 1917); Constitución de la República del Ecuador, tit. XIII (Ec. 1929).
25. For treatment of dignity in international law, see generally Paolo G. Carozza, "Human Dignity," in *The Oxford Handbook of International Human Rights Law*, ed. Dinah Shelton (Oxford University Press, 2013); Ari Kohen, *An Overlapping Consensus on Human Rights and Human Dignity* (Oxford University Press, 2014); Conor O'Mahoney, "There Is No Such Thing as a Right to Dignity," *International Journal of Constitutional Law* 10, no. 2 (2012): 551–57; Christopher McCrudden, "Human Dignity and Judicial Interpretation of Human Rights," *European Journal of International Law* 19 (2008): 655. For a range of views on human dignity in law, philosophy, antiquity, religion, and various cultures, see Marcus Düwell et al., *The Cambridge Handbook of Human Dignity: Interdisciplinary Perspectives* (Cambridge University Press, 2015). *See generally* Aharon Barak, *Human Dignity: The Constitutional Value and the Constitutional Right* (Cambridge University Press, 2015).
26. Oscar Schachter, "Human Dignity as a Normative Concept," *American Journal of International Law* 77, no. 4 (1983): 848–54.
27. Charter of Fundamental Rights of the European Union, art. 1, 2000 O.J. (C 364) 1.
28. Explanations Relating to the Charter of Fundamental Rights, 2007 O.J. (C 303) 17.
29. Ireland v. High Court [2023] IEHC 187 (Ir.); for an overview and a critique, see O'Mahoney, "There Is No Such Thing as a Right to Dignity."
30. Erin Daly, *Dignity Rights: Courts, Constitutions and the Worth of the Human Person* (University of Pennsylvania Press, 2021): 82–86.
31. C.E., § 10, cl. 1 (Spain).
32. S. Afr. Const., 1996, ch. 2, § 10.
33. Ústava České Republiky [Constitution], Preamble (Czech Rep., 1992).
34. For a biography of Frank Murphy, see J. Woodford Howard Jr., *Mr. Justice Murphy: A Political Biography* (Princeton University Press, 1968).

35. Korematsu v. United States, 323 U.S. 214, 242 (1944) (dissenting opinion of Frank Murphy).
36. Steele v. Louisville & N.R. Co., 323 U.S. 192, 208–9 (1944) (concurring opinion of Frank Murphy).
37. United States v. Screws, 325 U.S. 91, 135 (1945) (dissenting Opinion of Frank Murphy).
38. Duncan v. Kahanamoku, 327 U.S. 304, 324 (1946) (concurring opinion of Frank Murphy).
39. Spain Bradley, *Human Rights Racism*.
40. Patrick Thornberry, *The International Convention on the Elimination of All Forms of Racial Discrimination: A Commentary* (Oxford University Press, 2016), 29. *See also* U.N. Charter, Preamble; Warwick A. McKean, *Equality and Discrimination Under International Law* (Clarendon Press, 1983), 154.
41. *See, e.g.*, Universal Declaration of Human Rights, art. 1, G.A. Res. 217 (III) A (Dec. 10, 1948) ("All human being are born free and equal in dignity and rights."); Thornberry, *The International Convention on the Elimination of All Forms of Racial Discrimination*, 97 ("Equality and non-discrimination are intrinsic to the architecture of human rights law.").
42. Bell, *Faces at the Bottom of the Well*, 32.
43. Kevin Boyle, Anneliese Baldaccini, "A Critical Evaluation of International Human Rights Approaches to Racism," in *Discrimination and Human Rights: The Case of Racism*, ed. Sandra Fredman (Oxford University Press, 2001); Doug Cloud, *Arguing Identity and Human Rights* (Routledge, 2023).
44. Francis Fukuyama, *Identity: The Demand for Dignity and the Politics of Resentment* (Farrar, Straus and Giroux, 2019) (articulating this point with urgency, noting the power of dignity to craft a shared universal human identity that he views as most essential for our peaceful survival).
45. Gloria Steinem, *The Truth Will Set You Free, but First It Will Piss You Off*, xx (Random House, 2019).
46. Spain Bradley, *Human Choice in International Law*.
47. David Livingstone, "The Paradoxes of Dehumanization," *Social Theory and Practice* 42, no 2 (2016): 416–43. Jeremy Waldron, *The Harm in Hate Speech* (Harvard University Press, 2012), 105 (argues that dignity "is precisely what hate speech laws are designed to protect . . . dignity in the sense of a person's basic entitlement to be regarded as a member of society in good standing, as someone whose membership of a minority group does not disqualify . . . from ordinary social intercourse."); *see* Thornberry, *The International Convention on the Elimination of All Forms of Racial Discrimination*, 268.

48. Donna Hicks, *Dignity: Its Essential Role in Resolving Conflict* (Yale University Press, 2011).
49. Thomas Hobbes, *Leviathan*, Michael Oakenshott, ed. (Collier Books, 1962), 100.

CHAPTER 9

1. "Meet Marguerite Barankitse, Burundi," Nobel Women's Initiative.
2. Elise Harris, "Make Unity a Priority, Pope Francis Says at Reformation Anniversary," *Catholic New Agency*, October 31, 2016.
3. Nelson Mandela, Speech at Madison Park High School, Boston, MA, June 23, 1990, transcription Item 1569, The Nelson Mandela Foundation Archive at the Center of Memory, https://archive.nelsonmandela.org/index.php/za-com-mr-s-1569.
4. Diego Ribadeneira, "City Youngsters Heed the Lesson of a Legend," *The Boston Globe* (June 23, 1990), p. 1.
5. Recording available at GBH News, Nelson Mandela Visit Madison Park HS IN Roxbury in 1990, YouTube, https://www.youtube.com/watch?v=b66c6OkMZGw.
6. "Students Touched by Legend," *The Boston Globe* (June 23, 1990), p. 4.
7. "Weapon," s.v. Oxford English Diction (11th ed., Oxford University Press, 2006), https://opil.ouplaw.com/display/10.1093/law:epil/9780199231690/law-9780199231690-e447?p=emailAsUzpZWh66uXI&d=/10.1093/law:epil/9780199231690/law-9780199231690-e447.
8. ICERD Treaty, Article 7.
9. *Id.*
10. World Conference Against Racism, Racial Discrimination, Xenophobia and Related Intolerance, Declaration and Programme of Action ("Durban Declaration") (2002), para. 136.
11. Cecilia Barbieri and Martha K. Ferede, "A Future We Can All Live With: How Education Can Address and Eradicate Racism," UNESCO, June 29, 2020.
12. Alessandro Bergamaschi et al., "Blatant and Subtle Prejudice, and the Role of Teachers in Conveying Tolerance and Respect for the Other," *Intercultural Education* 33 (2022): 1. This study evaluated the influence of teachers in reducing racial biases among middle and high school students in the south of France. Of 2,906 students, schools were randomly selected, and the study sample consisted of 1,858 students. Overall, the study found that teaching about racial discrimination reduced prejudice (as reflected by questionnaires the students completed focusing on blatant and subtle forms of prejudice). The study additionally found

that student prejudice was correlated with parents' level of educational attainment.

13. Emma Arneback and Jan Jamte, "How to Counteract Racism in Education—A Typology of Teachers' Anti-racist Actions," *Race, Ethnicity and Education* 25, no. 2 (2022): 192–211. Study was based on interviews with twenty-seven high-school teachers in Sweden. Some of the teachers were organized in antiracist networks, some taught in schools where racism was a minor problem, and some taught in schools where racism was a manifest problem. The authors propose six approaches for teachers to counter racism in school, based on the different ways that racism manifests itself. In some schools, teachers must focus on verbal expressions of racism, in others, norms of exclusion may be more salient.
14. Iloradanon H. Efimoff, "The Impact of Education About Historical and Current Injustices, Individual Racism and Systemic Racism on Anti-Indigenous Racism," *European Journal of Social Psychology* 53, no. 7(2023): 1542–62. Two studies involved assessing the impact of five conditions on non-Indigenous students. The conditions improved Indigenous related knowledge, thoughts, and behaviors. Both studies involved students at the University of Manitoba (1,777 students); measures studied included demographics, modern racism scale, feeling thermometer scale, and political solidarity measure, among others. Conditions were (1) control, (2) historical and contemporary knowledge intervention, (3) historical and contemporary knowledge intervention and individual racism education, (4) historical and contemporary knowledge intervention and systematic racism, and (5) historical and contemporary knowledge intervention, individual racism education, and systematic racism.
15. Jason R. Soble et al., "Effects of a Brief Video Intervention on White University Students' Racial Attitudes," *Journal of Counseling Psychology* 58, no. 1 (2011): 151–57. The study looked at the influence of a video intervention (which described the scope of racism in the United States) on the racial biases of white undergraduates. The 138 participants either viewed the video intervention or an unrelated video. The treatment group experienced significant increases in racial awareness as compared to the control group but did not experience significant decreases in racial prejudice or fear of racial minorities; Kira H. Banks et al., "Examining a Community Intervention to Help White People Understand Race and Racism and Engage in Anti-racist Behaviours," *Journal of Community & Applied Social Psychology* 33, no. 2 (2022): 287–99. The study evaluated the effectiveness of community-led interventions in increasing white individuals' knowledge and awareness of racism. The study included 537

participants who learned about racism for forty hours over ten sessions. Participants reported increased knowledge after the study and increased confidence in discussions about race. Measures included antiracist behaviors and color-blind racial ideology.

16. Brian M. Donovan et al., "Humane Genomics Education Can Reduce Racism," *Science* 383, no. 6685 (2024): 818–22; Alessandro Bergamaschi et al., "Blatant and Subtle Prejudice, and the Role of Teachers in Conveying Tolerance and Respect for the Other," *Intercultural Education* 33 (2022): 1; Ellelan Degife et al., "Educational Intervention Against Biological Racism," *The Clinical Teacher* 18, no. 5 (2021): 542–46. Terry F. Pettijohn II and Amy S. Walzer, "Reducing Racism, Sexism, and Homophobia in College Students by Completing a Psychology of Prejudice Course," *College Student Journal* 42, no. 2 (2008): 459–68; Miriam E. Hill and Martha Augoustinos, "Stereotype Change and Prejudice Reduction: Short and Long-term Evaluation of a Cross-cultural Awareness Programme," *Journal of Community & Applied Social Psychology* 11, no. 4 (2001): 243–62; Laurie Rudman et al., "'Unlearning' Automatic Biases: The Malleability of Implicit Prejudice and Stereotypes," *Journal of Personality and Social Psychology* 81, no. 5 (2001): 856–68.
17. Jerry Kang, "Implicit Bias: A Primer for Courts," *California Law Review* 59, no. 3 (2009): 1123–78; Jerry Kang and Kristin Lane, "Seeing Through Colorblindness: Implicit Bias and the Law," *UCLA Law Review* 58, no. 2 (2010): 465–520; Jerry Kang and Mahzarin R. Banaji, "Fair Measures: A Behavioral Realist Revision of 'Affirmative Action,'" *California Law Review* 94, no. 4 (2006): 1063–1118.
18. Elizabeth A. Phelps, et al, "Performance on Indirect Measures of Race Evaluation Predicts Amygdala Activation," *Journal of Cognitive Neuroscience* 12 (October 2000): 729–38, https://banaji.sites.fas.harvard.edu/research/publications/articles/2000_Phelps_JCN.pdf.
19. Anna Spain Bradley, expert testimony, ¶¶ 118–37.
20. Save the Children, "Meet Eglantyne Jebb"; UNICEF, History of Child Rights.
21. Universal Declaration of Human Rights, art. 26, G.A. Res. 217 A (III), U.N. Doc. A/810 (Dec. 10, 1948); International Covenant on Economic, Social and Cultural Rights, art. 13, Dec. 16, 1966, 993 U.N.T.S. 3; Convention on the Rights of the Child, Nov. 20, 1989, 1577 U.N.T.S. 3; African Charter on the Rights and Welfare of the Child, July 11, 1990, OAU Doc. CAB/LEG/24.9/49 (1990); Additional Protocol to the American Convention on Human Rights in the Area of Economic, Social

and Cultural Rights ("Protocol of San Salvador"), Nov. 17, 1988, O.A.S. Treaty Series No. 69.

22. *See* data from World Bank (2024) and Wittgenstein Centre (2024), available at "Global Education," *Our World in Data*, accessed August 22, 2025.
23. "The Gender Gap in School Attendance Has Closed Across Most of the World," *Our World in Data*, accessed August 22, 2025.
24. UNESCO Global Education Monitoring Report "Out-of-School Rate" (2023).
25. UNESCO, "UNESCO: Global Number of Out-of-School Children Rises By 6 Million," press release (September 18, 2023). *See also* Veronika Samborska and Hannah Ritchie, "The Global Number of Children Not Attending School Has Declined by Nearly 40% Since 2000," *Our World in Data*, July 29, 2024.
26. UNICEF, "Primary Education," June 2022.
27. World Bank Group, *Population, Total*, accessed September 13, 2025; UNICEF, *Demographic Transition*, accessed September 13, 2025.
28. United Nations Department of Economic and Social Affairs, Population Division, accessed August 22, 2025. "Child Mortality and Causes of Death," World Health Organization, accessed August 22, 2025.
29. Anna Bonfert and Divyanshi Wadhwa, Tracing Global Trends in Education: A Tale of Old and New Gender Gaps, World Bank Group, April 18, 2024.
30. "The Gender Gap in School Attendance Has Closed Across Most of the World," *Our World in Data*, accessed August 22, 2025.
31. Audrey Axoulay, Statement by Director-General of UNESCO, "Afghanistan: Four Years On, 2.2 Million Girls Still Banned from School," UNESCO (August 14, 2025).

CHAPTER 10

1. David Marchese, "Nikki Giovanni Has Made Peace with Her Hate," *New York Times Magazine*, December 27, 2021.
2. UNESCO (United Nations Educational, Scientific and Cultural Organization), *The Race Question* (1950).
3. For debates over whether race should be retained, transformed, or abandoned in the fight against racism, see Henry Louis Gates Jr., "Writing 'Race' and the Difference It Makes," *Critical Inquiry* 12, no. 1 (1985): 4–5, rejecting biological race while affirming its cultural and historical force; Kimberlé Crenshaw, "Mapping the Margins: Intersectionality, Identity Politics, and Violence Against Women of Color," *Stanford Law Review*

43, no. 6 (1991): 1241–44; Kwame Anthony Appiah, *Color Conscious* (Princeton University Press, 1996), 30–34, distinguishing between race as a social fact and race as a moral essence; Paul Gilroy, *Against Race* (Harvard University Press, 2000), 1–5, arguing why race-thinking itself perpetuates racism; and Eduardo Bonilla-Silva, *Racism Without Racists* (Rowman & Littlefield, 2003), 1–4, emphasizing that racism persists even without overt racists or race-conscious actors.

4. Angela Y. Davis, *Women, Race & Class* (Random House, 1981), 1–3, treating race as politically indispensable yet analytically insufficient.
5. Subrena E. Smith and David L. Smith, "The Trouble with Race and Its Many Shades of Deceit," *New Lines Magazine*, March 29, 2023. *See also* Subrena E. Smith and David Livingstone Smith, *What Is Race?* (W. W. Norton, 2023), 215–20.
6. "Population, Total," World Bank, 2024. Tariq Khokhar and Haruna Kashiwase, "The Future of the World's Population in 4 Charts," The Data Blog, World Bank, August 5, 2015.
7. "Historical Estimates of World Population," U.S. Census Bureau, last revised, December 5, 2022, https://perma.cc/DQX3-ASFN.
8. Khokhar and Kashiwase, "The Future of the World's Population in 4 Charts". *See generally* "Global Issues: Our Growing Population," United Nations, accessed August 22, 2025.
9. Khokar and Kashiwasi, "The Future of the World's Population in 4 Charts."
10. Mark Dyble et al., "Sex Equality Can Explain the Unique Social Structure of Hunter-Gatherer Bands," *Science* 349 (May 15, 2015): 796–98. Andrea Migliano et al., "Hunter-Gatherer Multilevel Sociality Accelerates Cumulative Cultural Evolution," *Science Advances Issue* 6, no. 9 (February 28, 2020).
11. *See* Josine Blok and Andre Lardinois, eds., *Solon of Athens: New Historical and Philological Approaches* (Brill, 2006); Delfim Leão and P. J. Rhodes, *The Laws of Solon: A New Edition with Introduction, Translation and Commentary* (I.B. Tauris, 2016).
12. *See generally* C. Hignett, *A History of the Athenian Constitution at the End of the Fifth Century B.C.* (Clarendon Press, 1952); G. R. Stanton, *Athenian Politics c. 800-500 B.C.* (Routledge, 1990).
13. Alberico Gentili, *De Iure Belli Libri Tres*, John C. Rolfe, trans. (Clarendon Press, 1933), 67.
14. *Id*. at 68.
15. Johannes Morsink, *The Universal Declaration of Human Rights: Origins, Drafting, and Intent* (University of Pennsylvania Press, 1999), 36.

16. *Id.*
17. *Id.* at 37.
18. A/PV.1406, ¶¶ 79–87. Patrick Thornberry, *The International Convention on the Elimination of All Forms of Racial Discrimination: A Commentary* (Oxford University Press, 2016), 5.
19. Thomas M. Franck, *The Empowered Self: Law and Society in an Age of Individualism* (Oxford University Press, 1999), 1.
20. *Id.* at 5.

CONCLUSION

1. Tomas Tranströmer, "Preludes," *in Friends, You Drank Some Darkness: Three Swedish Poets*, ed. and trans. Robert Bly (Beacon Press, 1975).

Index

For the benefit of digital users, indexed terms that span two pages (e.g., 52–53) may, on occasion, appear on only one of those pages.